The Organization of Hypocrisy

The Organization of Hypocrisy

Talk, decisions and actions in organizations

NILS BRUNSSON
Stockholm School of Economics

Translated by Nancy Adler

JOHN WILEY & SONS
Chichester · New York · Brisbane · Toronto · Singapore

Copyright © 1989 by John Wiley & Sons Ltd.
Baffins Lane, Chichester
West Sussex PO19 1UD, England

Chapter 6 is a revised version of a chapter previously published in Wolff, R. (ed.) (1986) *Organizing Industrial Development*. Berlin: Walter de Gruyter. Reproduced by permission of Walter de Gruyter & Co.

Chapter 8 is a revised version of an article in press in *Accounting, Organizations and Society* and is reproduced by permission of Pergamon Press PLC.

Reprinted August 1991, June 1993, October 1994

Other Wiley Editorial Offices

John Wiley & Sons, Inc., 605 Third Avenue,
New York, NY 10158-0012, USA

Jacaranda Wiley Ltd, 33 Park Road, Milton,
Queensland 4064, Australia

John Wiley & Sons (Canada) Ltd, 22 Worcester Road,
Rexdale, Ontario M9W 1L1, Canada

John Wiley & Sons (SEA) Pte Ltd, 37 Jalan Pemimpin #05-04,
Block B, Union Industrial Building, Singapore 2057

Library of Congress Cataloging-in-Publication Data
Brunsson, Nils. 1946–
  The organization of hypocrisy : talk, decisions, and actions in organizations / Nils Brunsson : translated by Nancy Adler.
    p.   cm.
  Bibliography: p.
  Includes index
  ISBN 0 471 92074 6
  ISBN 0 471 93186 1 (pbk)
  Organizational behavior.   2. Corporate culture.   3. Office politics.   4. Hypocrisy.   I. Title
  HD58.7.B795   1989
  658.4'03 – dc20   89-14785
                                                                      CIP

British Library Cataloguing in Publication Data
Brunsson, Nils. *1946–*
  The organization of hypocrisy : talk, decisions and actions in organizations.
  1. Organisational behaviour
  I. Title
  302.3'5

  ISBN 0 471 92074 6
  ISBN 0 471 93186 1 (pbk)

Printed and bound in Great Britain by
Biddles Ltd, Guildford and King's Lynn

Contents

Preface

In a previous book, *The Irrational Organization*, I discussed some of the conditions for producing action in organizations and ways in which action can be coordinated by ideological means. The present book has a theme which could be described as the opposite: how organizations produce ideology, and how ideology and action can systematically conflict with one another to the benefit of organizational legitimacy and survival.

This theme emerged from a series of empirical studies which I conducted over a period of almost ten years. I am indebted to many people, from both the world of practice and the world of theory, who have helped me to produce this book—which does not mean that they should be blamed for my misunderstandings. A great many managers in numerous organizations have allowed themselves to be questioned, studied and analysed, thus giving me an insight into a fascinating reality. Many colleagues have helped me to refine these insights into meaningful analyses.

James March gave me the opportunity to work in the inspiring environment of his at Stanford University whenever I wanted to, and he never ceased to provide both encouragement and advice. John Meyer made extensive and very constructive comments that substantially improved several chapters and in particular Chapter 8. Richard Scott and Olov Olson also gave me advice, as did all the members of the F-section, who have also shown impressive tolerance of my lack of leadership whether I have been officially on writing leave or not. I made the empirical study reported in Chapter 4 together with Sten Jönsson. Nancy Adler not only undertook the heroic task of translating and interpreting a some-what chaotic original manuscript, but also helped to make it shorter and more coherent. Anne von Tiedemann patiently typed new drafts again and again, as well as helping to compile the index and taking charge of the list of references.

The Stockholm School of Economics gives me the opportunity to carry out my research. The Study of Power and Democracy in Sweden, the City of Stockholm, the Swedish Council for Research in the Humanities and Social Sciences, and Dafolo A/S have all provided financial support, in the case of Dafolo in the inspiring form of their prize for an earlier draft of the manuscript.

My thanks to all!

Nils Brunsson

Stockholm, December 1988

1
Organizations and Inconsistent Norms

Modern societies are becoming increasingly differentiated. The number of groups and special interests which can and do demand attention and consideration is continually growing. Many of these demands are mediated in some way by the state, which has consequently acquired increasing importance. More organizations than ever before are now supervising, supporting or impeding one another's operations. In capitalistic industrialized societies a strong 'bargaining economy' has emerged in which industrial success is becoming increasingly dependent on extensive contact between the business world and politicians, public officials and special-interest organizations. Traditional companies, local authorities or other producer organizations are subject to a rising tide of frequently contradictory demands. People as individuals are entitled to equal treatment, to physically and mentally acceptable working conditions, and to a high material living standard; other organizations are entitled to information; air and water must be spared pollution. As a result of all these demands, the situation of organizations and the conditions for organizing have been transformed. It is a long time since industrial companies could concentrate exclusively on manufacturing their products as efficiently as possible, and thus to survive and grow. They too are now involved in the creation, clarification, transmission and application of rules, norms and interests—all of which can greatly impede the prospects for efficient production.

All this has had a dramatic effect on organizations. Difficulties in handling this new situation may lie behind the loss of confidence and support from the public that many large organizations have suffered (Lipset and Schneider 1983). The developments also have important implications for organization theory. They question several assumptions which have previously been common in discussions of the way in which organizations behave and the way in which they should behave. These implications will be discussed in the present book.

Radical changes call for radical questions. Let us start by asking a question fundamental to any organization and any organization theory—what are organizations for? Why do they receive support and resources from their environments so that they can survive and grow? Certain organizations manage to survive by resorting to some form of force, compelling their environments to surrender the resources they want. But most organizations are denied this possibility; instead they have to depend on the fact that some part of the environment finds them worthy of support. So, what is it about these organizations and their activities that helps them to attract resources?

A TRADITIONAL VIEW

A common view is that organizations exist to generate collective coordinated action. Organizations, with their systems of rules and authority, can coordinate and steer the behaviour of their individual members towards the production of goods and services which could not be produced without such coordination. In industrialized societies enormous quantities of such goods and services are produced, which goes a long way to explaining why organizations have become so important.

If we assume that the *raison d'être* of organizations is to generate organized action, then the natural thing is to evaluate individual organizations according to their ability to produce such action. The action is supposed to result in products, and it is thus the products which have to be evaluated. Different organizations can be compared by reference to their efficiency in coordinating action. We who enjoy their products generally like the resource input to be kept to a minimum, at least if this organizational efficiency is reflected in the amount we have to pay. The concept of efficiency therefore looms large in macroeconomic market theory, which is concerned with the effects of different markets on resource allocation. Efficiency has also been a crucial element in the more hierarchic tradition which sees organizations as the instrument of the will of their principals. It has been assumed that shareholders, voters or corporate management are all interested in the efficiency of 'their' organization. Organizational structures and processes, i.e. how organizations are built up and how people behave in them, as well as the ideologies that organizations produce, are generally explained in terms of their ambition to achieve effective coordinated action.

But external stakeholders will be interested in more than effective action; they will also have something to say about the actions that should be undertaken, and consequently what products will result. In order to win the support of its environment, an organization has to supply products which fulfil needs or interests obtaining there. In other words the products must reflect values and norms in the organization's environment. Market theories tell us how the environment can influence the focus of production in an organization, while hierarchical theories tell us how principals and managements can select and decide what products will be produced.

Organizations are not the helpless victims of external demands for the efficient production of particular products. Demands for efficiency can be held in check to some extent, provided not too much information is available about other more efficient methods of production. And one way of limiting such information is by avoiding competition, perhaps by entering into price or production agreements or by creating monopolies. The way the environment evaluates individual products can also be influenced by various marketing expedients—advertising, for instance—which emphasize or underpin or even create values and needs.

But none of these manipulative approaches alters the basic assumption underlying the action perspective, namely that an organization provokes the support of its environment by supplying products which that environment regards as valuable. Thus normative theories based on the action perspective generally address three main issues: how to organize work as efficiently as possible, how to choose the right products (goods or services) and how to influence the external evaluation of these products. The theories then suggest organizational structures, processes and ideologies appropriate to the effective coordination of action, the choosing of products, and marketing.

INSTITUTIONAL ENVIRONMENTS

In the case of many organizations, however, the theories described above seem irrelevant in their focus on action and products. Some organizations generate very little coordinated action, and for them such action also means very little when it comes to attracting external support. To other organizations products are of no particular significance, because neither they nor their environments really know what they are producing. Schools and universities are typical examples of this type of organization. Teaching is largely a private activity undertaken by individual teachers and is seldom or never coordinated. The same applies to research. A school is of course meant to be producing a higher level of education among its students; that is its product. But it is difficult to prove that schools actually achieve this goal (perhaps the students would have learnt more if they had not had to spend so much time at school?) and it is difficult to compare results as between different schools. Nonetheless schools and universities survive, and they attract resources and support from their environments. And many other organizations which would find it equally difficult to demonstrate their products survive as well. They include management consultants, accountants, hospitals and many service organizations. The same applies to many sections or departments within organizations: staff units such as accounting, for instance, or top management. There must therefore be other ways of creating support outside the organization, apart from simply demonstrating a product.

Organizational structures, processes and ideologies are examples of such methods. Structures, processes and ideologies can reflect norms in the environment, just as products do. They too can answer an external demand. By structuring itself along lines that are generally regarded as reasonable, fair, efficient, rational, modern and so on, an organization can win the understanding of its environment. Conversely, if it fails to follow the current norms it may lose the support of its environment. To abandon curricula, subjects and lessons is a dangerous thing for a school to do. Schools which deviate from the recognized structures do not survive for long (Meyer 1983). Like many other organizations schools are supposed to include members of the appropriate professions on their staff; there may even be a law to this effect. Hospitals must employ fully qualified physicians, and companies must engage chartered accountants. Legislation may not be the only compelling factor; changing fashions are also a potent influence. At various times different types of organizational structure may be appropriate—centralized, decentralized, divisionalized or matrix—in order to inspire confidence in potential shareholders, bankers or the state. Input, too, can affect external support; it may be important to invest a reasonable amount of money in job satisfaction, environmental improvements, or cultural sponsorship.

There are also norms about the processes which organizations should or must employ. To a hospital the number of patients it actually cures is difficult to know and is not particularly important. What matters is that the physicians adopt the methods and stick to the norms laid down by the social service authorities for 'tried and tested scientific praxis'. The physician who does not obey these norms may be penalized as a quack, regardless of whether or not he has cured his patients, and hospitals which encourage such behaviour would soon lose their external support. Very specific norms calling for greater economic 'rationality' are becoming more common. Over the last twenty years or so big companies have been making increasing use of budgets; not having a budget would now stamp a company as extremely old-fashioned and evoke suspicion among potential financers. Corporate investment calculations grow more sophisticated from year to year (Lundberg 1957, Renck 1971, Tell 1974).

Ideologies, the views which an organization proclaims, can also affect its external support. Organizations may claim to possess a variety of positive qualities: they are efficient, they are service-minded, or they exist for the benefit of the public. Goals are even more useful in this context. If an organization cannot quite fulfil some particular norm, it may at least be a good idea to emphasize a firm intention to do so.

Structures, processes and ideologies are thus more than simply ways of coordinating action; like products, they are something which should be explicitly demonstrated to the environment in order to win its support. Consequently organizations must be open to public view, in a way that would not be necessary if their sole task was to produce organized action. They may also try to influence environmental norms about the 'right' structures, processes and ideologies, so that these agree more closely with their own situation.

But most real-world organizations are not judged solely on their products, or exclusively on their structures, processes and ideologies. Most organizations have to demonstrate products, structures, processes and ideologies—all of which reflect the norms of their environment. Naturally an industrial company has to manufacture products with reasonable efficiency; but it also has to obey the rules about the working environment, it has to employ professionals, make investment estimates, and espouse goals which show that it wishes the world in general well.

In the terminology adopted by Meyer and Scott (1983), we could say that most organizations have both a technical and an institutional environment. The technical environment evaluates and supports an organization in terms of its products and results; the institutional environment judges it on its structures, processes and ideologies. The institutional environment is not equally important to all organizations; it is presumably more important to banks and hospitals, for example, than it is to car repair shops and restaurants. But modern societies seem to spawn an increasing number of norms, telling organizations how they may or should behave. Laws are proliferating and fashions are growing increasingly changeable and influential. Politicians, bureaucrats, consultants and business schools are all reinforcing their roles in launching the trends and creating the norms by which organizations have to live.

External Norms Versus Efficiency

The norms concerning structures, processes and ideologies are often explained and justified on grounds that they should con-tribute to efficiency. Unfortunately, however, there is no guarantee that the demands imposed by the institutional environment are necessarily compatible with the demand that structures, processes and ideologies should contribute to effective coordinated action. On the contrary the very volatility of the norms of the institutional environment suggests that it must often be difficult to combine them with the requirements of efficiency; the conditions for efficient coordinated action presumably change more slowly than organizational fashions. When institutional norms fail to agree with the requirements for action, organizations will often try to create two sets of structures and processes, one for each type of norm. These sets should not interfere with one another, but should be separated or 'decoupled' (Meyer and Rowan 1977).

This means that two organizational structures evolve. One is the formal organization which obeys the institutional norms and which can easily be adapted to new fashions or laws, literally by a few strokes of the pen on an organization chart. A quite different organizational structure can be used in 'reality', i.e. in order to coordinate action. This second type is generally referred to as the 'informal organization'. Similarly two sets of organizational processes arise: one generates action; the other does not, but is kept for purposes of demonstration or display to the outside world. These second processes can be defined as rituals. Companies follow all the rules of joint consultation, for example, but this does not necessarily have any effect on subsequent decisions or actions; they produce sophisticated investment calculations, which have little impact on the final choice of investments (Jansson 1987); they make budgets but do not stick to them; they collect information and never use it (Feldman and March 1981). Organizations can also produce double standards or double talk, i.e. keep different ideologies for external and internal use. The way management presents the organization and its goals to the outside world need not agree with the signals conveyed to the workforce.

The separation of the formal and informal organizations, the rituals and the double talk are often important and even necessary ingredients in any modern organization that wants to act according to current demands for rationality, decency and fairness, while also efficiently generating coordinated action.

INCONSISTENT ENVIRONMENTS

Formal organizations, rituals and double talk all represent ways of coping with inconsistencies between institutional norms and the requirements of efficiency. But institutional norms about products, structure, process and ideology can also be inconsistent in themselves. Different interests in the environment demand different things of the organization, both regarding products and ways of producing them. Various professional groups inside and outside the organization have different ideas about how the organization should be run. All these demands not only differ from one another, they may well be difficult or impossible to combine: they are contradictory or inconsistent. The nature of the inconsistency may be logical, technical or resource-related. Some norms may call for a centralized organization and others for decentralization. Some groups may demand democratic management processes, others authoritarian. It may be impossible to combine the customers' product requirements with the related environmental rules. And there may not be enough money to pay all the groups which make economic demands on the organization.

Inconsistent norms are difficult to handle, difficult to reflect simultaneously, and difficult to combine with organizational action which is greatly dependent on consistency. Many organizations try to avoid the kind of situation which will expose them to conflicting demands. They try to specialize. They look for niches in the environment where reasonably consistent norms prevail; by satisfying the demands of this niche they then hope to win enough support and resources to survive. By defining themselves as a manufacturer of high-priced family cars, for example, the organization can weed out some of the many norms and avoid a certain amount of the inconsistency.

Another similar strategy involves trying to discover norms shared by all relevant external groups and to reflect these instead of the norms that conflict with one another. For instance, unions riddled with internal conflict have been observed paying much attention to the peace issue while de-emphasizing controversial wage questions (Micheletti 1987). Organizations can also try to follow the advice of the economists, creating a kind of preference function by trading off different norms against each other. They may form a dominant coalition of interested parties which can act according to an agreed set of values (Cyert and March 1963). However, attempts at avoiding inconsistencies are not always successful, and even if they succeed they are not always the most advantageous or viable strategy.

Many organizations cannot or do not want to avoid inconsistent norms; instead they become expert at generating support, resources and legitimacy from environments exhibiting just such inconsistency. Obvious examples are democratic parliaments or local authorities and other multi-party organizations. These spend their time trying systematically to satisfy a variety of groups, all making contradictory demands. And many of them are also expected to produce organized action. Thus in some way they must reflect inconsistencies *and* produce action. This is a fundamental problem for many organizations, be they large industrial companies or public agencies and whether or not they have sought this position themselves.

Thus organizations are being exposed to a growing number of inconsistent norms in their environments, and many are finding it increasingly difficult to avoid them. Yet at the same time most descriptive and normative organization theories assume either that external norms are uniform, or that they can be made compatible, or that conflicting norms can be avoided. The vast literature concerned with 'good' organizational management is chiefly concerned with organizational action, how to choose the right products and how to make organizations good at producing them efficiently. The purpose of the present book is instead to describe and analyse ways in which organizations handle inconsistent norms, and how this affects the rest of their organizational behaviour. We need to understand these aspects of behaviour better, particularly if we want to be able to influence and change them.

The theory presented here differs in several ways from other theories which regard organizations as systems for coordinated action, and analyse the organizations exclusively in this perspective. Integration and coordination, for example, are regarded in most normative organization theories as important to organizations. Coordination may even be conceived as synonymous with, the actual point of, organizing. And yet numerous observations of disintegration and a lack of coordination have been made in all kinds of organizations. In this book I shall not only try to explain the occurrence of systematic disintegration in organizations, but I shall also suggest that disintegration can have a positive effect on the viability of an organization that is exposed to inconsistent demands. Organizational structures, processes and ideologies have been regarded traditionally as important instruments of coordination, and necessary to the efficient production which ensures a satisfactory output. Here I shall describe these same phenomena not as instruments but as results; they are in themselves important organizational outputs.

Many researchers have advised organizations to avoid conflict if at all possible, to smooth them over if they do occur, or at least to conceal them from the rest of the world. I suggest that it may be useful for the organization to cultivate and demonstrate its conflicts. It is sometimes said that organizations are geared to the solution or avoidance of problems. I shall show that they also have good reason to create and maintain problems; to have problems is often a vital solution for an organization, whereas solutions can sometimes be a serious problem.

Organizational management has often been described as a series of processes aimed at controlling the actions of the organization; at the same time there are many descriptions of all the difficulties that arise when management does try to exert such control. In this book I shall examine another role that management can play, whereby it lets itself be controlled by the organization while projecting its own activities and influence outwards on to the environment. It is commonly assumed that the ideologies and expressed preferences of organizational management, and the various decisions taken within the organization, should all agree with the organization's actions, and preferably in such a way that the ideologies, preferences and decisions can be said to determine the content of the action. I shall show that it is sometimes important that the ideologies, preferences, decisions and actions of an organization do *not* agree with one another.

Many theories assume that organizations are or should be rational, although numerous studies have revealed systematic irrationality in organizations. Here I will argue that organizations can permit themselves more rationality when action is not fundamental to them. But the impetus behind rationality in decision-making is not necessarily the search for the right choice; other impulses may also be at work.

Thus there are plenty of theories which emphasize coordination, agreement, consistency and vigorous action in organizations. The point is not that these traditional theories or paths towards an understanding of organizations are wrong; it is simply that they are not enough. Theories emphasizing coherence and consistency do describe an important aspect of organizations, but one which alone fails to explain vital parts of organizational life. If we adopt the traditional theories we will find it difficult to understand why organizations often exhibit the disintegrative attributes I have mentioned here; we are too inclined to describe them in this light as dysfunctions, as signs that things are not working satisfactorily, and to advise the organizations to try to correct these 'faults' and to 'pull themselves together'. Both integrative and disintegrative qualities can be dysfunctional, but both can also be important or even necessary to the survival of an organization; it all depends on the situation, on the kind of environment, or on the tasks that the organization is trying to solve.

In order to understand why organizations have these disintegrative attributes, we have to study not only the attributes in themselves but also the processes by which they are created. It is also important to establish how far they represent the face which the organization chooses to present to the outside world, and how far they are part of its internal processes. We thus have to look carefully at the way organizations present themselves to the environment, and at events within the organizations. The events themselves, and the way they are seen by the actors involved, must be charted in detail before we can understand why the actors behave as they do, and what circumstances make a particular action possible or necessary.

The theory presented in this book is based on empirical studies of about a dozen organizations and many organizational processes in these organizations, and of the way in which individual actors perceived the various related situations. Some investigations were made while the studied processes were actually taking place, although several of them lasted for many years. But most of the study was undertaken retrospectively, soon after the events had occurred.

Some of the organizational processes observed in the empirical studies will be described in later chapters, to give substance and impact to the analyses. But first let us look at the basic elements in a theory of organizational behaviour in situations characterized by inconsistent norms. This will be the subject of the next chapter.

2
The Political Organization Principle

In the previous chapter I described how modern organizations are often exposed to inconsistent demands from their environments. In this chapter I shall try to explain how organizations can handle such demands. In principle the solution is to build the inconsistencies into the organization and into the organizational output, to let structures, processes and ideologies reflect the inconsistencies in the environment. But when organizations choose or are compelled to live with inconsistent demands, they will find it difficult to generate organized action, since organized action calls for consistency rather than inconsistency (as will be explained below). At the same time organized action is necessary to the creation of products, and products are usually important in attracting external support. Consequently, organizations which are highly dependent on organized action will be in particularly serious trouble when they have to face inconsistent demands. The conflict between inconsistency and action will also be discussed in this chapter.

As we have noted, organizations are dependent on environmental support in two respects: first, resources in the shape of money, labour, materials and so on should be put at the organization's disposal, and secondly the organization's existence must be accepted by the environment; its operations must not, for instance, be impeded by legislation. To use a very general term, we can say that the organization must enjoy a certain degree of legitimacy in the eyes of its environment. Legitimacy is the basis for the financing of the organization. Organizational legitimacy can be created in several ways. I shall be describing two principles of legitimation below, namely organizational action and the reflection of inconsistencies. The first principle is associated with the assumption that the survival of an organization depends primarily on an exchange of resources with its environment, i.e. the organization can supply certain goods or services for which it receives money to finance its continuing operations. The other principle is associated with the assumption that the survival of an organization also depends upon its ability to reflect and create a symbolical accord with its environment. I shall illustrate the two principles of legitimation in a comparison between two ideal types, one of which depends solely on action for its legitimacy and the other on the reflection of inconsistent norms.

Real-world organizations do not occur in these pure states; they normally have to be good both at producing action *and* at reflecting inconsistencies. But by looking first at ideal types we can see the differences between the two kinds of legitimation more clearly, which thus will provide us with a better basis for discussing the conditions of real-world organizations in a later section. The first ideal type can be dubbed the action organization, and the second the political organization.

THE IDEAL TYPE OF ACTION ORGANIZATION

Suppose we want to learn something about organizations. It will be easy to obtain the kind of knowledge that is based on the assumption that action is the main ground for organizational legitimacy. This is because most organizational research has been based on this assumption: action is assumed to be the fundamental goal of organizations, and physical products in the shape of goods and services are supposed to be the fundamental means of winning the support of the environment. In our terms we could say that much research has focused not on real organizations but on one of the ideal types, namely the action organization. It would obviously be impossible to summarize here all the knowledge that has been accumulated, so I shall simply mention a few of the essential features which distinguish this action organization from the ideal political type which I will examine later.

Structure—The Principle of Agreement

Agreement as a principle of recruitment and organization

The principle of recruitment in the action organization is agreement. This means that members are recruited on a basis of the express or implied condition that they share the general goals and purposes of the organization and its management, or at least that they behave as though they did (March and Simon 1958 p. 118, Brown 1978, Pfeffer 1981). The action organization does not employ people who say they will oppose the present management.

Agreement is also an important organizational principle; it applies not only to recruitment, but also to the ongoing work of the organization. The action organization puts a good deal of effort into maintaining agreement, into seeing that everyone is pulling in the same direction. The organization tries to avoid conflict, and if conflict does arise it strives hard to resolve it. A major instrument of conflict-solving is the hierarchy: someone decides what is right, and what the others should do.

The hierarchy is instrumental in coordinating the activities of the organization members, thus generating organized action. The organizational ideology is instrumental in the same context.

Strong organizational ideology

The action organization formulates rules to govern the behaviour of its members. The rules restrict the members' freedom of action, thus making it more likely that they will all behave in such a way as to generate organized action. Some rules are very concrete and firm. A conveyor belt, for example, assigns a definite task to each person on the belt, to be carried out at specific moments, with the result that the individual workers combine to produce extremely complex products. But rules of this kind only work in stable environments, where situations and tasks can be predicted. The conveyor belt is protected from external interference by an extensive administrative apparatus and an intricate feeder system. But if future situations cannot be predicted with such certainty and in such detail, the action organization requires rules at a higher level of abstraction—rules that can also be applied to situations which could not be foreseen when the rules were being made. The organizational ideology represents one such rule, which is useful to any organization in a variable and unpredictable environment.

An organizational ideology consists of ideas and values prevailing among organization members about the organization and its environment. The action organization tends to have strong organizational ideologies, i.e. its members tend to possess much the same ideas and values, and the ideas tend to be complex and conclusive rather than vague and abstract, and to exhibit a high degree of internal consistency. With an ideology of this kind behind them, members are more likely to react to a new situation in a similar way and to draw the same concrete conclusions about the actions that are required. There is thus a good basis for coordinated action without first having to go through a long process of analysis and discussion which can easily arouse conflict and uncertainty, which in turn will often inhibit action (Brunsson 1985).

Powerful organizational ideologies tend to evolve under their own steam; people who meet and work together easily come to think along similar lines (Argyris and Schön 1978, Starbuck 1976, Jönsson and Lundin 1977). But because organizational ideologies are such crucial instruments of coordinated action, organizations also make concrete efforts to create and maintain them. Organizational management defines goals and works out policies and business ideas; it tries to create a corporate spirit, a corporate culture and so on (Ansoff *et al.* 1976, Lorange and Vancil 1977, Starbuck *et al.* 1978). In this way the variety of ideas, perspectives, notions and opinions which members presumably represent when they join the organization is reduced and absorbed into the common ideology. In a complex world which can be comprehended in many ways, the organization circumscribes its members' understanding. To put it bluntly, the action organization makes people narrower or stupider than they were before they joined it.

Processes—Irrationality and a Solutions Focus

Decision-making

A powerful organizational ideology cuts down the need for making decisions. It is often obvious what action should be taken. The ideology chooses the action, and no other choice process is needed. If a decision is nonetheless taken, its purpose is to reinforce the willingness to act rather than to reach a choice between possible alternatives. The decision is meant to reinforce people's expectations that a given organizational action really will be undertaken, to motivate the relevant actors to carry it out and to commit them to the action.

Decisions with this kind of action-reinforcing function should not obey the norms of rational decision-making; action rationality is very different from decision rationality. Rational decision-making all too easily produces uncertainty and doubt; the decision process should instead be systematically irrational (Brunsson 1982). Ideally only one alternative should be considered, so that no doubt arises about what should be done. Two alternatives could perhaps be taken up, but the second should then be so obviously inferior that it simply serves to enhance the attraction of the main alternative. Ideally, only the positive consequences of the alternative to be chosen should be described, so that it appears in the very best light, as a goal obviously worth realizing. Preferences can be adapted to action, rather than the other way round. The action organization makes irrational decisions whenever the decisions refer to organizational action, particularly to difficult or complicated action which calls for the coordination of many people's activities.

Consistency between ideology and action

Organizational ideologies in the action organization are instrumental in coordinating action. Action will therefore largely agree with ideology. Action will reflect talk and decisions in the organization. To put it in another way: the action organization generally does what it says.

Specialization

The action organization specializes; it may limit itself to selling one type of product or addressing one market, or it may concentrate on one kind of technique. 'Business ideas' are often ideas about niches, or about special needs which the organization intends to satisfy. Industrial activity is based to a great extent on specialization. There are many reasons for specializing, the most frequently cited being to achieve advantages of scale. Specialization can increase efficiency. But technical arguments in favour of specialization are not the only ones; we can also cite ideological arguments. Organized action calls for a powerful organizational ideology, and if we subscribe to one such powerful ideology, then many otherwise possible actions are automatically excluded. Organizational ideologies should be precise, complex and consistent—which also makes them narrow and concerned exclusively with a limited section of reality; they restrict the number of possible actions. As we have already seen, powerful organizational ideologies limit the freedom of action of the actors, thus engendering specialization.

Solutions focus

The action organization is geared to solutions rather than problems. Only when we have a solution can we act, and shared loyalty to an organizational ideology will make it easier to find solutions. Industrial companies, for example, are based not on problems but on solutions. Once people have found a solution to some problem or problems, they can organize themselves and act. The car was the idea Ford had in mind, not the problem of transport; the ball-bearing was the business idea that launched SKF, not the problem of friction.

Firm confidence

Action is easier when a powerful organizational ideology obtains, and conflict is suppressed. Thus the action organization cultivates great confidence; the members of this organization are convinced that their view of the world in which they operate is the right one. This faith may conflict sharply with what appears reasonable to an outsider. The strong faith shown by some organizations in their own excellence can sometimes seem absurd, particularly if environmental conditions have been changing rapidly, and the organization has not been able to alter its ideology equally quickly. An outsider can afford to be more sceptical and critical, since he has no need to generate organizational action. Firm confidence affects the capacity for action, and it is difficult to see how it can be abandoned without reducing the ability to act.

Limited rationality

In conclusion we could say that the action organization is systematic in *not* adopting normative models of rationality. In a complicated world it cultivates a single perspective and a single idea about how it functions and about how its environment functions, and the confidence it attaches to this ideology is excessive in relation to what would seem reasonable. It seldom has to embark on long decision processes and the consideration of alternative courses of action. And if it does embark on such a process as a basis for organizational action, it anyway tends to be irrational, i.e. conflicting with normative theories of rational decision-making. The action organization cultivates a spirit of enthusiasm rather than criticism.

THE IDEAL TYPE OF POLITICAL ORGANIZATION

The ideal antipole of the action organization is what I call the political organization. This organization has no need at all to produce coordinated action; its only basis for legitimation is that it reflects inconsistent norms. Instead of seeking niches like the action organization and satisfying one need or interest at a time, the political organization reflects a variety of ideas and demands and satisfies the expectations of diverse groups in its environment. Groups in the environment support the political organization because they get their own demands satisfied (even if they are inconsistent), and because the political organizations can equitably satisfy the demands of other groups as well. The organizational structures and processes of the action organization are linked only indirectly to the environment; they are instrumental in generating products, and it is the products that are then supplied to the environment. Important structures and processes in the political organization, on the other hand, are aimed directly at the environment; the idea is to demonstrate them to the outside world, to show that the organization is attending to the inconsistent demands which are being made upon it.

I shall now examine the structures, processes and outputs of the political organization, illustrating my argument with a few examples. However, since the political organization is an ideal type, it does not correspond exactly to any real-world example that I can use. Instead I will use examples from organizations which are deeply involved in political behaviour, such as parliaments, governments, boards and top management. The illustrations refer to situations as generally described in the media. Examples from various empirical studies will be discussed in the following chapters.

Structure—The Principle of Conflict

The political organization recruits its members—or at least its management—according to a *principle of conflict*. People are attached to the organization because they do *not* share the same views as other members about what the organization should do. The composition of the organization is often ensured by recruiting members who represent different groups in the environment (or, in the case of management, members representing different groups in the organization itself). Thus in many countries trade unions are represented on company boards, for example, not because they are experts on technology or economics, but because it is assumed that they represent interests other than those of management or the other board members. For the same reasons parliaments consist of members of different parties.

But the principle of conflict does not stop at recruitment. The conflicts also have to be kept alive—something that is not always easy to do since strong forces are always working in the opposite direction; people belonging to the same organization easily come to think alike. The conflict between organizational members is important not only to the legitimacy of the organization but to the legitimacy of the individual members as well. If the trade union representatives on a corporate board always vote with management, for example, they will soon lose the confidence of their own members.

A good way for the political organization to maintain and demonstrate conflict is to develop several different *organizational ideologies*. The political organization is multi-ideological; it includes lots of ideas about the nature of the organization and its environment, and about what the organization should do. The organization reflects a complex environment full of inconsistent ideas in a series of ideologies that are also inconsistent.

But it is not enough to keep conflict alive and to embrace a variety of organizational ideologies. Since these conflicts and ideologies are directly connected with the legitimacy of the organization in the eyes of its environment, they also have to be demonstrated to the world outside. In view of the legitimacy requirement it is even quite acceptable to demonstrate to the outside world conflicts and ideologies which do not actually typify the internal operations of the organization. 'Objective ideologies' do not have to agree with 'subjective' (Brunsson 1981).

While the action organization adopts various techniques in order to create unity and to generate a powerful organizational ideology, the political organization employs techniques intended to sustain conflict and a variety of ideologies. Their members often like to see themselves not primarily as members of the political organization, but as members and representatives of other preferably single-ideology organizations, such as political parties. They try to keep in regular contact with their own party while avoiding too much contact with actors in other parties; ideally such cross-party communication should take place in some visible setting such as a public debate, which promotes conflict and discourages mutual understanding. The concepts of the 'ruling majority' and the 'opposition' helps in parliaments to keep the organizational conflict alive, as the very purpose of the opposition is to criticize the policy of the majority and to suggest alternative courses of action. This is greatly facilitated by the fact that the opposition knows their suggestions cannot by definition be carried out, just because they come from an opposition. It is always easy to find alternatives that need not work and for which one will not be held responsible.

Conflict as a principle of recruitment and organization, and the cultivation of diverse ideologies, are thus two attributes of the political organization which lead to the reflection of inconsistent environmental values in the organizational structure. But this reflecting role is also evident in the processes of the political organization.

Processes—Intellectuality and Depression

The political organization is 'intellectual' in three respects. To begin with, it embraces *several ideologies*. Thus its members' ideas are not regimented; instead countless ideas and opinions are exploited and elaborated. A series of ideologies tends to use more information than a single one. Analysis often benefits from diverse approaches. An abundance of ideologies and conflicts provokes criticism, and lively criticism reduces the risk of coming to the wrong conclusions. Thus the political organization should be better equipped than the action organization to understand a complex and change-prone world.

Secondly, the political organization is intellectual in the sense that it tends largely to follow the norms of *rational decision-making*. The political organization devotes a good deal of time to decision-making, i.e. its members describe much of their activities in these terms; they indicate clearly when a decision has been made, perhaps by voting on it and recording it. There are several reasons for this insistence on decisions in the political organization, two of which will be discussed later. For the time being it is enough to note that the political organization really is confronted by choices which ideologies do not solve and which sometimes have to be resolved by decisions. If an organization has several ideologies, there will be no obvious way to act, no obvious ideology to invoke in judging a situation, and no self-evident conclusions to be drawn. And because of the conflicts inherent in the organization, several different alternatives are certain to be suggested.

The political organization can afford decision rationality, since it is not dependent on action or action rationality. Its need to demonstrate conflict also explains why its decision processes are relatively rational: rational decision processes provide an excellent way of demonstrating conflict. Establishing different goals, handling many alternatives, describing all possible positive and negative consequences of the alternatives and discussing which one is best—all these are activities in which conflicts and different ideologies can be clearly demonstrated, activities which give the organization an opportunity to reflect inconsistencies in its environment.

The political organization is also intellectual in that it is largely concerned with *problems*. Problems, not solutions, are its strength. It also entertains a special affection for tough or insoluble problems. Some problems are insoluble because in themselves they embrace conflicting interests, e.g. how to keep unemployment and inflation at a low level at one and the same time. Others are insoluble by definition, e.g. how to treat violent criminals in a humane way while also guaranteeing the rest of the population protection from violence. Yet others are insoluble simply because nobody (up to now) has found a solution to them, e.g. how to prevent criminal behaviour or the abuse of drink and drugs. The 'problem of the young', which local authorities try to solve by providing recreation centres and supporting youth clubs, is at least four thousand years old, if we are to believe Socrates.

Insoluble problems are a splendid vehicle for the reflection of many ideas and values. They can be endlessly discussed from all sorts of angles and without ever reaching a conclusion. Solutions that can reflect an equal variety of ideas are rare indeed.

Instead of specializing, the political organization tends to *generalize* itself. The reflection of inconsistent values is in itself an expression of a generalizing strategy. But any political organization that wants to grow will do more than this; it will actively seek to incorporate new ideas in the environment into its own organization. No group need be left outside its domain. The organization grows by reflecting an increasing number of inconsistencies.

Moreover, the political organization is eager to reflect ideas on a widening range of topics. Problems are discussed in European parliaments today which fifty years ago were thought to belong exclusively to private or business life and to have nothing to do with the political system. The introduction of an economic policy in the Keynesian sense in the 1930s is one example; the introduction of industrial policy whereby the actions of individual companies become a political issue is another. Local government no longer limits itself to building councils and local education authorities; it also boasts leisure councils and committees for traffic safety. The generalization of these organizations, in our sense of the term, has of course led to enormous expansion.

Generalization does not only trigger growth; it can also enhance the legitimacy of an organization. The greater the number of ideas the organization reflects in a wider range of fields, the more important it will be to its environment and to individual people or groups there. We could say that the political organization tends to spread into every corner of its environment and to complement events and actions there with ideological reflection, symbols and meaning.

In the political organization *mistrust* and scepticism are encouraged. Freedom of thought is not hampered by any need for common action. The organization systematically cultivates criticism of the status quo. It is the job of the opposition to criticize the policy of the majority. It is easy to absorb new ideas quickly. Where several ideologies co-exist, people daily hear a lot of criticism and are more likely to be sceptical about all ideas, including their own. The only thing they can be quite sure of is that they are wrong. Such scepticism often seems well founded; it is certainly difficult to know how the organization and its environment work, and what they should be doing.

Freedom of thought can be greater when it does not have to be subjected to the demands of common action. It is difficult simultaneously to promote free, visionary and innovative thinking and free, visionary and innovative action.

The intellectuality of the political organization means that organization members get a lot of practice in analysing and discussing difficult problems, and are therefore often good at it. But people in highly political organizations seem more disposed to uncertainty, more inclined to lack self-confidence than their colleagues in more action-oriented organizations. There is an element of depression in the political organization, since it is engaged in problems which it cannot solve, its members are uncertain about the nature of their situation, and they do not know what should be done; they know or believe that much of what they do is wrong, but it is difficult for them to change their behaviour. And anyway criticism is a major activity in the organization.

In view of all this it is not difficult to understand why top local government administrators and politicians, for example, often seem so depressed, so pessimistic and self-critical. Politicians frequently refer to politics in derogatory terms (Brunsson and Jönsson 1979) and municipal administrators describe their organizations as inefficient and inert. People who work in more action-oriented organizations or who operate closer to production, on the other hand, appear more optimistic and self-confident. This contrast may reflect differences in organizational structures, processes and ideologies and in the difficulty of the tasks people have to tackle. A strong conviction that everything we do is right, a conviction shared by our environment, combined with a narrow range of understanding and work that leads to solutions, all add up to a situation which promotes happiness, while a more realistic view of the world, with a predilection for insoluble problems and limited scope for manoeuvres, is far more likely to promote frustration and anxiety.

The popular notion that the public administration is inefficient while industry is efficient may be due partly to the self-perceptions of those concerned: people working in organizations where politics is particularly important or visible regard their own organizations as inefficient, while those who work in organizations that put more emphasis on action see them as efficient (or if they are not, they can easily be made so). These convictions seem to have strong roots; when things were going badly for much European industry at the end of the 1970s, the blame was in many countries attributed to world depression and the price of oil rather than to any weakness in corporate production and marketing. The great subject of discussion was instead how to make the public administration more effective, smaller and cheaper as befitted a stagnating economy, so that it would be possible to regain the financial equilibrium which had been undermined by grants to unsuccessful companies.

Outputs—Talk, Decisions and Products

What, then, are the outputs of the political organization? It clearly has great difficulty in generating products that call for organized action. On all the points mentioned above, the political organization reveals qualities that are the direct opposite of those in the action organization, and which are necessary if the organization is to be good at generating action. But there are other products which require very little coordinated action, for instance when the organization pays money to external groups.

Further, an organization's production and promotion activities need not be limited to physical products; organizations can also produce and promote ideologies. The political organization tends to give a good deal of attention to producing and promoting ideology. One of the ideological outputs of organizations is *talk*. The political organization sets great store by what it says, orally or in writing. Talk, in the broader sense of the spoken or written word, is produced not only for internal purposes but also and more importantly for the environment. Another output consists of *decisions*. Decisions are a form of talk important enough to warrant classification as a separate category. The political organization makes decisions which it is then anxious to demonstrate clearly to the outside world. A parliament or a local council does very little other than talk and make decisions.

Thus talk, decisions and physical products can all be used to reflect inconsistent norms in the environment. Organizations can sometimes try to meet inconsistent norms by way of inconsistent products, for instance by producing actions to meet different demands sequentially over time (Cyert and March 1963), or by letting special units in isolation specialize in producing different actions. Organizations may also reflect inconsistent norms in talk and decisions. This is what I have called double standards or double talk in Chapter 1. Double talk is particularly popular in the political organization because inconsistent ideas can often be reflected more easily by way of ideology than by way of products. To supply products that satisfy conflicting demands is generally difficult and almost always expensive. Particularly when money is in short supply, the political organization can be expected to rely even more than usual on inconsistencies in talk and decisions as its way of reflecting inconsistencies in the environment. To talk inconsistently is not difficult; it is a natural output of the political organization whose members base their talk on different ideologies. Nor is it particularly difficult to make inconsistent decisions, at least so long as the decisions are not implemented, as is by no means always necessary.

Organizational Hypocrisy

Talk, decisions and products are mutually independent instruments used by the political organization in winning legitimacy and support from the environment. In the action organization talk and decisions are instruments for coordinating action which leads to products. Thus talk, decisions and products tend to be consistent. In the political organization the talk, decisions and actions do not have to be connected in this way. On the contrary we can expect to find inconsistencies between them: in order to reflect inconsistencies in the environment the political organization can employ inconsistencies, not only within the separate areas of talk or decisions or products but also between them. In other words hypocrisy is a fundamental type of behaviour in the political organization: to talk in a way that satisfies one demand, to decide in a way that satisfies another, and to supply products in a way that satisfies a third.

It is easy to find examples of organizational hypocrisy. Let us take some examples from national government policy in various different countries. When a Swedish referendum on nuclear energy was held in 1980, people had to choose between two identical alternatives and one different one. A decision in favour of either of the first two alternatives would mean deciding to discontinue nuclear energy 25 years later, but doubling the nuclear capacity over the next few years. In other words the idea was to discontinue nuclear energy by decision, and to expand it in actual production. In this way the widespread belief that more electric power was needed as well as the equally widespread fear that nuclear energy is dangerous, were both efficiently reflected. It is not surprising that these alternatives triumphed over the third one, in which decisions and products were consistent, i.e. it was proposed both that a decision should be made to close down the nuclear power stations now, and that action should actually be taken to implement the decision. Of course Swedes didn't want dangerous nuclear energy, but how were they to acquire more current? It is also significant that there was no alternative in which decision and product were consistent in the other direction, although some politicians personally believed that nuclear energy was harmless, but here a strong awareness of the need for inconsistency seems to have come into the picture.

Action takes place in the here and now, while talk and decisions are often associated with the future, particularly if they are to be inconsistent with existing production. Thus the future can be exploited to compensate particular interests for an absence of production, or for products which favour other interests. Nuclear power, for example, was to be discontinued at a date 25 years from now. When the Swedish state was really short of money during the 1980s, the government appointed a special Minister for the Future, i.e. a minister who by definition should engage not in action but in ideology. A demand for an increase in child benefit was difficult to satisfy with money; instead in the course of a few critical years the government arranged a series of conferences on the situation of families and promised publication of a book on the same subject.

It is a common observation that liberal governments can introduce changes that are more socialistic than any measures of a socialist government, and vice versa. The most extensive socialization of Swedish industry in the post-war era occurred during the brief period when the liberal parties rather than the socialists were in power. In Britain during the 1980s a government much given to extreme right-wing rhetoric has spent unprecedented sums on social welfare. The American president who re-established diplomatic relations with communist China was known for his firm anti-communist stance. All these cases can be explained by the fact that it is easier to be inconsistent between ideology and action than to be consistent. Liberal governments can compensate for socialization by talking about the 'free economy' and 'free markets' and possibly even by making decisions on such questions. Socialist governments can compensate for real tax reductions which favour high income-earners or a restrictive wage policy by talking and making decisions about helping low wage-earners and the working class in general.

In the autumn of 1987 Volvo suffered a scandal. The company's transport department publicly announced its intention of transporting car bodies between some of its plants in western Sweden by road rather than rail, which meant that a few more trees would die of air pollution. Criticism of the statement on the part of the Volvo management and the business press was harsh: the statement, it was pointed out, was both stupid and inappropriate. Management declared that operational staff should not make public announcements of this kind; it was management's job to present the company and its plans to the outside world. Management also pointed out that Volvo was very environmentally aware. Over the next few months full-page spreads in the press advertised the company's concern for environmental issues and the large sums of money it had spent on the environment. But nobody denied the facts of the case, namely that the car bodies were going to be transported by road. What was being demonstrated was management's intentions, which were particularly important of course when the actions of the operative units conflicted with them and—what was worse—had come to the knowledge of the general public.

There seems to be a good deal of hypocrisy at the societal level as well. Major material changes in societies tend to take place in areas about which there is little public debate while situations that are much discussed tend not to change (Edelman 1971). Talk seems to make action less needed.

Inconsistencies in the outputs of organizations reflect inconsistencies in the environment and can therefore help to establish the legitimacy of the organizations. This does not necessarily mean, though, that double talk and hypocrisy are the result of a conscious tactic adopted by individuals, groups, parties, managements or ruling majorities. It may simply mean that individual people in an organization do have inconsistent values, interests and ideas, and that this sometimes affects their actions without there being any conspiratorial intention. When we remember just how inconsistent we are—we, who constitute their environment and whom some of them are supposed to represent—this is not a particularly surprising idea. Even if their personal inconsistency is subjected to the standardizing influence of suborganizations such as parties and departments, it is not unlikely that it will sometimes break out.

But double talk and hypocrisy are also a natural result of interactions between representatives of the diverse interests and ideas reflected by the organization. Inconsistencies in talk arise just because each person speaks for his or her own interests and ideas. Inconsistencies in decisions and production may be the result of compromises, whereby the demands of each side are partially, but only partially, fulfilled. Further: talk, decisions and production may be inconsistent with one another, since different groups take part in them at different times, and their strength and external situations can also vary on the different occasions. Also, talk and decisions may be an expression of wishful thinking, and production an expression of what is feasible.

Inconsistencies in talk, decisions and products can also arise as a result of organizational differentiation and independence. Different units in the organization can be expected to talk, decide and produce independently of one another and therefore with mutual inconsistency. The sales department has different interests from the production department, the social welfare board works for interests and ideas that are different from those of the technical office or the street maintenance board, the board for consumer polices has interests different from those of the department of agriculture, etc. (Lawrence and Lorsch 1967).

The fact that most inconsistencies probably arise from interactions between individuals, parties, departments, etc. whose behaviour is otherwise reasonably consistent is probably important to organizational legitimacy. Conscious or planned inconsistencies may easily be interpreted as conspiracy, manipulation or dishonesty. This applies particularly to hypocrisy. The environment can certainly be very exacting: demanding inconsistencies but not planned inconsistencies, demanding organizational inconsistency but not personal or suborganizational inconsistency. Organizational leaders in both government and business often spend a lot of time explaining that their personal behaviour has been consistent even though the overall result of the organization may not be. They do this by showing either that their decisions have actually been the same throughout, or that the external situation has altered in such a way that their consistent adherence to the same interest has given rise to apparently inconsistent utterances, decisions or products. It seems to be a strong article of faith that politicians and other organizational leaders should not have been wrong, i.e. they should not be inconsistent over time.

Politics

This description of the ideal type of the political organization suggests that certain structures, processes and ideologies which organizations display to their environment and which represent dissolution and disintegration within the organization are particularly appropriate to the reflection of inconsistent norms. The kind of organizational structures, processes and ideologies and the relationships between them, which together have been described here as constituting the political organization, will be subsumed below under the designations 'politics' and 'political'.

'Politics' generally refers to the handling of conflicting interests, and in this respect I use the term in its traditional sense. The terms 'politics' and 'political' are often also used to describe a special way of handling conflicting interests, or rather a special perspective on the way they are handled, namely that different groups with diverging interests interact with one another in various processes—bargaining, sabre-rattling, blackmailing, etc. Each group acts in its own interest, and the result of the interaction between them is a certain distribution of resources, advantages, or power. It is a sort of politics by exchange.

The perspective I bring to bear on politics here is slightly different, since I focus on the way in which the individual organization can handle different interests within its own body. This may involve interaction between various special-interest groups within the organization, but regardless of the way things are handled 'politics' means that the organization as a whole reflects many conflicting interests. It wins legitimacy and acquires resources not by fighting for a single interest but by associating itself with several interests and demonstrating their incorporation into its own being. The organization justifies itself as a vehicle for the reflection of these multiple interests. This is politics by justification rather than by exchange.

ORGANIZATIONS IN THE REAL WORLD—
POLITICS AND ACTION

So far I have distinguished between two ideal types of organization: one which relies solely on organized action for ensuring the support of the environment, and one whose legitimacy is based solely on its reflection of inconsistencies. They differ sharply from one another. Organized action calls for coordination, integration and uniformity, qualities which will imbue organizational structures, processes and outputs. The reflection of inconsistencies calls for politics: for dissolution, disintegration, isolation and variety in structures, processes and outputs. Obviously both descriptive and normative theories about political organization must conflict in fundamental respects with theories about organizing for action. But both kinds of theory are necessary to an understanding of real-world organizations, in which both action and politics are important.

How, then, do real-world organizations compare with the ideal types? Although there are no organizations which agree fully with the ideal types, there are certainly some which come close to them. National parliaments approach the ideal political type. Parliaments almost exclusively produce talk and decisions. They practically never take action; they may perhaps undertake one or two study trips, but such things are generally regarded as marginal or even unnecessary. Inconsistent values are cultivated and demonstrated, in that members are recruited according to the principle of conflict; different ideologies are produced and elaborated; rationalistic decision processes are used to reach decisions, and discussion often touches upon difficult or even insoluble problems in the surrounding world. An example of an organization which would come pretty close to the ideal action type would be a factory in a big corporation, where the corporation management handles most of the factory's dealings with banks, customers, trade unions and politicians, and corporate management evaluates the factory solely in terms of its ability to produce certain specified products cheaply.

Both these examples refer to units which could be described as suborganizations in a larger one: parliament is part of the state, and the factory is part of a corporation. There is no coincidence about this; the kind of units which are generally regarded as whole organizations generally have a dual basis for their legitimacy, both politics *and* action. It is expected that they should reflect a variety of values and that they should run reasonably efficient operations. For example, a municipality is not only supposed to demonstrate conflict; it is also expected to build towns, a task which calls for a great deal of coordination both within and between different organizational units as well as over long periods of time.

Both state and municipalities have long experience of basing their legitimacy on a combination of action and politics. Business companies have long experience of basing their legitimacy very strongly on action. But in modern societies, as was noted in Chapter 1, the ability to handle inconsistent norms is becoming an increasingly vital skill for companies as well.

If we could create, manage, and work in organizations which legitimized themselves exclusively by politics *or* action, it would in a sense be simple: each base has its own fairly special clear-cut requirements as regards organizational structure and processes. And if our exclusive base is action, we can also enjoy an abundance of books and articles, all telling us just what we ought to do to produce organizational action efficiently without considering politics.

But in real organizations which have to reflect inconsistent norms as well as producing action, things are more complicated. As we have seen, diametrically opposite structures and processes are required by an organization which is expected to be good at acting and another which has to be good at reflecting inconsistencies. The double basis for legitimacy presents the organizations with a dilemma. If they try to satisfy one legitimation base, they will mismanage the other. The demand for action requires an integrative structure; the demand for politics requires dissolution. This is a genuine dilemma, an insoluble problem. It is not possible to be good at both politics and action. It is not possible to solve the problem, only to handle it.

The basic method for handling these conflicting demands is to separate and isolate politics and action, to 'decouple' them, in the terminology of Weick (1969). There are four ways in which organizations can separate action from politics: chronologically, by subject matter, in different environments, and in different organizational units. In the following pages I will describe these four methods and illustrate them with a few examples mainly from local authorities—organizations which are particularly experienced and skilful at handling simultaneous demands for politics and action.

Separation in Time

The separation of politics and action in time means that the organization responds to the demand for politics at certain periods and to the demand for action at others. During the political periods the organization becomes an arena for the public demonstration of conflict between individuals, parties or other kinds of group. The organization's ideologies are clearly inconsistent. There is no common consistent ideology on which to base decisions and action. Instead, the inconsistencies in ideas and values among organizational members are strong and clearly displayed, perhaps in debates and votes. It is important to discuss problems. All this means that the organizations can reflect and display a broad spectrum of environmental values. But the ability to produce organizational action is slight. Talk and decisions replace action.

At other times the organization responds to demands for action. Disagreement is repressed if it threatens to interfere with organizational action. The organization tries to maintain a consistent common ideology, to be able to reach agreement. There is more willingness to compromise. The organization seeks solutions. It becomes clever at taking action, but poor at reflecting inconsistencies.

In the next chapter I shall describe the experience of Runtown, a municipality which adopted this method. During the 1970s Runtown lived through successive cycles from periods of high integration with little politics and energetic action to periods of advanced dissolution with a lot of politics and an inability to act. Similar cycles are easy to spot at the national level as well. During election campaigns politicians usually exhibit an extremely high level of conflict, and a whole series of real or fictitious conflicts are loudly displayed. After the election it is time to act, and there is then a lot of talk about 'reconciliation' or government declarations about 'the interest of the country as a whole'. After the election, coalition governments are often formed to produce strong majorities. Before elections coalitions are often dissolved, which of course makes it easier to reflect and demonstrate conflicts during the campaign. Similarly, companies can concentrate on action when the demand for their products is strong, but when demand is weak they often turn to the state for subsidies and try to prove that apart from their physical products they stand for other values such as employment and knowledge as well.

Recently Swedish municipalities have been passing through cycles at roughly ten-year intervals, during which time they swing from integration to dissolution and back again. During the 1960s most municipalities were small; local politicians argued that they were working for the interest of the whole municipality, and party politics were weak or non-existent. In the large municipalities there was a spirit of cooperation between the parties. This was a situation that favoured the solution of what many people saw as the major urban problem, namely the urgent need to abolish the housing shortage as quickly as possible. The municipalities were able to maintain their action-oriented legitimation base but were criticized for mismanaging the political side. There were complaints about all the 'secret goings-on' and the 'rule of the moguls', and demands that real political differences should be brought out into the open. The result was more party politics and majority rule in most municipalities. This process of politicization was probably reinforced by the big municipal mergers that led to conflict between different parts of the same municipality and made politics more abstract; this further emphasized the conflicts and reinforced the ideologies. During the 1980s, when the economic climate has become harsher, the municipalities are being criticized for 'party-political bickering' and politicians are held in contempt. Decentralization to small and more coherent districts within the municipality has become popular. Demands are being made for greater efficiency. The model is no longer parliament, but idealized images of business companies in the manufacturing and service industries.

Separation by Topic

Politics and action can also be separated into different topics or issues. Some issues are used for conducting politics, others in an attempt to produce action. Some issues require little or no organizational action, which makes it easier to proceed in the political mode. This often applies to redistribution questions, for example, i.e. how much money should be paid in subsidies to different groups: monetary disbursements are simple to carry out and can generally be initiated quite easily by a majority decision. But a lot of politics can be made out of deciding the size of the sums. In other cases, the interest in generating action may be non-existent or at any rate very weak, so that politics can easily be made of them.

While some issues can be used for politics, others lend themselves to a stronger action orientation. Such an orientation is appropriate when action is greatly desired but is also organizationally difficult and complicated. Town planning is an example of this: there is generally a strong desire to reach agreement, and conflict can seriously jeopardize any chance of realizing the plans (Sahlin-Andersson 1986). For companies it is easier to allow union influence in discussion on wages than in discussions on how production shall be organized.

Separation by Environments

The organization can also opt for politics or action, depending on the environment with which it is interacting. When local authorities have to deal with other organizations such as industrial companies, they usually create special industrial committees whose meetings and discussions are held behind closed doors, and conflict is repressed. Such measures are necessary if the local authority is not to undermine its own bargaining position. Small countries try to reach internal agreement on their foreign policy. But when it is a question of dealing with something as disorganized as the electorate, then it is possible to act in a more disintegrated way. If the electorate organizes itself into village communities, lobbies, or occupation forces, then the politicians also tend to organize themselves, i.e. becoming more united and less political.

Separation by Organizational Units

Lastly, politics and action can be separated organizationally: some units can respond to political demands and are organized in such a way as to resemble the ideal political type, while other units can respond to demands for action and are organized in a way that closely resembles the ideal type of the action organization. Municipalities and the state typically possess a number of variously politicized suborganizations. As we have seen, parliaments and local councils are strongly political units which produce talk and decisions in public arenas. Governments and committees hold closed meetings and are more action-oriented.

The organization can also be divided into one part run by politicians and one part run by the administration. Politicians are recruited according to the principle of conflict, while administrative officials are recruited according to the principle of unity. In other organizations boards can be politically composed, while management and production departments are based on the idea of unity. In this way the organization as a whole can respond to demands for both politics and action—so long as the two units really are isolated from one another. If the politicians' or the board's decisions are not followed by the corresponding administrative actions, for example, then the top level's reflecting function will be all the simpler, since isolation favours inconsistent decisions. If the actions of the administration are independent of the debates and decisions at the top, and are chosen instead according to the administration's own preferences, it will be all the easier to implement them.

The political and administrative dichotomy becomes more problematic if the organization tries to link the political and administrative suborganizations together, i.e. if the decisions of the political unit are to be made consistent with the actions of the action unit, or vice versa. This problem arises when it is claimed that the decisions of the leadership should steer administrative action—which is not an unusual idea.

Naturally these four ways of separating politics from action are not mutually exclusive. Most organizations can be expected to use more than one or even all the methods, although the emphasis may be different in different organizations. In the following chapters I shall describe what forms the methods take in practice, how they arise, and what their possible consequences may be.

POLITICS IN ORGANIZATIONAL PROCESSES

In this chapter I have described in theoretical terms how organizations handle inconsistent norms with the help of various measures which I have subsumed under the designation 'politics', and how politics conflicts with demands for effective organizational action. In the next five chapters I will describe political aspects of organizations in more detail.

In the next chapter I will discuss how the political aspects of organizations actually arise, and what dynamic forces are involved. It will be seen that organization members have great difficulty in controlling the extent to which they display political behaviour.

Decisions are fundamental to organizations in which politics play an important part. Decisions unite or separate talk and action, leaders and led. In Chapters 4 and 5 I shall examine the design and nature of decisions in control processes. Decisions as a form of control are best suited to the kind of control imposed by the led on the leaders, to the adaptation of ideology to action. Decisions will be more concerned with *responsibility* than with influence. Responsibility is important for organizational leadership as well as for organizational legitimacy. The concept of responsibility will be elaborated and its importance to an understanding of organizational processes will be described in Chapters 4 to 7.

Politics in organizations involves an openness to external demands. Organizations are dependent on reflecting these demands but it may also be important for them to control the way in which this reflection is to be achieved. In Chapters 6 and 7 I will discuss how open organizations can actively handle external demands.

The argument in this book conflicts sharply with the many rational models of organizations. It also has implications for our understanding of organizational decision-making. Both these themes will be elaborated in Chapter 8. I will also describe hypocrisy in operation at a different level from the one discussed hitherto: organizations tend to present themselves in a way that is inconsistent with the way in which they function. This is one of the themes in Chapter 9, where I shall also discuss the spread of political behaviour in modern organizations. Finally I shall look at the implications of politics for the internal or external stakeholders who want to affect and control organizations.

3
Politics in Practice

In the previous chapter the basic characteristics of what I have called the political organization were described from the outside. The emphasis was on political behaviour as it is evident to external observers—behaviour which can thus explain how such organizations win external support. The explanations suggested were largely functional rather than causal, in other words related to the results rather than the causes of the behaviour. Thus if conflict, depression and hypocrisy succeed in evoking the support of the environment while the opposite behaviour does not, then we are likely to find a certain measure of such characteristics in the organizations that have survived. It may be possible to combine this functional explanation with a causal one. If we assume that individual actors seek to ensure the survival of their organizations, and that they believe this kind of behaviour favours survival and, further, that they are in a position to pursue it, then we also have a causal explanation as to why organizations do act in such a way. We are basing our explanation on people's intentions, and these intentions are concerned with the survival of the organization rather than with other more personal interests on the part of those involved. We could call this special kind of causal explanation a strategic explanation.

Presumably strategic explanations do sometimes represent reasonable reflections of reality. But politics by itself tends to make such explanations less useful. Politics implies that organizations are relatively loose-knit, with their leading actors representing external groups rather than the organizations themselves;

moreover the emphasis will be on conflicts between the various actors rather than on any kind of common organizational goals. There is an endemic shortage of people prepared to put the survival of the organization first. And even if there were any such people, the conflict structure would make it difficult for them to realize their intentions. Finally, it seems that the nature of politics is little understood by organization members; in the cases I studied, the actors commonly assumed that their organizations fitted the action model. In view of all the theories devoted to the action model this is hardly surprising, but it naturally caused both confusion and frustration.

However, there are other causal explanations that do not come under the strategic heading. The behaviour of the organization may be the result of many people's individual efforts to influence either their own situation or that of some external group. Various individuals may each be trying to steer the behaviour of the organization as a whole in a particular direction, perhaps in order to promote their own specific goals, but the overall result of their disparate efforts may be a type of organizational behaviour that no single person intended. For example, we can assume that certain political aspects of an organization, such as its inconsistent environment, its conflict structure, its problem orientation and the hypocrisy it practices, will all affect and reinforce one another. Although this is an important argument to which I will return in Chapter 9, as an explanation it remains on a structural rather than a process level. In this and the four following chapters I shall instead describe some organizational processes in which the various political characteristics are produced and maintained.

I shall also be approaching the issues from a slightly different angle than before. The discussion below will be based on a number of fairly detailed empirical descriptions of real-life organizational processes. Such an approach has several advantages. For understanding the argument of the book it is necessary to look behind the official façades of organizations and describe processes that are part neither of these façades nor of popular descriptions from external observers. The empirical descriptions also make it easier to see how the theoretical concepts have been generated, and how they can be used to analyse real-life situations and events in organizations. Moreover a discussion based on descriptions of real cases can morè easily capture the typical complexity of organizational processes.

Most of the case studies that will be used in these chapters concern Swedish local authorities. The reader may think that these are a rather special kind of organization. And—like all organizations—they do of course have some characteristics specific to themselves as well as many others which are common to a great many organizations. I have chosen them here, however, because many of the characteristics they exhibit are of special interest to the theme of this book.

If we are interested in how organizations cope with inconsistent demands, then we do well to study some organizations which are exposed to such demands and which are used to handling them. And if we are interested in learning how the situation can be handled successfully, we do well to study successful organizations—organizations whose legitimacy has not been undermined by their exposure to inconsistent norms. Swedish local authorities represent a type of organization which has long experience of handling inconsistencies and which has still managed to maintain a remarkably high degree of legitimacy. They are independent organizations, formally disconnected from the state, having their own elected politicians and a right of their own to charge taxes of any size on the inhabitants' personal incomes. They are the producers of an extensive range of public services from housing and road construction and maintenance to the care of children and the elderly. In Sweden as in many other countries local authorities have been growing rapidly over recent decades; altogether Swedish municipalities employed more than 660 000 people in 1986 as compared with less than 100 000 in 1950. Their revenues have increased at a similar rate; in addition to fees for services, they raise taxes amounting on an average to 30% on personal incomes. And all this has been achieved without protest or rebellion of any significance; in fact groups favouring higher taxes have sometimes been more popular than others. Furthermore, local authorities are interesting in the present context because they are used to being exposed to inconsistent demands in their environment, but also because they are actively engaged in exploiting them, while managing simultaneously to produce plenty of organizational action.

Inconsistencies, together with the problems they cause and the way they are handled, are all perfectly visible in these organizations. By studying them we can find a basis for understanding the same phenomena in other organizations where the inconsistent demands are not equally obvious or predominant, or where there has been less experience of handling them, or where they have not been handled successfully enough for the organization to survive. Private companies in modern societies have a great deal to learn from local and national governments, and are in fact learning from them, trying to imitate many of the methods which these organizations have long been using in the handling of inconsistencies.

In the present chapter I shall illustrate several kinds of political behaviour and look at the different ways in which they have arisen, by examining an organization with pronounced political features over a ten-year period. In particular this case helps to illustrate how different political characteristics reinforce each other and how political behaviour may arise unintentionally as the result of organizational members striving for action rather than politics.

ATTEMPTS AT ACTION PRODUCE POLITICS

Runtown is a small municipality in southern Sweden consisting of a central place and several outlying communities. The municipality employs about 600 people; 49 local politicians make up the municipal council. Runtown is the result of a merger of two former municipalities in 1970. It has a population of about 10 000.

Throughout the 1970s the municipality alternated between periods of some action orientation and periods of a markedly political nature. Short periods during which leading politicians were largely in agreement and the organization was energetic in producing action were succeeded by long periods of sharp conflict and an inability to act. During the political periods the organization as such tended to disintegrate: it acquired such a strong element of conflict and debate, and its capacity for action was so reduced, that it seemed more like an arena for the operations of individuals and parties than an organization in the usual sense. In the periods of action the actors were more successful in sticking together and in getting things done.

At the beginning of the 1970s the general situation of the

municipality was perceived as very threatening, and this could only be handled by a reasonably united organization. But dissatisfaction with the internal situation soon made itself felt, and not long after an election in 1973 the disintegrative political tendencies became stronger. The political behaviour culminated in 1976, when the organization more or less collapsed with the departure of several leading administrators. Once again the pendulum swung back, and during the autumn of 1976 and the spring of 1977 Runtown was once again characterized by unity and a belief among the actors that together they could cope with the problems. But the political processes again became more powerful, culminating during 1978 and 1979. Let us look more closely at how these alternations and the highly political states came about.

From Agreement to Disagreement

In the two smaller municipalities which were merged to create Runtown in 1970, the municipal administration had been a modest affair. Municipal operations had not been generalized to a great many areas, and the politicians dealt with several practical matters themselves without any help from administrators. Some activities which later became important municipal concerns were still being handled by the main local companies, which owned a lot of land. The companies thus planned and managed most housing construction, and they administered residential property. Local politics were characterized by broad agreement across party boundaries; the municipalities were run by an informal coalition between Socialists and Conservatives in happy collaboration with the big companies.

The capacity for action was considerable. This was demonstrated in an employment crisis. A few years before the merger one of the large companies was closed down. The municipality managed to get state support for emergency employment schemes on a scale that, for the times, was quite unique. It also launched an innovation—a successful publicity campaign to attract new companies to the area with the promise of cheap premises subsidized by the municipality. The campaign was successful; new companies moved in.

The merger of the two municipalities made it more difficult to act in unison. Furthermore the merger coincided with a move towards much more 'generalization', whereby an increasing number of functions came to be regarded as local government responsibility. The new municipality felt compelled to increase its administrative staff. On the political front the Socialist bloc and Centre-Right bloc, consisting of the Conservatives and the Agrarian Party, enjoyed roughly equal strength. The balance between them was held by two small local parties. After the merger the political conflicts acquired a new dimension; the politicians no longer saw themselves simply as representatives of different parties, but also as representatives of different communities. A coalition government of the former kind was now considered impossible or at least inappropriate. The Centre-Right bloc appointed the chairman of the executive committee, and formed a fragile majority with some support from the two small parties of the middle ground.

The new municipality was created just as a further employment crisis broke. Two of the new companies closed down their local plants and the situation called for strong municipal action, which in turn engendered a spirit of internal agreement and cooperation. Once again the municipality tried to attract new business into the area. This time, however, things moved more slowly, and the campaign dragged on for a long time.

The agreement on location policy, established immediately after the merger, soon gave way to disagreement over various important internal problems. Investment was urgently needed in new and better installations for water and sewage, and in new schools and administrative offices. One major source of conflict concerned the choice of area for a planned expansion of the central place. Before the merger the politicians in one of the old municipalities had agreed that certain areas were to be built. This decision was not accepted by the new majority in the merged municipality. Instead the administration was instructed to investigate two options. The question remained unsolved for nine years. The time was spent on extensive investigations, lively debates and squabbling. The long uncertainty also made it very difficult to implement parts of the investment programme during this period: nobody knew where new investment would be appropriate or where repairs were called for.

More Action Wanted—Less Action Achieved

The 1973 election resulted in much the same balance between the political parties. The municipal leadership again faced a number of new tasks. The water supply was now so inadequate that some areas suffered acute water shortages during the summer. The sewage system could not cope with peak loads. Many school buildings were substandard, and the standard of recreational facilities and equipment was also poor. The local government offices had been condemned by the public health authorities, and the state was demanding that new day nurseries be built.

Despite all these urgent calls for action, the municipality found it hard to get anything done at all. Everyone could agree that action was needed, but not exactly what should be done or in what order. It was easier to reach agreement in the executive committee than in the municipal council. Quite often the same people who voted for a proposal in the committee would vote against it when it came up before the council—which generally meant that the proposal was rejected there. As well as having an inhibiting effect on action, this behaviour caused a lot of irritation and confusion.

The only action on which leading politicians and administrators could agree concerned action aimed at the world outside. They appealed to the state again, calling for a new system of state grants that would favour the municipality. They also continued to pursue an active location policy, trying to persuade more business to establish in the area. Neither of these efforts were successful, which in the second case was hardly surprising: the advantages that could be offered to industry in the area were now far less than before, if they existed at all. Not only was there a shortage of labour and of homes for those who might move into the area, but it was also uncertain whether there was any land available for industry as the area for expansion had still not been fixed.

This situation caused deep dissatisfaction among both politicians and administrators. People began to feel that perhaps something was wrong with their own organization, which could explain why nothing was done about the internal difficulties, and why no results were achieved from attempts to tackle the external problems. Towards the end of the mandate period two attempts were made to change the internal situation: an organizational reform was considered and an attempt was made to introduce long-term economic planning. Both failed. Let us take a closer look at one of them, namely the attempt at organizational reform. It provides a good illustration of the difficulties that impeded top management's efforts to bring about some action.

An Attempt at Reform

The idea of an organizational reform came first from the administrators, who were generally dissatisfied with the way the municipal leadership was working. It was felt that top management should delegate more, and that there should be some general political guidelines regarding operational objectives. Furthermore, many administrative routines led to a lot of duplicated work.

A number of the leading politicians were also dissatisfied. They were pretty sceptical about the administrators. There were accusations of inexperience and inefficiency. Ever since the new administrators had been appointed, the politicians had felt remote from practical action, and they were dissatisfied with the information they received from the top administrators about what was happening.

The budget applications from the administration in 1975 included requests for a great many new posts which would cost the municipality a lot of money. This made it easy for the politicians to agree on the launching of reviews which were to consider how to organize the politicians as well as the administrators. For the first task, however, no money was granted, and only the work of reviewing the administration was ever officially launched.

In order to tackle the organization of the politicians as well, the Conservative and Social Democrat members of the executive committee began to work on their own. They worked out a recommendation for a new organization for the politicians. This would mean dividing the functions of the present executive committee between three committees, so that more members of the present committee would be able to help to prepare reports, which would give them a better overall view and understanding of the various issues. The present chairman would head only one of the new committees. When the recommendation was put before the working group of the executive committee, the chairman, his

Agrarian party colleagues, the administrative manager and several other administrators all reacted violently. The suggestion was interpreted as a personal attack on the chairman and the administrative manager.

In April 1976 the consultant who had been hired as investigator submitted his report. It was sent to the local government office, and was then passed on by the research officer to the members of the executive committee and representatives of the staff unions. The Conservative and Social Democrat members objected strongly to this procedure. They composed an official protest in which they claimed that until the executive committee had seen the report and made a decision on it, 'there was no recommendation for the staff to react to'. They also demanded that the oral presentation of the report should be cancelled.

However, the report was presented orally a few weeks later. Some changes in routines were recommended, and it was proposed that the administrative manager should be given more coordinating functions. The Conservatives and Social Democrats were dissatisfied both with some of the main proposals and with the investigator's general confidence in the administrators.

The report was sent for further analysis to the 'steering group' which had been appointed to lead the investigation. The proposal for a new political organization was also submitted to this group. Both were sent out for comment to political parties, administrative units and staff unions. Not until October 1976 was the steering group able to meet, and then all it did was to recommend that one new post should be created.

The organizational recommendations were overshadowed by the protest, which was discussed countless times in the executive committee during the spring. The members of the Agrarian party moved that the protest be put before the council, where they were sure it would be voted down and they would be proved right. Those who had formulated the protest were no longer interested in it—it was no longer relevant—and they moved that it should be dismissed and no action taken. In August it was at last discussed at a meeting of the council, where the protesters won the vote. The chairman of the executive committee resigned, on the grounds that he no longer commanded a majority in the council.

By now most of the municipality's leading administrators had also resigned, one of their main reasons being their dissatisfaction with the events connected with the organizational review. During the autumn and winter the five chief administrators all left the municipality.

Developments in Runtown thus far show clearly that political characteristics do not necessarily become strong as a result of conscious efforts. Leading politicians and administrators were striving throughout this period to achieve some action, but the result was the opposite. The explanation is to be found in the political aspects themselves—they reinforce each other: particularly important in this case were the conflict structure, the fact that talk and decisions often became independent outputs and the presence of ideological inconsistencies that made it difficult to form a common ideology. Let us look at these factors in somewhat greater detail.

The Conflict Structure

Runtown's organizational structure was based on conflict. The leaders of a municipality are meant to represent the various shades of opinion obtaining in the local population. In Runtown there was conflict not only between political parties but also between representatives of the different communities. Because of these powerful conflicts most decisions were reached only by a bare majority and after much debate, during which the negative effects of the decisions would have received an emphatic airing. And even then the decisions could be changed later, often because individual actors or parties voted differently on different occasions.

This meant that the administrators, whose job was to carry out the various actions, felt they had little support from the decision-making politicians. Besides, it was difficult to feel much commitment to the measures decided, when there was no guarantee that the decisions might not be changed later. And in the case of any long-term action, the risk of a decision being changed was of course even greater, since new elections could mean that new decision-makers came into power.

Since the composition of the ruling majority was always an uncertain factor, conflict was all too likely to result in inconsistent action in the end. It was often impossible to decide on an action at one go; instead it could be the result of a chain of decisions, some of which were never actually adopted. Furthermore, the opposition might succeed in pushing through some decision that contradicted an earlier one. There was then little likelihood of the particular action ever being carried out in its entirety. This is what happened to the organizational review, which achieved a single concrete result, namely one new appointment.

There was thus a good deal of acute conflict, even though people were actively seeking to contain it in certain cases or at certain times, or in some suborganizations. But their attempts were counterbalanced by the fact that on other occasions the same people were actually expected to demonstrate conflicting opinions. This made it difficult to act, since few actions were independent of other issues in this way, few could be carried out quickly, and few could be handled by a single suborganization. On the contrary the handling of many actions lasted through several periods with swings between an action orientation and a political orientation; they were also often handled by several different suborganizations, some more oriented towards action than others; at the same time these actions were intimately related to a variety of other issues. The difficulty in achieving action resulted in hypocrisy, i.e. in talk and decisions that did not correspond to any action.

Talk and Decisions as Independent Outputs

The Runtown organization obviously found it much easier to talk and to make decisions than to act. Decisions were taken on countless important questions; contradictory decisions were adopted, so that a decision to do something did not stop a decision being taken *not* to do the same thing. This was possible because the decisions were not necessarily followed by action; the constraints of action did not have to hamper either decision-making or talk. The freedom thus attaching to decisions and talk made the politicians' work easier: they did not have to spoil the organization's image by saying 'no' to proposals for action, when such action was required. Hypocrisy was not only the result of the difficulty in achieving action but was also reinforced by other factors.

One reason for the presence of so much hypocrisy was the role that had been forced upon the politicians. Whereas the politicians in the two smaller municipalities had previously been involved in many practical activities, their work now consisted of ideological tasks: arguing and making decisions. Their debates and discussions were supposed to lead to decisions, but once the decisions were made it was the administrators' turn. And so, on many issues and in many areas, they decided to concentrate on their own part of the job; they became more decision-oriented than action-oriented. Furthermore, this proved to be the only sensible alternative in view of the failure of all attempts to get the organization to act. It was much easier to succeed at producing arguments and decisions.

The actors who voted one way in the executive committee and another way in the council had a strong intuitive recognition that some parts of the organization should contribute to action and others to politics. At the closed committee meetings they felt compelled to see that something was achieved and were therefore prepared to compromise with their convictions. At the council meetings which were reported in the local press, it was important to say what they really felt.

Another example of talk and decisions emerging as independent outputs and thus helping to produce hypocrisy was the investment planning conducted during 1976. Up to that point the organization had avoided the problem of setting explicit priorities, i.e. of declaring their willingness to abstain from or to delay certain measures. They had thus been able to talk and decide on many measures, but very little action had ever been achieved. During 1975 the number of essential or at any rate highly desirable large-scale investment projects was increasing. A great many projects, in fact far more than could reasonably be undertaken during the year, were included in the budget for 1976. At the beginning of that year the county employment board insisted that investment projects should be ranked in order of priority. The working group of the executive committee was asked to produce a list of possible priorities, which they did. Projects were classified into three groups according to their urgency. The first and most urgent group consisted of 44 projects representing a total of £14 million, the second contained 11 projects to a total of £1.5 million, and the third 8 projects amounting to £250 000. This list was approved by the working group, while the executive committee said it would 'decide later on the urgency gradings of investment projects planned and decided upon (!)' (my exclamation mark).

The municipal treasurer also drew up a list of the investments which were most needed. This memorandum was reported in the press and all the parties published their support for it. One of its proposals, namely that a youth recreation centre should be built, became an all-party election promise in the election campaign of August and September that year.

After the elections, when the budget was being prepared in November, a new list of priorities was drawn up for major investments, this time ranked from 1 to 7. Everyone agreed it would be financially possible to realize two or three of these only. But the building of the youth recreation centre was placed sixth, and last of all came the building of a warehouse, which had already been decided at a meeting of the executive committee in July 1976. Other projects also included the extension of the water mains to the area where the present water capacity was inadequate and water had to be transported in tank trucks during the summer months. This project was listed fifth out of the seven, but was nonetheless included in the budget resolution for 1977.

While priorities were being listed, decisions were also being made in the executive committee about several investment projects, some of which had not been included in the first priority list at all, or had appeared only in one of the low-priority categories. During the summer of 1976 the public health authorities threatened to close the administrative office building. In July the executive committee decided to build new offices. The office building later proved to be the only major project which was actually started and completed during 1977.

The ranking of these investment projects made for hypocrisy: the organization talked about some investments (projects were included in the lists of priorities and promised in the election campaign); it made decisions about others (in the budget or elsewhere); and in one case it acted (administrative offices were built).

The project which featured most prominently in the election manifestos was later given the lowest priority rating: a project which has been presented in an election campaign has already been largely dealt with; the politicians have gone on record as being keen to do something about it. When priorities were being established a few months later, it was easier to spotlight other projects. Setting priorities was easier the second time round; the first time it seemed necessary to put almost all the projects in the top category, which meant that when the second list was made six months later a great many projects had already been talked about, and it was easier to select one or two to head the list. The projects that were decided on in the meantime, or later in the budget, were not among those that had been given priority. Nor was the only project that was subsequently realized.

This focus on talk and decisions contrasts sharply with other periods and other issues, when the politicians saw action as the important end-result of their work. The question of choosing the location for the expansion of the central place was an issue of this kind. It was so uncertain whether a decision would hold that the politicians themselves postponed it for nine years. Even if there was a majority on every separate occasion favouring a particular location, there was never any guarantee that the majority would survive for the four or five years needed to implement the decision. So no decision was taken until there was reasonable certainty on this count. This was a case in which inconsistent decisions were avoided and consistency between decision and action was sought—which simply meant that it became extremely difficult to make any decision at all.

Striving for Ideological Unity

In order to achieve greater force in action, attempts were made during certain periods to agree on a common conception of the situation and of possible ways of improving it. They were all—politicians and administrators—in the same boat, and it was important to work for the good of the municipality as a whole. They tried to build on a common 'objective ideology', a common set of assumptions and norms that could be used in all their internal discussions. The main thrust of this ideology was a recognition that the situation was certainly difficult, in particular since jobs were in short supply, and a determination to try to 'sell' the municipality to companies which might be persuaded to move in. However, all this agreement had been achieved at the cost of keeping the ideology very simple and vague. It could describe the situation of the municipality in a few limited dimensions; it could suggest a few reasons for the current state of affairs, and it could cite at most one or two factors which might be expected to affect the future. It is easier to agree on a weak ideology like this than on one which is more complex and precise. But because of the same weakness, the ideology was unable to provide a good basis for the joint production of any actions which were not simply repetitions of previous behaviour.

The achievement of a certain measure of ideological unity had also been helped by a strong environment attribution, a propensity to blame the environment: it was not the municipality but the world outside which determined what would happen. Again this made it easier to agree on the chosen ideology, since it did not involve blaming oneself or one's colleagues. People did not have to blame one another when something went wrong, as they would have done in the purely political case. But blaming the environment does not provide a good basis for action either. If crucial determinants lie outside the organization's control, then all the organization can do is to try to foretell the future; it cannot mould it. This environmental attribution explains the feelings of uncertainty about the future, feelings which were largely realistic but which did not provide a good basis for action.

Thus the ideology itself did little to motivate action in general; it made it difficult to mobilize support for specific measures. And, in addition, the ideology then explained why there was very little point in taking actions of one's own.

The unity that was achieved with so much effort also served to conceal the diversity of opinion which did in fact exist. It was thus difficult for people to know what line their colleagues would adopt on the various issues when it came to the crunch. If they had all been better informed on this point, it would have been easier to reach some kind of compromise, or to scotch the frequent rumours about the evil intentions of the adversaries—rumours which were an important part of the 'information' both sides were receiving.

POLITICS AGAIN

Between 1973 and 1976 external crises were succeeded by internal troubles—which did not mean, however, that the external problems had gone away. The 1976 election did not produce any major change in the relative strength of the parties; the small parties still held the balance and the loose non-Socialist coalition had a majority in the executive committee and on the various boards.

There were certain signs that attitudes were changing. At the first meeting of the executive board after the election the former president was elected once more. Many new politicians were elected to important positions in the boards. The leader for the Social Democrats argued that now was the time to make a new start—to 'let bygones be bygones'. There were several new top administrators. Everyone wanted to see a new kind of behaviour and more action.

At the beginning of the period there were even a few results. Although at the beginning of the year all parties but one had expressed keen support for a new organizational structure involving the creation of new committees, a unanimous decision was taken at the end of the same year in favour of the opposite solution: no new committees—a decision which was easy to implement because it meant no change. The new administrators energetically pursued the question of long-range economic planning and eventually persuaded the politicians to agree to a document specifying municipal goals. This, they felt, would put their own operations on a firmer basis, since the politicians would have to become a little less volatile. The politicians had no difficulty in agreeing to these goals, which were expressed in very general terms and seemed unlikely to have much impact on their own activities.

As well as these decisions about goals and organizational structure, work also started on building the new administrative offices. Things moved quickly, and the offices were ready by April 1978. In this case, as in others, the administrators were the real drivers. And finally a decision was reached, after nine years, about the new area which was to be built. Ironically, the decision was to build in exactly the same area as originally planned in 1969.

But the peaceful mood of 1977 was short-lived. By the spring of 1978 it had been succeeded once more by stormy conflict, arising from a desire to produce quick concrete action. One example was the effort made to speed up the housing construction programme.

The building of new homes had been severely delayed due to the continual uncertainty about where to build, and there was now a housing shortage. In discussing the housing construction programme for 1978–1982, people's patience ran out. The opposition demanded that the building start-up in one particular area should be brought forward by a year. After much argument in the executive committee and an extremely lively debate in the council, the opposition's proposal was finally adopted by a large majority, and the council appointed a special unit to ensure that their directives were observed.

Inflamed argument about this decision, and not least about the supervisory unit, continued to infect the atmosphere at several subsequent meetings. The chief effect of all this was that relations between the various political groupings deteriorated, thus further reducing future chances of getting anything done. The supervisory unit was never appointed and the decision was declared illegal by the county administration board.

This was not the only example. In other cases politicians tried to intervene in negotiations with various external organizations, in order to speed up agreement and consequently actions as well. But such interventions not only weakened the municipality's bargaining position; they also increased internal conflict and delayed action even more.

Conflict and the Incapacity to Act

By the early summer of 1978 events of this kind had resulted in acute conflict and mistrust. The various parties involved had little confidence left in one another. The council was highly mistrustful of the executive committee. At council meetings any suggestions critical of the committee's recommendations were almost always approved. The politicians often combined in groups that did not match the election-based composition of the executive committee. The Conservatives agreed more often with the Social Democrats than with the parties of the middle ground who were their 'natural' allies, although at the same time the leading Social Democrats on the committee frequently agreed with the parties of the centre and against the rest of the municipal council. Moreover, regardless of their official party affiliation, politicians from the central place often opposed politicians from other parts of the municipality.

Consequently decisions were often made which would be difficult or even impossible to implement in the way the council intended. Thus many decisions were never put into effect or were delayed by the political bodies who were immediately responsible for their implementation.

As a result many projects were held up; the necessary action simply never occurred. Most of the actors spoke openly of the general incapacity to act and recognized that the municipality was suffering because of it. The situation also triggered a good deal of aggression. People accused one another of creating problems on purpose. The politicians were in acrimonious mood and morale was low. Rumours followed one another thick and fast and conspiracy theory flourished.

The administrators had also begun to form a special-interest group of their own. Unlike their predecessors the new administrators were in broad agreement among themselves. At first, too, most of the new top administrators were fairly satisfied with their work situation. The conflicts among the politicians which came out into the open during the spring of 1978 somewhat spoilt their dawning enthusiasm, although they soon found that the political conflicts did not really stop them getting things done their own way. On the contrary. It had been possible to get the new administrative offices completed very quickly and easily, as well as the clarification of goals. And this last could even be expected to strengthen the position of the administrative corps *vis-à-vis* the politicians. The objectives, formulated in the language of the administrators but approved by the politicians, could imply certain future commitments on the part of the politicians. Some administrators at this time were quite open about their desire for a stronger power base, from which they could promote such changes as they considered were necessary to the good of the municipality.

Nor were the administrators the only ones to be building up their positions. Several external actors were equally busy. Business companies in the area stood to gain since their various demands for housing and so on were always taken up by people who wanted to oppose the municipal leadership. This gave the demands added clout, and encouraged the municipal leaders to meet them as quickly as possible. Up to a point the administrators were using the same mechanism to increase their own power, i.e. their views often won extra support from opponents of the municipal leadership.

Discontent and Conflict

All the actors agreed that they had failed: their efforts to produce action had once more ended in an incapacity to act. They could all see that the conflict had been excessively severe, that the politicians had lost a lot of influence, and that the municipality was not being properly run. Many of them even found it difficult to justify their own behaviour, and admitted it had not been appropriate. Although they knew they were doing the wrong thing, they went on doing it: aggravating the conflict and making it more difficult than ever to act. The conflicts became so acute that it would be difficult to see any positive function in them at all; they had become far stronger than the conflict between the disparate environmental demands they were actually supposed to be reflecting. Developments in Runtown show how difficult it can be to keep conflict at a suitable level. The conflicts became not only unnecessarily acute but also what the actors called 'personal'—they referred not only to different ideas but also to the people standing for those ideas.

Politics and action gradually became organizationally divorced from one another, so that some capacity to act was maintained despite the sharply rising level of conflict among the politicians. This was possible partly because the administrators acquired greater scope for action by demanding that goals be clearly formulated, and partly because like various external actors they were able to exploit the intense politicization for their own ends.

These developments can be explained to a great extent by the powerful inconsistencies that characterized both organizational ideologies and roles. Let us look at these factors in a little more detail.

INCONSISTENCIES IN IDEOLOGIES AND ROLES

The actors in Runtown had now developed a great many clearly inconsistent ideologies. People held inconsistent views about the nature of the situation and about how to tackle it. Politicians from different parties or on different boards, or those living in different parts of the municipality, all had different views. The ideologies were political in the sense that they were characterized by great inconsistency, not only in that different actors had different ideas, but each actor cherished several ideas that were inconsistent with one another.

Ideological Inconsistencies

Over the last few years the common platform consisting of an objective ideology had been gradually undermined. One step had been a growing awareness that some things simply could not be blamed on external forces. Another step was taken when the new administrators suggested that the employment situation was not as terrible as it had seemed. Slowly people began to realize that trying to attract business to the area and appealing to the state for help was not the whole solution to their problems. No new objective ideology emerged to replace the old one. Rather, there was now virtually no common picture of reality to start discussions from.

By now people's private opinions clearly reflected an action perspective *and* a political perspective with respect to the organization. Everyone recognized that politics was important: politicians should disagree, but their disagreement should be based on ideological and political differences; conflict should be between parties, not between people or groups within the parties; there should not be alliances between non-Socialist and Socialists; the job of the opposition was to criticize the majority party or parties. But at the same time the same people also cherished a number of action-oriented beliefs: problems should be solved by consensus; there was no intrinsic value in developing a political profile; and debate should be rational, not 'political'!

Because the actors' ideas about the way the municipal leadership should work were incompatible, it was impossible to develop working routines to satisfy all demands. Thus whatever the routines happened to be at any given moment, people would be dissatisfied with them and frustrated by their own inability to suggest any solution. Almost all routines were open to criticism, and no one could ever reject the criticism as based on faulty grounds. During periods of violent politics, the politicians felt most strongly that they must produce action. During the action-oriented periods they felt a greater urge to demonstrate their own opinions—to 'be political'. Thus both the extreme states of politics and action-orientation gave rise to frustration and to attempts at introducing more of the other state. It was difficult to find stable states, which could be regarded as representing an acceptable mixture of politics and action.

All the leading actors also recognized the many unacceptable elements in the current situation: the in-party conflict, the conflict based on where people happened to live, the alliances between the non-Socialist and Socialist parties, and the 'personal' nature of many conflicts (interperson conflict rather than disagreement on the facts of a case). People were also dissatisfied with their own behaviour; the routines they followed rarely matched their own ideas of the best way to do the work.

But inconsistencies between things as they are and things as we would like them to be do not necessarily deprive us of any ability to act; on the contrary such disagreement should be an incentive to action. The problem here, however, was that the actors badly wanted to change both work routines and the municipality's overall situation (what they worked at and how they did it), and on both counts solutions were difficult to find. This meant that actors were compelled to exploit any attempts at changing the situation as a way of improving procedures, and vice versa. Almost every issue could be perceived as a way of changing the overall situation, or as a way of altering internal procedures. Thus some people saw the proposed organizational reform mainly as a question of better working procedures, others as a way of reducing costs; and the housing construction programme became in some ways a fight about the competence of the council and the executive committee. In such cases people drew their arguments from two completely different directions, which made it difficult for them to foresee or understand each other's attitudes. And this made it particularly difficult to find solutions which were acceptable from both angles, and which could command the agreement of many of those involved.

People had different ideas, but one thing they did have in common: goals. They all had the same idea about general municipal goals, about the direction in which they should be going. This did not agree with some of their ideas about appropriate procedures: most actors thought that they could or even should sometimes agree on means, but that their very role was to disagree on goals; politicians should represent different values. Because people of opposing views did not also have opposing goals, their disagreements and conflicts seemed even harder to understand.

Faced by this confusion people began constructing goals for each other, with the result that people's genuine views and the views which they believed each other to hold, i.e. their subjective and perceived ideologies, became inconsistent with one another. People thought that other people were chiefly interested in their own power, and in undermining everyone else's. They saw themselves as the only ones who were working for the good of the municipality. These misconceptions of each other's intentions seem to have been used as a way of trying to explain the common failure to produce action. But the misconceptions reinforced the conflict, which in turn made it even more difficult to get anything done.

Thus the actors in Runtown recognized both the action task and the political task of their organization. But this very recognition is in itself an ideological inconsistency and it tended to produce more inconsistencies and more conflicts, thus reinforcing the political behaviour of the organization and weakening its ability to act. The same effect was produced by the inconsistency between the politically oriented norm that decreed disagreement on goals and the action-oriented reality of agreement on goals. All this serves to show how very easily political behaviour can come to dominate action-orientation. Once again the actors themselves strove for more action but achieved more politics. But it was not only the ideological inconsistencies that determined this result; it was also the inconsistencies in the role constellation. This will be discussed below.

Inconsistent Roles—A Bewildering Spectacle

The diverse ideologies described above contained a variety of views about whether actors should tend towards politics or action in their behaviour. As we shall see, these different ideologies were also manifest in different roles, so that inconsistencies in ideologies were also generating inconsistencies between roles. Runtown was like a theatre company planning to give several plays but when some actors fail to show up deciding to combine different plays into one. Several plays are performed on the stage at the same time but in each play only some parts are represented. The mismatch between the parts played in Runtown goes a long way to explaining the flourishing production of inconsistencies and the high level of intractable conflict that so inhibited action.

Some actors were playing the opposition role, a role well suited to the political aspects of the organization. The task of an opposition is to criticize the decisions of the ruling majority: it is not expected that their own suggestions will be realized, and it is therefore possible to formulate them without much thought for the economy, for the administration, or for consistency with any other decisions. The critics' job is rather to indicate other ideological alternatives, other policy directions. While the majority party addresses its proposals mainly to the administrators who are supposed to implement them, the opposition is really addressing the general public, the media, and ultimately the electorate. 'People can see what I'm against', as one of the main opposition members put it. And indeed the opposition role and those who were playing it received much support from the media.

The opposition role thus presupposes someone to play against. We cannot imagine an opposition role in a solo performance. The opposition role is determined almost entirely by the other side, the ruling majority. If the opposition role is to be meaningful, there must be a majority which gets its own way by means of its superior voting power.

Runtown largely lacked the kind of counterpart that the opposition role requires. The opposition players complained that there was no 'political leadership'. The members of the majority coalition were not tackling their role in a way that would have suited the opposition, because they were attending to a different part of the ideology, namely the more action-oriented idea that decisions should be made on an 'objective basis' and (consequently) by consensus. They sought the advice of the opposition role-players on 'questions of fact' and tried to adapt their own proposals to these views, provided they found them justified on 'objective grounds'. For the opposition members who sat on the executive committee, the situation became particularly awkward. They were compelled to play a double role; in committee they were often unable to take up an oppositional stance. It was easier in council, where debates were not so firmly geared to facts. They voted differently in the two assemblies.

Another reason why the opposition role became so difficult to play was that the ruling coalition was uncertain of itself. There was always a risk that the opposition's proposals could win the votes. Proposals made as part of the opposition role could suddenly become decisions. The opposition accordingly found themselves responsible for decisions which it was not always possible to implement, or which were inconsistent with earlier decisions made on the same issue. One way in which the opposition could protect itself against this—one which was adopted quite often at a later stage—was to call for a fuller examination of the relevant issue rather than demanding concrete measures. But this actually increased their chance of winning the vote, and several questions were delayed for a very long time as a result of this mechanism. At the same time these lengthy processing procedures were one of the major targets of the opposition's own attacks.

The action-oriented role which members of the majority party, and some others too, were trying to play can be called the *objective role*, a role which does not belong to the same play as the opposition role; it belongs to a more action-oriented play. This made it difficult for these actors to interact with those playing the opposition role, and vice versa. But the assumption of the objective role also complicated relations with the administrator role. According to the existing ideology, the administrators had an indisputable right to the objective role, and they also had better opportunities for playing it: the objective role demands a lot of knowledge and a lot of time and is therefore better suited to administrators than to politicians. Politicians who play the objective role risk making themselves redundant. In Runtown they helped to promote the power takeover by the administrators.

The opposition and objective roles are both difficult to play when there are no objective ideologies, as was the case in Runtown in the latter part of the 1970s. The objective role presupposes agreement on fundamental values which can be used in assessing suggestions, i.e. there should be agreement about 'the facts'. If the opposition role is to function satisfactorily, there must be several objective ideologies which can confront one another. At least there should be one objective ideology to oppose.

The third role which was played by politicians in Runtown was the *intriguer role*. The occupants of this role tried to get their own way by canvassing votes from all possible parties. This role provided a way of acting against the occupants of the objective role, without assuming that role oneself. The intriguer role was thus a result of the mismatch between the opposition role and the objective role. Unlike the other roles, the intriguer role had weak ideological roots; it did not agree with the way people felt that the work should be done; it did not conform with their view of how either politics or action ought to be conducted. One effect of this was that most of the intriguers' work was done in secret, hence the name. Consequently the results took the other actors by surprise. Rumour and private goals often triggered action, in a way that was impossible in the public dramas where the other roles were being played. The intriguer role was an alternative to the opposition role; it was a way for non-majority actors to get their own proposals accepted. Some players alternated between the opposition and intriguer roles. This made it even more difficult to predict what decisions would actually be adopted.

The intriguer role presupposes the existence of an abundance of easily persuasible 'extras', i.e. actors who have very little connection with the main play, but who are nonetheless important to the outcome. A great many members of the council fitted this bill; with their votes they decided the outcome of important issues, and yet politics was really very peripheral to their normal operations. Consequently they felt little commitment to any particular party or to the executive committee, and they were often ill-informed on matters of fact. And yet they were almost all dissatisfied with the behaviour of the municipal leadership. These extras were obviously a thorn in the flesh of the objective role occupants, but they were pretty useful to the opposition players. And yet it was still the others—the occupants of the objective role—whose proposals were supposed to be winning the votes.

But it was not only the existence of inconsistent roles that complicated the situation in Runtown. A struggle was also going on about what roles to include at all, and what drama should be played. This struggle was connected with something that is always crucial to any organization in which politics is an important element, namely the struggle for influence.

The Struggle for Influence: Choosing the Play and the Roles

Conflict and a diversity of ideologies in an organization lead to internal struggle. The ideology and interests that are to steer organizational behaviour have to be established. The struggle for influence can be pursued in every single issue; each action launched is preceded by a struggle for influence, and this in turn decides the ideology that will determine the particular action. These constant struggles for influence obstruct organizational action, since they undermine people's commitment and confuse their expectations. And the various resulting actions are unlikely to be consistent with one another. Thus when consistent action is desired, people will try to avoid struggling for influence in this way, perhaps by making package deals that cover several actions at one go. But there are also certain solutions that have no direct connection with any specific action or actions; rather, they consist of the distribution of organizational roles. Some roles provide more opportunities than others for exerting influence. The struggle for roles is therefore important in determining which special interests acquire the most influence.

However, no special-interest group is free to choose whatever role it likes, since few roles are independent of the roles that others are playing. And not all roles fit into all dramas. Certain roles or pairs of roles complement one another, for instance the majority role and the opposition role. A different kind of play calls for consensus. Here the roles are based on the idea that all parties should influence the design of an action, and that all parties should be committed to it. The objective role is appropriate here.

It means toning down the ideological differences and giving little outlet to individual wills. Consensus roles arise most naturally when the ideological differences do not appear too acute. Where differences nevertheless exist, the roles imply a kind of agreement about future compromises.

Thus the struggle for influence is largely expressed as a struggle associated with roles. And the roles shape the conditions of influence. The struggle for roles is basically three-pronged. It concerns what drama is to be played, who should play the roles in any given drama, and what influence each particular role should possess. The struggle is conducted within the framework of the organization's normal operations. These operations are the arena in which roles are created and allocated. For this reason the treatment of individual issues is determined on a basis not only of the issues themselves, but also of the effect it will have on roles, and thus on the various groups' prospects of acquiring influence in the future. Decisions and actions are important not only in themselves, but also as weapons in the struggle for future influence. This is one of the main reasons why the interactions often become very complex in organizations.

Since the struggle associated with the different roles is conducted within the very framework of the organizations' normal operations, these operations will also be affected by the struggle. The struggle can influence the organization's orientation towards politics or action. It may sometimes have strong political or 'disintegrative' consequences, i.e. leading to obvious conflicts and inconsistencies and to problems in coordinating action, or it may have 'cohesive' consequences, i.e. leading to greater unity and consistency, thus providing a better basis for action.

The majority-opposition play and the consensus play represent different ways of handling the tension between the political and action-oriented demands to which the organization is exposed. We could say that the plays represent different agreements about the balance between the different forces. A given drama with a given allocation of roles thus constitutes a cohesive impetus to action in itself. When the play or the distribution of roles is called in question, it means that greater scope is being given to the disintegrative, political demands.

The struggle over what drama is to be played tends to have political consequences. A good way of acquiring influence over the choice of drama is to play a role that fits one's own favoured drama. If others want to play other dramas, they will adopt roles which suit 'their' drama, with the result that the roles adopted will not fit one another. Any attempt to play roles from different dramas contradicts the basic idea of organized action. Furthermore, there will be less chance of being able to predict the behaviour of the organization or of other actors, and this leads all too easily—as we have seen in the case of Runtown—to confusion and conflict. This in turn also reduces any hope of achieving organizational action. The struggle for roles within a given drama has similar although perhaps weaker political effects. The struggle can sometimes be avoided by transferring the decision of role allocation to the world outside the organization, for instance to an electorate which by its votes decides who is going to be playing the majority part.

Finally, the struggle for influence can be conducted within the established role system. This struggle is an essential part of the behaviour that constitutes the roles and dramas, and these are thus reinforced by the struggle in the role system itself. In this struggle politics and action can be better controlled; when the majority-opposition drama is played, politics are more likely to emerge; when the consensus drama is played, action more readily results.

The struggle for influence among the politicians in Runtown was mainly connected with the question of what drama should be played. Some actors were playing the objective role while others were playing the opposition role. In this second play there was also some confusion about who was in opposition and who was not. Since the struggle for influence in Runtown was concerned with the drama to be played and the roles to be adopted, rather than with the influence attaching to certain given role occupants, its effects were disintegrative in the extreme.

As organizational norms, action-orientation and politics thus give rise to different dramas and roles in association with the struggle for influence. When the pursuit of influence includes attempts at defining or changing the game or the allocation of roles, it will favour politics and discourage organizational action. Even if people strive for both politics and action-oriented roles, politics is likely to be the end result. Once again, politics tends to dominate action.

THE DOMINANCE OF POLITICS

If we examine events in Runtown over the whole period described above, two political behaviours emerge with particular clarity: first, a tendency to handle problems rather than to solve them, to administer rather than to change things, and secondly an inclination to swing sharply between periods of politics and periods of action.

Problem Administration

A striking feature of events in Runtown during the 1970s was the low level of change. At the end of the period things were not very different from the way they were at the beginning. External and internal problems were both much the same. For instance, the problem of substandard buildings and the inadequate infrastructure persisted throughout the period; so too did many problems connected with the workings of the organization.

And yet there had been strong incentives to look for solutions and to change current behaviour. People had been very much aware of the problems, and therefore of the urgent need to solve them. There had been crises which in themselves could have provided an opportunity for big changes. Furthermore, several new leading administrators and politicians had joined the organization during the period.

However, these incentives were counterbalanced by powerful forces favouring inertia, chief among them being the political behaviour. Change calls for action, but it is just the kind of action that involves change which is the most difficult to produce in organizations. When it comes to change, the old patterns of coordination cannot just be repeated; people have to decide what change is to be made, to agree on it, and then to coordinate their actions. There is both a choice problem and an action problem—something which makes coordinated action very difficult indeed (Brunsson 1985). And organizations with powerfully political characteristics find it difficult to produce action in general, and change in particular.

Much Activity—Little Action

There was not much change in Runtown but there was variation. During the 1970s the organization oscillated between a proclivity for action and politics. The oscillations were affected by the nature of relations with the environment at different times. The organization was most firmly geared to action when it was a question of interacting with external interests. Location policy was one example; the appeals to the state were another. External crises such as company closures aroused some unity, while quieter external circumstances coincided with highly politicized states.

The swings between politics and an action-orientation also had strong internal causes. Both tendencies were reflected in organizational ideologies and in the different roles that the actors played. Most of the time politicians and administrators in Runtown strove for action, but what they achieved was mostly political behaviour. Political behaviour can be anything but strategic; it may be the unintended result of the interaction between political characteristics. Here it was the struggle for action and the struggle for influence which constituted the strategic processes—what the actors were working for most vigorously. And these struggles in turn generated a powerful dynamism that served to maintain and reinforce the politics in the organization. In this way ideological disunity led to acute conflict and made it difficult to generate action, which then served to strengthen the conflict even more. The incapacity to act encouraged the production of talk and decisions as independent outputs, which in turn simply made action more difficult than ever. The organizational ideologies and the various roles and games the actors tried to play were inconsistent; they reflected the idea of an action orientation as well as the idea of politics. This is what produced the alternation between politics and action, but the confusion between the two ideas then tended to reinforce the politicization and to weaken the capacity to act. Politics tends to dominate action.

The Example of Runtown

Because of their extreme nature, the developments in Runtown were clearly visible; but this does not mean that they are typical. Many organizations manage to achieve a better balance between politics and action, mainly by separating them more efficiently. One way of separating them is to let politics and action correspond to the division of labour between leaders and led. At the beginning of the 1970s there was hardly any such division of labour in Runtown, but it became increasingly important later, partly because talk and decisions became independent outputs, 'decoupled' from action. The decoupling of ideological output from action gave the new administrators a chance to act, leaving the politicians to get on with their talk and decisions. Thus the task of taking action fell to the more highly action-oriented administration, which somewhat alleviated the overall incapacity to act; the new administrative offices, for example, were actually built. But the administration did not become wholly independent of the political apparatus, so that later events again had an inhibiting effect on action, although not quite as dramatically as before.

Thus the struggle for action became conducted mainly by the administrators. By leading the struggle for action they also enjoyed the most success in the struggle for influence. In the end they assumed more of the traditional role of the administrator, initiating and executing municipal activities, while the politicians discussed their proposals and made decisions.

In the next chapter I shall discuss politics and action in a situation with a clear organizational distinction between politics and action.

4
Decisions as Transition Between Politics and Action

Organizations are commonly divided into two parts, the leaders and the led. One of the leaders' most important tasks is to take care of the organization's external relationships and to ensure that it obtains support from its environment, while the led can handle the production of goods and services. The leaders have a special role in creating legitimate structures, processes and ideologies, while the led can concentrate on products. The leaders deal with the organization's legitimacy and the led with its efficiency. This kind of division is particularly useful when the demands for legitimacy and efficiency clash, e.g. when politics are important to legitimation. The leadership or management system can be isolated from the production system. It becomes easier to exercise hypocrisy: the leaders' talk and decisions can satisfy one set of norms, while the products satisfy others.

But the terms 'leaders' and 'led' refer to more than just a difference in status between two sets of tasks in the organization; they also suggest that the two suborganizations are coupled together in such a way that the leaders' ideas find expression in the actions of the led; the leaders do not normally participate directly in production, but they are supposed to control it. The leaders can employ a variety of control instruments. It is a common belief that decisions are one such instrument: the leaders consider what will be for the best, they make up their minds and convey their decision to the led, whose job is then to put the decision into effect, to realize it in action. Decisions are particularly important if the leaders are not in full agreement and represent different ideologies among themselves; the decision then clearly shows which ideas, and whose ideas, are to apply in the action. Decisions are a common instrument in managements to whom politics are important. In this chapter and the following one I shall therefore be discussing decision processes as 'coupling' and 'decoupling' mechanisms between politics and action.

Many decision-making theories correspond nicely to this division into leaders and led, in particular all those theories that describe rationality as a major norm for decision processes, or as a good description of such processes. In rational decision processes the decision represents the choice of a particular action. It is assumed that the process starts by establishing the preferences which are to steer the evaluation of the various action alternatives and the choice between them. Thus rationality implies the existence of a hierarchy between decisions and action whereby decisions control action, and of a similar hierarchy between preferences and action alternatives. It is then a natural step to translate this into an organizational hierarchy: those who specify goals also control decisions, and decision-makers control those who translate decision into action.

But the idea of the coupling of leaders and led, with decisions acting as the coupling mechanism, is not restricted to the abstract world of rational decision models. The association of leaders with control is often codified in law. It then is a common notion in company law and in national constitutions that the board or the government or some other superior body is and should be in control of operations. Decisions are often regarded as an important—or even the only—legally binding means of control.

That decisions should provide a means of control is also expected by actors inside and outside many organizations. The leaders may have other purposes for their operations than simply to create legitimacy for the organization. They may be interested not only in asserting their own views, but also in transforming these views into action—particularly if they see themselves as representing special interests, opinions or values. Thus the leaders want to control the led; they want to exert influence. One way of doing this is by getting decisions passed which embody their own values or give these values a prominent place, and by trying to see that the decisions are actually put into effect.

External interests may demand that the leaders should make their mark on the action. These interests may not be content to see the organization reflecting their ideas in talk and decisions; they may also demand action that agrees with their views. And there is further justification for such an attitude, in that many organizations are described by their own representatives as being geared to the production of desirable organizational action.

However, the coupling of leaders and led is certainly not without problems. It may be difficult to get the leaders to make decisions about planned or realized actions, and it may be even more difficult to see that their decisions steer action. And if we really do succeed in linking the leaders with the action, then both legitimacy and efficiency may be imperilled. It can be particularly difficult to exert control through decisions if the political element in the leadership is strong, and control through decisions can interfere drastically with politics. If action is to be effective, we have to curb politics, and if politics are to be strong, there is less basis for action. Consensus on a particular line may control action more powerfully, but it reduces the organization's capacity to reflect inconsistent norms. For a political leadership which is eager not to renounce too many of its conflicts, decisions of a vague or contradictory kind are desirable (Baier *et al.* 1986), but such decisions are not particularly efficient when it comes to implementation.

With the help of an empirical example I shall discuss in this chapter how leaders and action can be linked together by way of decisions in organizations where politics are important, and what effects the decisions may have on both politics and action. The example I have chosen concerns an attempt by the ruling majority in a local council to control the actions of the administrators.

THE CASE OF GREATON

The following case deals with the leadership of Greaton, a fairly large town in Sweden. The leaders were elective politicians, who were seeking control over an administration consisting of public officials. More specifically I shall be discussing events connected with the urban transport system, how it was designed and how it was changed. These issues were not only extremely controversial; they also called for extensive and complicated coordinated action on the part of the organization. We shall be looking at a period immediately following the emergence of a new Socialist majority in the local council. It is only to be expected that a new ruling majority will want to introduce some new measures—at least this is generally what has been promised during the election campaign. And such was the case here. An important election promise had concerned a new transport policy: collective transport was to be given priority over car traffic. The collective transport system was to be made better and quicker, while car traffic should be reduced 'to the great benefit of the air and environment of the inner city'. It was also clear that the leading politicians in the new majority party wanted to implement their programme, which would mean persuading the administrators to accept some quite radical changes in the way they had been running things.

It was hardly to be expected that the administrators would be keen to participate in these changes. They had a well-established tradition of planning for better 'accessibility' and 'navigability' for car traffic. The last twenty years had been spent on extending the road network for car traffic, regardless of whether non-Socialists or Socialists were in power. One large administrative section was therefore engaged in planning routes for car traffic. There was no reason to imagine that the administration would change the thrust of its transport policy of its own free will, and the situation was thus ripe for the exercise of influence.

The established procedures followed by politicians and administrators were perceived by these actors as control procedures, and they were in fact presented as such in official descriptions of the organization. The politicians' forum for controlling transport policy was the local building committee. This committee made all decisions about investments and regulations which might affect urban traffic. Under the building committee was a large administrative unit, the town-building office. This unit's job was to prepare and later to implement the decisions of the committee, i.e. to supply the committee with the factual information needed for their policy-making, and to see that the decisions of the committee resulted in the intended action. This follows common organizational principles which assume that decisions are the major instrument of influence; since decisions are made by top management, it is also top management which determines the organizational action. In the case of governments the principle of majority rule is applied, so that the action is controlled by the majority party or coalition formed after an election. In such cases the principle is associated with the concept of democracy as a sequential chain, whereby the will of the people is injected into the action that is ultimately taken. The idea is that the politicians become the representatives of the people, whose decisions are made at election time; then, through their own decisions, these representatives of the people control the administrators, who in turn control the concrete actions undertaken by the organization itself. If the chain is not to break, all the links must hold, and the organization of the relationship between committees and administrators is presented as an attempt to guarantee one of the links.

The official description of the relations between leaders and led in Greaton, and the way in which the interaction between them was organized, thus corresponded pretty well to the situation in most large organizations. Superficially it looked as though the leaders were in firm control of operations. But when we look more closely at the way control processes work in practice, the picture may seem rather different.

In Greaton most issues did not involve any link between the leaders and the action taken: these issues were delegated to the administration, which handled them without any interference from the politicians. The questions handled by the building committee were mainly concerned with broad planning issues: the general lines of development for a period of 10–30 years, as well as more detailed short-term issues stemming from the long-term plans. For instance, the decision-makers went through a couple of decision processes concerning rearrangements of traffic in the city, which were part of the administrators' normal planning activities. In these planning processes, the administration produced a large number of detailed analyses. Various studies were submitted to the committee over long periods, either as oral reports or preliminary findings. The process ended, normally after several years, with the politicians making a decision which was later to be implemented by the administrators.

The division of work that obtained in Greaton between decision-makers and those in charge of operations is not unusual, and there are valid reasons for it. If you are to make a good decision, it appears perfectly reasonable to utilize the expertise of the operational side. It is thus difficult to envisage any very different overall role for the decision-makers: their job is to make decisions and to acquire as good a basis as possible for them.

How far, then, were the politicians able to control the administrators through their decisions? The new ruling majority made vigorous efforts to realize its ideas for a new transport policy. Two possibilities were open to them. Either they could work within the framework of the regular procedures, asserting their views as the planning proceeded and making a series of decisions which would ultimately create a new transport situation. The other way would mean working outside the regular routines. The new majority party chose both methods of attack, but without success. Its failure illustrates how difficult it is to exert influence by making decisions.

DECISION-MAKERS AS DEFENSIVE SCRUTINEERS

To be able to exert influence in the role of decision-maker, three conditions must be satisfied. The first concerns an independent will: the decision-makers' opinions and the actions they want to carry out must be moulded independently of those over whom they are to exert influence. If the led have a determining influence on the decision-makers' beliefs, then the decision-makers may of course find it easy to implement their ideas, but they will not have exerted any influence. The second condition is that the decision-makers' views should influence the decision in such a way that views and decisions agree. And the third condition is that the decisions are actually realized, that decisions and actions agree. All these conditions will be illustrated below, with the help of the Greaton case. In this subsection I shall start by discussing the second condition, namely that the decision-makers' views do influence the decision. The other two conditions will be discussed in the two following sections.

The Role of the Decision-makers

The role which the decision-makers can play in the decision process is largely determined by the role of the led, and vice versa. In Greaton the administrators were in a very strong position. In terms of resources they were the stronger. In most cases the contribution of the politicians was very modest in relation to the work put in by the administration. The led, i.e. the officials preparing the issues to be put before the building committee, numbered more than fifty times as many as the regular members of the committee. A study of the way major issues were handled in committee showed that the administrators spent about a hundred times longer than the committee members on the issues. And the administrators had a sound educational background in the field of traffic planning, and most of them had had long experience of handling traffic issues; they were experts—the politicians were laymen. On the resource side the administrative machinery thus clearly dominated the people's politically elected representatives.

However, more important than their purely resource-related dominance was the active leading role assigned to the administrators at several stages in the decision process. We can distinguish four important steps in this process: the initiation of a case, i.e. an idea, a suggestion, or a problem is brought up for discussion; preparation, or the production of a decision base; decision; and finally implementation.

Most cases were initiated by the administration. This applied particularly to the larger and more important issues, which were normally brought up as part of the administration's (and thus the committee's) current planning. Cases initiated by any other parties were anyway submitted to the administrators for investigation, and in the relatively few instances when such initiatives were not simply rejected they were almost always incorporated into the regular planning process.

Initiating a case also means defining it in a particular way, i.e.

by presenting a problem to be solved, thus also largely indicating the criteria for evaluating proposed solutions. For instance, the same case can be regarded either as a way of saving money, or as a way of improving the environment, or of increasing accessibility; the same problem can be looked at from the point of view of collective travellers, car drivers, or residents. Moreover, a solution in principle is generally suggested right at the start. It has been found in studies of investment analysis that the original definition of a proposed project is very rarely altered during the decision process (Bower 1970). Thus the initiation phase in the handling of a case is very important to the decisions which will ultimately be made. Nor was there any redefinition at later phases in the cases studied here. On the other hand, cases initiated outside the administration were often at least partly redefined by the administrators, in that the issues were incorporated into the regular planning process, and were thus adapted to the prevailing view of the particular problem. Redefinitions of this kind can be extremely important to the end result of the decision process.

The preparation of cases was the responsibility of the administration. It was the administrators who collected the information and produced the base on which the decisions were to be made. During this preparatory stage, however, the politicians were able to scrutinize sub-results, to ask questions about them and to put forward their own views.

Finally the administrators formulated a proposal for a decision by the committee. Whenever there were conflicting postures among committee members, the administrators strove to limit the decisions to questions upon which agreement could be reached, and to postpone controversial questions to a later occasion. Thus plans could be adopted and action started in spite of conflicts.

The politicians' own planning base consisted of the various programmes for transport which the political parties had drawn up. But these programmes were very brief and expressed in extremely general terms. They gave little idea of how the parties would act on any concrete transport question.

The final decision was made exclusively by the politicians. But the moment of decision had little significance in terms of influence: the real choices had all been made long before, when the issues were selected and defined, and during the preparation process. The decision did not involve a choice between alternatives. Once a common view of a solution had been achieved, which by now had all the characteristics of a compromise product, there was no longer any need for alternatives. They had already been incorporated into the final proposal. The procedure did not really allow for dealing with alternatives at later stages in the planning process. The administrators regarded it as wasteful to spend precious planning time on alternatives, when they thought they knew what the politicians wanted. And presumably the decision-makers did not want alternatives during the final phase, since the tacit agreements and compromises now embodied in the proposal might be jeopardized if a political discussion of alternatives were to precede the decision. From the point of view of implementation, it was also better to accept a consensus-based solution than to start discussing a variety of solutions, which could mean that those responsible for implementation might misinterpret the conclusion or feel uncertain about what action was really intended.

The implementation of the decisions was the task of the administrators. It was often difficult for the politicians to check whether decisions had been carried out, and if so whether they had been carried out as intended.

Defensive Scrutineers

It can be seen from this account that if the decision-makers had any influence on action, it was during the preparatory stage, when their role was to go through the suggestions submitted by the administrators as carefully as possible, and to comment on them. Because of the way their role was designed, it was generally negative criticism that emerged: weaknesses in the suggestions could be criticized but there was very little opportunity for the decision-makers to make suggestions of their own. Naturally they could sometimes produce an idea for a solution in principle, but this would then have to be processed by the administrators and possibly reformulated as a fuller proposal. The decision-makers were thus expected to act as defensive scrutineers; and it was largely in the exercise of this role that they influenced the decision process.

Many of the politicians also regarded the role of defensive scrutineer as the role which politicians *should* play. It was commonly felt that the politician's job is to represent the public interest in the planning process, so that the experts do not wander too far away from the values and wishes of the electorate: 'To protect the citizens against the experts'.

The politicians were less aware than the administrators of the procedure by which different issues were handled in committee. The politicians did not distinguish so carefully between what the administrators called 'issues'. Instead they thought in terms of various politically interesting problems that kept recurring in connection with several issues. The politicians saw themselves as handling transport policy. To them an 'issue' was more in the nature of a framework for their talk and decisions, rather than something which, after being handled, emerged as a complete and finished whole.

The role of the defensive scrutineer also implies that the decision-makers deal mainly in solutions rather than problems. Only to a very minor extent are they engaged in problem-solving in the course of handling an issue. Instead the problem-solving activities are transferred to the led. This has implications in a theoretical perspective, since many decision-making theories describe the decision process as a problem-solving process. Thus these theories are not particularly well suited to describing the decision-making of leaders acting as defensive scrutineers. The important choices are normally made in early phases of the decision process, when problems are formulated and proposals presented. If participation is restricted to the later stages in the process, the chances of influence are smaller and the methods for wielding influence will have to be very different.

Thresholds to Leadership

As a result of this defensive scrutineer role, the individual decision-maker could to some extent choose the issues, or the aspects of a particular issue, to which he was prepared to devote his time. If no politician had any particular comments to make on an issue, then the decision would follow the recommendations of the administration. If a politician expressed his disagreement with the administration's proposal, this meant—according to the politician's own definition—that he was making politics of the question, i.e. he invited debate and conflict. The final result was often that a vote was held, and reservations were sometimes registered against the decision of the majority. The only exception would be if all the politicians were of the same opinion in opposition to a proposal from the administration, but this seldom occurred.

All this impeded any decision-maker who wanted to oppose a proposal from the administration. There was simply not enough time to make an issue of everything. Controversial questions took much longer to deal with in committee. They also had to be prepared in much greater detail. In addition, the politicians had to fight on unequal terms: the administrators had a certain advantage, simply because they had submitted their solution first.

Those who first submit a proposal need only argue in its favour. The opposers not only had to show that their own proposal was a good one; they also had to prove that the administrators' was not. In producing proof of this, the politicians were at a huge disadvantage, since they did not have access to anything like as much factual information as the administrators. Moreover they had smaller resources. A suggestion from the decision-makers, which could not usually be expressed other than as a rough alternative solution backed up by a few arguments, had to stand against a well-elaborated and carefully prepared proposal from the administration.

There was thus a threshold to cross for those who wanted to pursue their own line on an issue. And unless a politician crossed the threshold and questioned the proposals, the administration's line would be followed. To some extent, too, the administrators could determine whether or not an issue would become controversial: they could decide whether to propose several alternative solutions, or only one. If they suggested alternatives, the politicians were compelled to adopt an active approach, and there would then generally be political disagreement. Sometimes, on the other hand, the administrators' proposal would be intentionally designed to allow for compromise or package solutions which no party would be likely to question. By launching compromises of this kind they were in fact often determining which parts of the various party programmes would be realized.

In Greaton the administrators were never openly in disagreement when they submitted their proposals. They reached agreement among themselves before presenting their material to the committee. Should any disagreement nonetheless remain between different departments of the administration, the issue concerned would probably not be included on the committee's agenda. Thus any committee member who wanted to pursue a line in opposition to the administration always found himself facing a solidly united corps of experts, who had been able to devote far more time to the issue than he had.

And indeed most politicians expected and wanted the administrators to present a united front, since this undeniably reduced the complexity of the problems and thus the time the politicians needed to spend on them. But it did not perhaps increase their influence.

Various other ideas and ideologies also made it difficult to question certain issues. Some problems were regarded as technical, and it was then the job of technologists and experts to find solutions; politicians were not expected to involve themselves in such things. Quite often everyone was agreed that the questions were technical in this sense, but some issues lay in the borderlands between those that were technical and those that the politicians should handle; it was not clear which area they belonged to. Here the very legitimacy of an independent stance on the part of the politicians could be called in question. The politician who wanted to pursue a line of his own then had the double task not only of proving that his own proposal was better than the administration's, but also of justifying the legitimacy of his intervention. Sometimes the administrators in Greaton might question the legitimacy of the politicians' stance, but accusations of illegitimacy were more generally heard from the political opposition. One of the differences between the previous and present ruling majorities was that certain questions which could formerly be left to the technical experts now had to be decided by the politicians on a basis of other non-technical values. The new ruling majority then faced the difficult task of changing accustomed ideas about what was technology and what belonged to the domain of the politicians.

Politics or Action-orientation

A related problem concerns interactions among the politicians themselves. As defensive scrutineers they were likely to set great store by consensus rather than conflict. The very design of the kind of decision process described above is oriented towards action. It does not start from various goals of the decision-makers, thus making different values, alternatives and consequences explicit and visible. Rather, it is based on the notion that even controversial issues can ultimately be solved by finding 'one best solution', i.e. a solution that is good from all points of view, or that there is a single overriding criterion such as 'the best interests of the people'. Perhaps this is simply another way of saying that the questions are technical: a good solution is the result of 'right thinking', not of efforts to satisfy the particular interests that they represent. In this light 'politics' acquires negative overtones and 'action' positive ones. Building committee members often assumed that anyone who 'made politics' of a question must be acting against their own better judgement, and doing so for the not altogether respectable purpose of capturing votes.

Because of their defensive scrutineer role, this view of politics probably had a particularly inhibiting effect on the politicians. If the politicians had possessed more initiative, i.e. if they had been making the proposals, the effect of such a view would not have been so great; it would have been possible to accuse possibly critical administrators of conducting politics.

The sceptical view of politics that was rife even among the politicians themselves naturally served to enhance the status of the administrators' professional values. In Greaton the status of the administrators was already high: all the politicians praised them for their efficiency and the excellent standard of their investigations and reports. On the other hand, several politicians described themselves as 'simple opinion-makers' or something along those lines. Some of them compared the 'objective' and 'factual' approach of the administrators with the nature of their own action: if the politicians wanted to improve the quality of their work, they should strive for greater objectivity. Of course, this type of ideology makes it even more difficult to legitimize any independent political stance.

The politician's role as a defensive scrutineer thus implies a heavy emphasis on action rather than politics. The views of those whose job it is to act are allowed great impact, something which favours implementation but reduces the chance of exposing conflict in the issues handled. It also makes it more difficult for the decision-makers to exert any influence over the led. In view of this it is easy to see why the politicians in Greaton generally sought to exert influence at an early stage, when the final decisions were still being worked out. The role of defensive scrutineer acquired its greatest importance in discussing the preliminary proposals as they were put forward by the administrators. This did not make it possible to avoid the problems described here, but at least at this stage the administrators had a better chance of adapting to the politicians.

Thus if leaders acting as decision-makers hold views which disagree with those of the led, it may be very difficult for them to see these views reflected in the decisions, and the difficulty is particularly great if at the same time they are supposed to be exposing conflict. But how much opportunity is there for the decision-makers ever to acquire the kind of independent views likely to trigger such a control problem? This will be the subject of the next section.

OPINION-MAKING

In many hierarchic models it is assumed that decision-makers' preferences or opinions are exogenously determined, i.e. independently of those whom their decisions are to control. When the decision-makers represent other people or groups of people, they are expected to inject these other people's views into the decision process; the politicians' function is to assert the views of the electorate. But what are the decision-makers' chances of developing independent ideas? When the decision-makers enjoy a close relationship with the operational experts, and if this relationship is also of considerable importance to them, we would expect them to be greatly influenced by these same experts. It is difficult to create or maintain opinions of one's own in intimate confrontation with expert knowledge; it might be easier if there were an opportunity to associate with other groups apart from the experts and to find arguments and support from these other parties. For anyone who acts as the representative of a particular group, it would seem natural to turn to this group. In the case of the politicians in our case, the voters constitute a possible support group of this kind; they were the formal principals of the politicians.

Principals as Opponents

The politicians represent the voters, but the Greaton study suggests that the politicians' situation in relation to the actions of their organization was only minimally affected by the way they believed the voters would react. The politicians believed that very few of these actions ever came to the knowledge of the ordinary citizen, and that the citizens were anyway unaffected by them when it came to voting in the local elections.

Moreover it was difficult for the politicians to take the voters' views into account, since according to their own statements they knew very little about the voters' values and found it difficult to discover what they really thought. Certainly the voters sometimes reacted against a decision on some particular action, but these reactions generally became evident far too late—usually when the decision was to be carried out, or even when it had already been implemented. And in any case the voters' views might not be the same when the decision was adopted and when it was to be implemented. Further, the politicians felt that the voters lacked any overall grasp of the issues at stake and that they put their own interests first. The politicians had the advantage of their greater knowledge, and this made for difficulties in the transfer of information from voter to politician. This difference in knowledge as between principals and decision-makers is to some extent inherent in their roles, and is therefore a common phenomenon. It corresponds to the knowledge gap between decision-makers and actors, and it explains some of the difficulty that principals encounter in acquiring influence.

The knowledge gap explains why very little use could be made of the comments received when proposed solutions to the traffic problem were put before the public. Exhibitions and other informative activities were sometimes arranged on the initiative of the administrators, dealing with various aspects of the building committee's sphere of operations. The idea was not only to inform the public about the ideas and activities of the committee, but also to get some idea of what the general public thought. Visitors to the exhibitions could express their views on special question-naires. But committee members found it difficult to let these views influence their operations.

One of the exhibitions produced a great many answers to various questions posed by the administration. An analysis of the answers revealed that about 95% demanded more investment in collective transport at the expense of private car traffic. In so far as committee members noted this result at all, it was felt that the answers could not be allowed to affect the related decisions—partly, it was argued, because these views 'were not repre-sentative of the general public'. And in fact the answers to the questionnaires had no influence on the decisions made.

One reason why it was so difficult to consider the opinions of the electorate was that the voters demanded action before the organization had any chance of taking action. The public dis-regarded the fact that decision and implementation processes took a long time. Another and more important reason was that voter opinions were independent of the system as a whole, i.e. they were concerned with concrete desirable measures, but they did not also look at these measures in relation to a whole host of other measures. The politician, on the other hand, was compelled to see every suggestion as part of a total plan and thus found it much more difficult to make up his mind on any individual item.

The politicians found it particularly difficult to take the views of one special type of voter into account, namely the organized pressure groups which sometimes roused a powerful body of opinion against some action on which the politicians had already decided. The problem was that these reactions generally arose at a very late stage in the decision process, often when implementa-tion had already begun. The politicians had very little scope for considering such reactions at this stage and were forced instead into defending their decision. Many politicians regarded these pressure groups as a threat to themselves.

Interaction with the voters thus had little impact on the politician's choice of issues to support or oppose. Instead it was the interaction between politicians belonging to different parties which was the determining factor. The background to this situation was that all the politicians believed unanimously that the general public reacted readily to anything negative in the actions of the municipal government, i.e. to any mistakes which might have been committed. At the same time it was difficult to get the public to recognize the organization's good deeds. The picture which the public formed of the politicians' activities was largely moulded by people who were critical of them, and particularly by parties who were their political opponents. It was the criticism voiced by these opponents which so powerfully reinforced the picture of the politicians that it reached the man in the street. It was thus the opposition that determined which actions of the ruling majority became visible to the general public. The individual parties were quite simply being marketed by their opponents.

Thus in deciding what line to pursue or what questions to take up, it was necessary to take into account the probable reaction of one's political opponents—whether or not they would exploit the issue. The politicians often had to feel their way carefully, deciding in stages what to do next according to how they read the reactions of their opponents. This explains why the politicians found it so difficult to answer questions about what they might or might not do in some possible future situation: their behaviour would be determined not only by the facts of the case—which would have made it quite easy to predict their behaviour—but also by their opponents' actions, which were more difficult to foresee.

Thus the politicians did not know the voters' views on specific questions, nor did they feel that they had much chance of discovering them. And when any opinions did reach them as a result of direct enquiries into people's views on a particular question, the politicians were either unable or unwilling to consider them. Nor were they able or willing to be influenced by various more spontaneous protests against decisions already made.

The risk in this situation was that the politicians would confuse the electorate with their own political opponents. Lacking any real knowledge of the voters' values, the politicians too readily assumed that critics represented the views of a large section of the electorate—which was not necessarily so. Or they might assume that the criticism would anyway convince the voters or the public in general that their party was wrong. In either case it made it more difficult to pursue a line of one's own.

All this meant that the politicians ran the risk of acquiring a systematically distorted picture of the opinions of the electorate. They were also often convinced that the general public was always against change, or at any rate against any major change. A change that improves the lot of one group often means that others may suffer in some way, and we have already noted that the politicians always heard much more about the negative results. Groups that suffered from a change were naturally against it, and it was their protests which reached the ears of the politicians, or which at any rate dominated any debate. When another change came up, which benefited the previously disadvantaged group, the protests would come from another quarter, and so on. Almost all changes brought down protests on the heads of the politicians, who would naturally assume that people in general were against change— even though on each occasion the opposition represented only a small proportion of the electorate.

All these mechanisms helped to conceal the real views of the electorate from the politicians, who thus found it difficult to claim that they knew what the voters wanted, which in turn reduced the legitimacy of their arguments. They were appointed to watch over the interests of the public, yet they obviously had little idea what these interests were. Many administrators claimed that their most important task was 'to protect the people from the politicians'.

The politicians tried to make up for their lack of contact with the electorate by cultivating good contacts with their own party members. They arranged meetings with their members in different districts to discuss transport policy. But these groups had little capacity for discussing detailed technical questions or solutions. Their time and their knowledge sufficed only for the more general questions. At the meetings the Socialists received continuing support to pursue their new transport policy. Above all, however, this contact between leading politicians and the grassroots of the party gave the politicians an opportunity to explain why it was difficult, or impossible, or inappropriate to realize various ideas which were popular at the grassroots level.

It was now the politicians' turn to act as experts, in this case towards the uninformed people.

Some leading politicians even tried to acquire support on a private basis, by making secret contact with administrators of the 'correct' party sympathies, and this helped them to some extent to pursue their own line. But these politicians were running two risks: first, that they would simply get the same expert opinion they had already been given, since political sympathies do not readily override factually based conclusions; second, their chosen expert might not be as knowledgeable as the administration's leading expert on the particular question, in which case his arguments would be unlikely to prevail.

There were thus two main reasons why the views of the principals made little impact on the leaders. One was the very general problem of the knowledge gap between them. The second stemmed from the inconsistent norms in the organization and its environment, which tended to strengthen the role of the internal opposition at the expense of the principals.

Freedom of Opinion or Influence on Decisions

The opportunities for adopting independent positions differ as between the ruling majority and the opposition. The opposition does not always have to engage in talk and decisions which must agree with—and protect—the organization's actions. Members of the opposition can make suggestions and adopt attitudes on politically controversial questions more as a way of registering the ideas for which they stand; and their target is not so much the administrators as the general public. The opposition need not feel so dependent on what the administrators or the ruling majority think about the planning process or about the way various questions may be related to one another. Rather, it is important for them to look at things from the point of view of the individual citizen, who often sees the relationship with other questions quite differently from the administrators.

In Greaton the present opposition had been the ruling majority for about ten years until the changeover after the latest election. The parties had not yet had time to readjust their policies to their new roles. But these earlier roles appear to have had a considerable influence on their policies. The politicians who represented the former ruling majority showed much stronger commitment to the planning process and the administrators, than those who had represented the opposition. Those who had long been part of the ruling majority were more inclined to regard many of the committee's activities as 'technical' than those who had represented the opposition. In other words the former ruling party left more decision to the administrators than the then opposition would have liked. One leading politician belonging to the former majority party spoke of 'our' administrators, unlike the new majority party which spoke of 'self-appointed experts'. Proposals stemming from the former opposition would often involve radical deviations from what was regarded as 'technical' principles by the administrators and the former majority party.

This situation may of course have depended on ideological differences between the parties. But a comparison with similar municipalities where the opposite situation between ruling majority and opposition obtained does not provide much support for such a hypothesis. It seems more likely that the differences depended largely on the very fact that one group is in the majority role and the other in opposition.

The close relationship with the administrators explains not only the difference between majority and opposition policies but also the difference between the politicians who were on the building committee and those who were not.

During the period studied more suggestions within the committee's area of responsibility came from the councillors who were not members of the committee than from the committee members themselves. Naturally this may be partly because committee members have more opportunity to influence operations in the course of their regular work on the various issues, and perhaps they have no great need to put forward any special suggestions besides this. However, it may also have been because it is more difficult for people strongly committed to the planning process and the way it works to make independent suggestions. Committee members possess more information, but this information tends not to be much help since most of it comes from the administrators, which restricts the politicians' chances of discovering any problems or possibilities apart from those which occur to the administrators.

Thus it seems that the leaders who find it easiest to adopt an independent stance, namely the opposition politicians and non-committee members, are those who are not involved in decision-making or who do not enjoy a majority in decision-making, while those who formally support the content of the decisions, i.e. the politicians representing the ruling majority on the committee, are those who have most difficulty in exerting influence from an independent stance.

An added complication here is that the individual decision-maker may not even recognize his own difficulty in forming independent preferences. The organizational actions agree with the decision-makers' opinions and he may perceive such a state as one of perfect control. This makes his control problem even more difficult to solve.

IMPLEMENTATION

Much has been written about the difficulty managements experience when it comes to influencing their organizations or the environment. Chief among the problems discussed in this literature is that of putting decisions into effect. Decisions made with great ceremony and every finesse are quite often never implemented; actions and consequences fail to agree with the import of the decision. In the literature concerned with implementation this is regarded as a problem of control, a problem for those in charge.

When the normal decision process was followed in the building committee, there was no such implementation problem. Not that every decision was actually carried out, but this was not blamed on administrative obstruction. Either there was not enough money, or minor uncontroversial adjustments were made to new facts or evaluations in the course of implementing a decision.

Unlike what is often assumed in implementation literature, the leaders in our case frequently found the *agreement* between decision and action to be so strong as to be frustrating. Decisions once made were meant to steer actions for a long time to come. The whole idea of long-term plans was to commit the decision-makers (and others) to a particular line of action, in other words to limit their freedom of action. Such commitment was necessary to ensure that various actions were mutually consistent. But in any period of transition such commitment tends to be extremely awkward. In this case criticism often arose first when an action was actually being carried out, and could sometimes be surprisingly strong, although no one had foreseen it long ago when the decision was being made. And of course during the long delay between decision and action, circumstances had time to develop quite differently from what was once predicted. Moreover, the general public might have changed its ideas, even if the decision originally agreed with what most citizens thought at the time. Or ideas and values which underpinned an action might even have been abandoned by the politicians themselves. In the building committee politicians quite often found themselves wanting to change the actions of the administration, or at least to alter their own decisions, but in practice they were compelled to defend these very actions to the outside world. In view of all this it is not surprising that the politicians unanimously emphasized a thick skin as a politician's most important asset.

But the majority in our case also tried an implementation strategy. They tried to order the administration to behave according to decisions that the majority had made by themselves. Let us see what happened then.

A Case of Implementation

Most of the decision-making by the new majority in Greaton followed the pattern that has been described above. The politicians were placed in the role of defensive scrutineers, and they had great difficulty in forming or defending any opinions of their own on concrete issues that differed from those of the administrators. At the same time they had to defend the realization of plans that had been decided during the previous mandate period.

Thus it was not clear how far the handling of these new traffic schemes, for instance, could be regarded as an expression of the new transport policy. The questions would almost certainly have been handled in much the same way by the previous ruling majority. Politicians and administrators agreed that the traffic system was to be revised, and as a result of all the preparatory work they were also largely agreed about how it should be done.

The history of the traffic issue repeated a pattern already familiar from previous experience: it was difficult to assert and pursue a definite political stance in the course of such investigations. By the end, administrators and politicians of varying party affiliations generally found themselves in broad agreement. Proud slogans were easily translated into practical and unconventional solutions. There was also a considerable time lag between an idea and its realization; the preparatory investigations could take up to two years, and realization could well take several more.

All this helps to explain why, in its eagerness to do something radical about the traffic situation during its mandate period, the new ruling majority sometimes tried to act outside the usual investigatory procedures. The politicians tried to create 'issues' of their own, by tackling a series of concrete details and issuing direct instructions about making changes in them–they tried an implementation strategy. The most important example of this was the so-called tramway issue.

Greaton had long been famous for its far-sighted policy whereby traffic lights gave priority to collective transport. The only exception was along the main thoroughfare, where the rapid flow of through car traffic was guaranteed by a synchronized 'green wave'. Now the new ruling majority wanted to give priority to the tramway here too, which would seriously interfere with through car traffic. On the grounds that they did not want the question to get bogged down in the usual investigatory procedure, the ruling majority in the committee simply ordered the introduction of the new system without a special investigation.

The reaction was fierce. The proposal was roundly criticized by the opposition and by the administrators concerned. It was claimed that the proposal conflicted with basic (non-political) technical principles for the design of good traffic systems. Moreover it would drastically disturb the flow of car traffic, to no particular advantage for passengers on the trams. The ruling majority replied that no great technical difficulty was involved and the cost would be small, so the measure could easily be imposed without any necessity for a special preparatory study. And this was what the committee decided. But the minority group registered the protests they shared with the administrators, who questioned the right of the committee to call for action without any preceding investigation. The opposition politicians and the administrators both regarded the questions as strictly technical, and objected to the ruling majority treating it as political. Leading opposition politicians felt that the issue should be decided on objective grounds, not by 'political opinion-making'.

The administration now faced the job of implementing the decision. Before doing so, however, they decided to submit a report to the politicians describing the consequences of their decision. For instance, exhaust fumes would increase by 25% in the area concerned. The administrators also suggested making a start at two crossings (where they had in any case intended to suggest priority for the tramway), leaving the other crossings to be considered later. This recommendation was submitted to various other bodies for their comments; when the answers had been collated, it was decided to launch the first stage. The whole process took three years, i.e. from beginning to end of the mandate period.

Thus this issue too shows how difficult it can be for a leadership to exert influence by virtue of its decision-maker role. In some other similar cases the new ruling majority tried to implement its policies, every time with equally meagre results. Throughout their mandate period the transport situation remained essentially unaltered; the only major change was the continuing increase in car traffic, in Greaton as in the rest of the country. And there were only three years in which to act. The Socialists lost the next election—as might seem reasonable, since they had promised in the previous election to do something about the traffic situation and had clearly not kept their promise, thus providing grist to the mill of those who believed in the 'dishonesty' of politicians.

DECISION-MAKERS AS BEARERS OF RESPONSIBILITY

It is thus obvious that in their decision-making role the politicians in Greaton found it very difficult to steer their organization's behaviour. But, in most cases, it was not simply that the decision-makers' decisions were never carried out. It was rather that the politicians found it difficult to make the decisions they wanted, or to find the will to make any independent decisions at all. Only when the decision-makers tried to avoid these two problems, by making decisions without contacting the administration, did they have any problem in implementing what they had decided. Their difficulties stemmed from the conviction that decision-making gives rise to control, and from the very structure of the decision process. The case shows all too clearly that taking part in formal decision-making is not likely to endow the decision-maker with much influence.

In the introduction to this chapter I argued that it is natural for leaders to engage in decision-making in organizations with a strong political slant. Now we have seen that decision-making represents a very limited instrument of control. Many of the difficulties facing decision-makers are independent of the presence or absence of a strong political element in the organization. As we have seen in Greaton, the obvious political ingredients can have both positive and negative effects on the control capability of the decision-makers. The fact that the leaders demonstrated powerful conflicts among themselves was a disadvantage only when they tried to implement their own ideas about the tramway system. If the leadership wants to implement a decision whose content it has determined quite independently, it will have an easier task if its members are united. On the other hand the existence of an opposition meant that it was easier for at least part of the leadership group to formulate ideas independently of the led. And in Greaton the relatively strong action orientation of the decision-makers obstructed rather than favoured control.

Although the politicians exerted little control, they did not themselves perceive this as a major problem. When interviewed about their personal situations, none of the politicians ever suggested that they had come to the job with a view to acquiring influence. The most common motivation for wanting to be a politician was the chance it offered to see how society functioned and to be involved in its development. Both the politicians and the administrators believed that the politicians should bear the responsibility for the decisions—which they did, in that the formal decisions were made by them. And since they bore the responsibility, they had to defend the decisions to the outside world.

The Receiver Role

The picture of decision-making which emerges from this empirical study is far removed from the descriptions of the traditional hierarchic rational decision model. Actions were normally initiated here not by the leaders but by the led. The leaders issued no clear goals which could be easily operationalized; instead operational norms evolved gradually during the early stage when different sub-solutions and consequences were being investigated. It was typical of the leaders that they did *not* know very precisely what they wanted, that they were flexible and receptive to impressions. A decision involved not a choice between alternatives but the end point in a discussion which had gradually carved out a solution based on compromise. The tramway issue illustrates an attempt to introduce a different order; to use a decision model that resembled the hierarchic-rational model: the politicians in this case had definite ideas of what they wanted. The initiative came from the politicians, and the action (so they thought) would satisfy their goals; the job of the administrators was simply to effect it. It was no coincidence that the attempt failed.

The interaction between leaders and led can be better described by a communication model. Communication calls for a sender and a receiver. Experiments in social psychology (Zajonc 1960) have shown that a person wanting to send information has a more highly differentiated, a more complex and a more organized cognitive structure, i.e. a mental image or notion about the subject at hand, than an intending receiver. The receiver has a more open and simple cognitive structure. The sender finds it easy to weed out irrelevant information but more difficult to change his picture, since any change in a well-organized whole will trigger other changes. The receiver, on the other hand, can accept and integrate a considerable amount of new information and can thus let his picture grow successively more complex.

Tests on the cognitive structures of politicians and administrators in Greaton showed clearly that the administrators' cognitive structures in connection with the issues handled were far more differentiated, complex and organized than those of the politicians. The administrators were able to describe the issues in a very detailed manner, while the politicians' ideas about them were extremely simple in comparison. Anything else would have been most surprising; the administrators were after all experts in their various fields as a result of long training and much experience, while the politicians, although perhaps experts at managing, were there to represent laymen. The administrators' structures were also less balanced, i.e. they tended to be unequivocally positive or negative in their ideas about various solutions, while the politicians' views were in this sense more balanced.

A well-developed cognitive structure provides a stronger base for definite normative ideas than a less well-developed structure can. The administrators had strong views about what they wanted; the politicians' views were much weaker. The administrators thus possessed the requisite qualities for functioning as good senders, and the politicians had the qualities of receivers. These differences between leaders and led can be expected to exist in all the more and more common cases when leaders are experts in general management and in handling external relations important to organizational legitimacy rather than experts in the technical tasks of the organization.

The interaction between politicians and administrators in Greaton can be described as a 'transmission' from administrators to politicians. The administrators repeatedly presented material to the politicians, sharing with them their expertise and their views. The politicians gradually learned more and more about the frame of reference presented by the administrators and about the facts which were relevant to that frame. Tests showed that the politicians' cognitive structures were substantially more developed after the long process of handling an issue than they were at the start, although they were still far less developed than the administrators'. By the end of the process their cognitive structures were also less balanced than they had been at first: 'You can make a decision once you've formed an opinion', as the actors put it themselves.

To make decisions meant assuming responsibility for a particular action, which also meant that outsiders regarded the decision-makers as 'responsible' for the action taken. If someone were to be bold enough to assume this responsibility, he had to be sure he could defend both decision and action to other people, i.e. to act as a 'sender' *vis-à-vis* the grassroots in his own party and the general public. To be able to do this, a reasonably well-developed cognitive structure is needed—or at least one that is better developed than the public's. The politician must be a little bit more of an expert than the laymen he represents, which is why the decision process is important and why it takes a long time, particularly when an issue is complex or likely to arouse opposition, so that an active marshalling of the defensive arguments will be called for.

Hierarchic-rational models assume that the leaders or decision-makers are senders and the led are receivers; the decision-makers know what they want and they transmit the relevant information to those concerned with operations. When the conditions appropriate to this division of labour are not present, we cannot expect the model to work. It is unrealistic to expect those who know a great deal about operations to let themselves be convinced by other people who obviously know much less. People who know exactly what they want will find it quite easy to persuade others to support them; it is not as easy for those whose goals are more abstract and vague.

It is not difficult to see that the senders have influence, but how can receivers acquire any? Not, anyway, by specifying concrete goals or guidelines. The receivers' ideas about an issue are not normally sufficiently well-developed for them to be able to do this. Rather, criteria for 'good' or 'bad' solutions emerge in the course of the decision process. It commonly happens that when leaders are asked for goals and guidelines in the absence of an adequate decision base, their offerings are so general as to be useless for work in production. When the administrators in Greaton wanted usable guidelines, they preferred instead to adumbrate alternatives which suggested the possibilities inherent in a problem. By reacting to these outlines the politicians helped to narrow the field down to a few alternatives. Thus, with a relatively small investigatory input, a viable alternative could be achieved. The method used for working on the administrators in this situation was 'nagging', which often meant constantly reiterating the impossibility or necessity of certain concrete solutions. When such nagging succeeded, it implied that the administrators had accepted the politicians' views as their guidelines for a new solution, and sometimes they even learned to use arguments derived from their own frame of reference to support the new solution.

If senders choose to let themselves be influenced, they must adopt a listener strategy: by presenting their outlines and deliberations appropriately, they can detect intentions while also helping their receivers bit by bit to form a view of the problem.

The tramway case was an attempt on the part of the politicians to acquire influence in another way. With a vague feeling that it is easier to exert influence as a sender, the politicians tried to act as senders do. But the administration was not used to the receiver role, and with their much more highly developed picture of the issue they were unable to adopt such a role. Instead two senders confronted one another, each trying to send messages to the other, and communications simply broke down.

The politicians came up against similar problems on several occasions when it came to implementing their decisions. The principals sometimes refused or were unable to act as receivers. The politicians sometimes faced protests from organized protest groups. These groups consulted experts on traffic questions; they made their own analyses of the situation and suggested solutions which were almost as complex and well developed as those of the administrators. Thus, when politicians tried to explain their measures to the public, the information was greeted not by receivers but by other senders with cognitive structures better developed than those of the politicians themselves. It was not possible to communicate on these conditions, and the politicians were compelled to push ahead without being able to build up an understanding for their actions among the people at large. On several occasions this required the use of force and the help of the police. According to the politicians, situations like this were the most distressing aspect of their work; you really had to be 'thick-skinned' to be able to cope. If you give way, you are breaking an important part of your 'contract' with the administration. You are abandoning a planned implementation, and disturbing a complex weave of diverse measures. The very rare cases in which the politicians capitulated were referred to with horror by the administrators, as occasions when the politicians failed to do their job and ducked their responsibility.

Influence and Responsibility

A decision process of this kind links the decision-makers to the action, but the nature of the link does not agree with many decision theories or with the official picture of the organization. Outwardly, decision-making is normally seen—as in Greaton—as a question of control: the decision-makers control the action. But the type of decision process described here generates very little control or influence of this kind; rather, the led control the decision-makers.

The significant link between decision-makers and action appears instead in the shape of responsibility. The responsibility committed them to the action and to defending it against critics or opponents. This close relationship between decision and action made action very much easier to achieve, and in some cases the politicians' responsibility was probably even necessary, if there were to be any possibility at all of implementing the action. Many of the actions decided by the building committee were very controversial; they also took a long time to carry out and demanded a great deal of cooperation between different units. It would presumably have been difficult if not impossible to impose many of the major controversial changes in the urban scene, if there had not been firm responsibility and a strong commitment to the necessary measures on the part of the leading politicians.

It was just because the decision process was described as a control process that it generated responsibility. In our culture those who are perceived as 'causing' something are also regarded as responsible for it (see also Chapter 8), and those who control are undeniably 'causing'.

The processes described here show how not only decisions but also talk are made to agree with action by adjusting opinions to it and by presenting these opinions when carrying out actions. The opinions which the action-oriented administrators represent find expression in action. In the course of the decision process, opinions and talk are adjusted, so as to protect the action and promote its realization.

The role of the decision-makers is then to buffer the organization's actions, assuming the responsibility for it and coping with the world's criticism. The role of the organization members directly engaged in action is exposed to much less interference. There is less variability, more predictability; once the decision-makers have been persuaded to ratify the plans, things can proceed much as intended. Any interference from outside falls on the decision-makers: they bear a lot of responsibility but have little influence, while the led have a great deal of influence and little responsibility.

Action-oriented Decisions Provide Scope for Politics

The division of labour between decision-makers and actors paves the way for action. This action orientation is possible because the decision-makers systematically avoid the prescriptions of the rational model about how decisions should be made. As far as the decision-makers are concerned, we can say that the sequence of talk–decision–action has been reversed. The action provides the conditions for the decision, and talk is used to defend the implementation of the action. The decision process is concerned with responsibility and commitment rather than with choice, with action rather than the choice between alternatives.

Most of the conditions and processes described are not limited to organizations with strong political leanings but are more generally valid whenever leaders and led are coupled via decisions. But the decision idea seems to be particularly useful in political situations. In Chapter 2 it was argued that political behaviour in organizations and rationality go well together. The procedure described here exemplifies the way in which forces for action are created by avoiding rationality, even when there are strong political ingredients in the organization.

But vigorous action is generated at the expense of the leaders' influence. The leaders' role is to allow themselves to be controlled rather than to control in their relations with the led, and to exert influence rather than allowing themselves to be influenced in their contacts with those whom they represent. The control chain has been reversed in relation to the rational and official pictures. The principals or the leaders do not steer the led. If leaders do exert control, it is rather because they can sometimes refuse to accept responsibility by postponing or refusing to make a decision. And principals may be able to refuse to accept certain actions, or at least to replace leaders who have accepted them.

But these restrictions on the leaders' influence not only serve to create consistency between the three factors action, decision and talk; paradoxically they also provide an opportunity for separating the three and producing hypocrisy. Of course the leaders have to produce talk and decisions which are consistent with major organizational actions. But they can also talk and make decisions about things which are not to be carried out, and because of the restrictions on their influence they need not even risk any possible implementation! General slogans will rarely lead to action. And so the leaders can talk freely about what they want and intend to do, without having to adjust to what is actually possible. They may of course be forced into defending certain actions which have been or are being carried out, but they can compensate for this by talking about the future. Sometimes, too, they can make a decision and then try to assume the sender role—an obvious way of signalling what they would like to do, without much or any likelihood of the decision leading to action. If the rational model had worked in practice, it would not have provided the same opportunity for decoupling idea and action, politics and practice. The politicians' talk and decisions might then have steered the actions of the administration.

Thus the division into leaders and led, combined with the system of decision-making described here, obviously fails to produce what it claims in the way of decision-maker influence on action. But decision-maker and top management influence is not a problem that is crucial to the survival of organizations. Rather, decision-making helps to solve two other problems which are fundamental at least to organizations in environments characterized by inconsistent norms. In such environments it is often very difficult to win acceptance for individual actions; different groups call for different and contradictory actions. In this kind of situation an organization will need strong ideological support for its actions, and it is just this support that the organizational leadership provides by its assumption of responsibility in the kind of decision process I have been describing here. In this way the legitimacy enjoyed by the organizational leadership can be transferred to the sphere of action. And since the leaders' influence is weak and that of the action-oriented led is great, the prospects are also good that the chosen actions will be easy to implement. The decision model thus helps to solve the problem of producing vigorous action.

The other problem which this decision model helps to solve concerns the reflection of inconsistent norms. It can on occasion compensate somewhat for the sacrifice of politics to an action-orientation, by providing the organizational leadership with an opportunity to produce talk and decisions corresponding to norms which can be mutually inconsistent as well as being inconsistent with the actions performed. In so far as such talk and decisions can compensate for action, they can also help to make action easier to achieve.

5
Responsibility as an Impediment to Influence— The Case of Budgeting

In Chapter 4 I described what can happen to the relationship between politics and action when the coupling between the two depends on decisions. As a result of the decision processes, talk and decisions tended to be adjusted to action, while action was largely determined by the administrators; the decision-makers' task was then to assume responsibility for the action and to defend it to the rest of the world. We found that involvement in decisions can bring more responsibility than influence to the decision-maker concerned. In the present chapter I will demonstrate that decision-makers may be more interested in the responsibility effects of their decisions than in the decision content, one reason being that there may be a connection between responsibility and influence: the assumption of responsibility can mean a loss of influence. An organizational management can increase its influence by avoiding decisions and the responsibility that goes with them. It is this relationship which will be exemplified in the following description of a common type of decision process, namely budgeting.

BUDGETING

Budgeting is a common form of decision process in organizations.

Like many other organizational techniques it stems originally from the public sector. The importance of budgeting in this sector depends partly on the fact that a good deal of the funds available for distribution are derived from taxes and are thus independent of the production of individual goods or services. This means that the money is usually collected in a central unit, which then has to distribute it to various production units before production can occur. This type of redistribution problem does not necessarily arise in organizations where the production units acquire money direct from sales. However, this has not stopped the rapid spread of the budgeting technique over the last 20 years or so, even in organizations—private and public—which do acquire their revenues in this way.

But budgeting need not be concerned exclusively with the solution of a technical redistribution problem; the budgeting processes may have other causes and effects. The great importance of budgeting in the public sector suggests that it may have a role in politics: 'Budgeting lies at the heart of the policy process', as Wildavsky (1975) put it after studying national budgeting in a number of countries. In a study of municipal budgeting Olsen (1971) found that the budget process mainly fulfilled a symbolical function. In normative budgeting theory and in Wildavsky (1974, 1975) the budget seems to be regarded as an important instrument of control in organizations. As we shall see in the following discussion, the budget process can fulfil all these functions.

The budget is a decision on a grand scale: on one single occasion the organizational leadership makes decisions about virtually all operations over a future period, generally the coming year. The link between decisions and operations consists of money: the content of the decisions is the promise of money to various units or programmes. Instructions of a more or less concrete nature about the activities for which the money is to be used can be attached to the decisions. But compared with the type of decisions discussed in the last chapter, the coupling between budget decisions and action is a very loose one.

Budgeting and Hypocrisy

Because of its relatively loose links with action, budgeting

provides a good instrument for conducting politics and producing hypocrisy. Inconsistencies can easily arise between the budget
decisions and the action performed during the year. The fact that
money has been allocated to an operation does not necessarily
mean that the operation will take place; obstacles may well appear. Up to a point the inconsistencies can be regulated, depending on how much weight is given to budget control. If no great
effort is made to check how the money is being used, or very little
store is set by this kind of budget control, then inconsistencies are
more likely to arise. If inconsistencies are discovered and
criticized, the criticism can be dismissed on the grounds that
management has done what it could by making the money available, and that it is the operational side which has failed to use it,
or has wasted it, or has used it for something else—all of which
can be blamed on operational incompetence or contrariness.

The budget is a plan concerning the future. It therefore also
provides excellent opportunities for hypocrisy in the form of
discrepancies between present and past behaviour and promises
for the future. The budget also offers a good opportunity to
produce talk and decisions along the lines that 'everything will be
better in the future', particularly if the past or the present leave
little to boast about. Many organizations appear to be much more
interested in discussing their budgets than analysing their accounts (Brorström 1982, 1985). They often base their new budget
on the figures in the previous one rather than on any accounting
data; figures for current or even the previous year are not usually
available when the new budget is being prepared. This often leads
to big discrepancies between budget and accounting data
(Høgheim et al. 1989). By concentrating on budgets rather than
accounts, an organization enjoys greater freedom in presenting its
chosen image, not only internally but also to the outside world, so
that even its environment may begin to confuse facts with fiction.

The budget decision usually comes as the final stage in a long
budget process. In very open organizations such as public agencies at the national or municipal level, the whole budgetary
process as well as the final decision usually receives a good deal
of attention in the media; this is often the most important forum
in which organizations can talk about themselves to an audience
that can really hear them, and that hears them clearly. It is also
easy to conduct politics in the budget context, i.e. to produce

inconsistent talk. By definition a budget is concerned with the future, and it is not embarrassed by realities which may be difficult for people to disagree about. It is also easy to disagree in connection with the budget, since it is concerned with a continuous variable, namely money, about which there are as many views as there are coins.

In many public agencies budgeting really does lie at the heart of the policy process. A great deal of interest is devoted to the budget by the organizations themselves as well as by the media. Much of the debate both inside and outside these agencies occurs within the framework of the budget process, and much of the work of the administrators and the decision-makers is concerned with it. Work on the annual budget often continues for most of the year. The link between budget and operations is often weak; neither actual performance nor actual outlay necessarily stick very closely to the budget. But in the organization and the media any interest in actual outcomes as reported in annual reports is often extremely slight. Quite often the administration is unable to use all the money allocated to it. For instance, during the great expansion of the public sector in Sweden during the 1960s and 1970s, this was often the case simply because it was physically impossible to build as quickly, or to employ as many people, as the budget required. The budget provided a platform for promises, and on that platform there was no reason to limit staff numbers or restrict the scope of the promises. In fact the best sort of promises were those which would be impossible to fulfil, since they involved no real consumption of funds.

Thus the chief importance of the budget often seems to have been symbolical. Work on the budget provided an important platform for the reflection of inconsistencies in talk and decisions, while actions remained pretty loosely linked to the budgetary decisions. But the usefulness of the budget process to politics and its symbolical value both depended on the availability of more money than would be possible to spend. In more recent years, however, this has not been a typical state of affairs in the public organizations of Western Europe. On the contrary, the low level of general economic growth has also limited the growth of tax revenues, turning money into an increasingly scarce resource. In this situation the kind of behaviour described above tends to create financial difficulties. For national governments whose institutional arrangements permit them to spend more money than they have coming in, the result has almost without exception been a budget deficit. In other public agencies without the ability to generate long-term deficits, and where the shortage of money has thus been more tangible, the results have been different.

The lack of money has made it harder to satisfy a variety of demands by taking concrete action. It has thus become more important to produce inconsistent talk and decisions; the debate has become increasingly lively. But it also became more difficult to exploit the budget as an arena for politics, since it was necessary to limit the number of decisions which might call for big outlays. On the contrary, there was every reason for accepting a common interpretation of the role of the budget, namely that it can be used as a way of controlling action and containing expenditure. This would also imply a closer link between budget and action. Below I shall discuss the role of the budget in a case of municipal budgeting under perceived conditions of scarcity.

BUDGETING UNDER STAGNATION

Ulston is a small municipality in Sweden. The authority employs a workforce of roughly 5000 and at the beginning of the 1980s was reporting a turnover of around £65 million. Local taxes were high and the municipality had a heavy public debt. Like all Swedish municipalities Ulston set their own local tax rates in the form of a proportional rate on incomes, which in 1980 in Ulston was a little over 17%; if the county council tax is included, the rate was over 31%, and this meant that Ulston had one of the highest tax rates in the country. The residents also had plenty of experience of tax increases, most recently in 1980. A great many services were still inadequate: child care had fallen badly behind, many buildings and whole districts in the centre of the town needed renovating or rebuilding, the administration was scattered among innumerable different locations often in dilapidated buildings, and the care of the elderly was expected to make heavy demands in the future.

The political situation in the municipality had long been unstable. At election time only a few hundred votes separated the non-Socialist and Socialist blocs. The ruling majority in the council was always changing; after a period of Socialist government, the non-Socialist bloc won the election in 1979.

During the election the non-Socialist parties had promised to cancel the tax increases planned by the Socialists. Their intention was to hold the tax rate at the (high) level it had reached under the previous régime—although the current five-year plan already adopted indicated the necessity of an increase with 1.25 percentage point.

The first budget to be prepared entirely by the new ruling coalition was the budget for 1981. At least three reasons have already been mentioned why it should have been done without raising taxes. First, the tax rate was already the highest in the country. Secondly, most politicians in the ruling coalition wanted to avoid tax increases, and thirdly they had committed themselves to such a policy during the election campaign (a promise which had brought them victory; the Socialists had said they would introduce an increase).

Leading politicians and administrators were all firmly convinced that it should be possible to control the economy and municipal operations by means of the budget. If every effort were made in preparing the budget, they thought, it should be possible to keep taxes at their present level, and to produce a budget that really did control developments, i.e. one that restricted disbursements during the year so that tax revenues at the present rate would provide sufficient funds.

There seemed to be good reason for this conviction. The tax rate is traditionally established in the budget, and like other decisions the budget is often presented in the normative literature as an effective means of controlling developments in practice. In the normative world the budget has a number of qualities which make it seem like a good instrument of control, particularly if its task is to curtail expenditure. To begin with, the budget is a plan. It is intended to limit the administration's economic freedom of action, so that spending on day-to-day operations is restrained by a lack of money. Secondly, the plan is also supposed to exert control over the purposes on which the money is spent. At the same time the budget is intended to affect what happens in other arenas: it provides the economic limits to what people can plan and do.

Thirdly, the budget to some extent abolishes the chronological or sequential aspect of organizational operations; it imposes a sort of simultaneity; actions which will be realized at different times are balanced against one another at a single moment. When resources are scarce, this means that certain activities will appear to be mutually exclusive. If we do A we cannot do B. There is thus a strong incentive to exclude some activities.

This highlights the minus side of the budget operation: it is not only an enabling instrument, making it possible to produce something; it also imposes the sacrifice of something else. The expenditure-orientation of the budget has much the same effect; expenses rather than results are described and measured.

The leading politicians in Ulston soon realized that budgets in the real world can look very different from this, and can have other effects. They sent directives to all departments demanding a cut in costs. The budget negotiations then began, lasting as usual for almost a year. But the result of the process was very different from the intentions of the leading politicians. The budget finally presented implied heavy cost increases that made it necessary to raise taxes again. The budget included a 0.5 percentage point tax increase, bringing the total rate up to around 32%. At the same time public borrowing rose again. Nonetheless the budget indicated a predicted loss of liquidity amounting to about £1.5 million.

The new ruling coalition had failed. The budget process in Ulston did not put a stop to further expansion or to tax increases. Nor did it lead to any cost reductions. And what was more, the result was a budget that proved to be too capacious: when the budget year was over the financial accounts showed a budget surplus of more than £1 million, which was a record, as well as being the equivalent of a tax *reduction* of over 1 percentage point. Thus, although it turned out that taxes could have been cut, they had nonetheless been increased. In the next two subsections I will explain how this result could come about.

ROLES AND ACTORS IN THE BUDGET PROCESS

The budget process in Ulston was not particularly unusual. Its most uncommon aspect was perhaps the general conditions of the organization, which was wealthy (empowered to raise taxes from fairly rich taxpayers) but operating in a situation of uncertainty (as will be shown below). In other words it illustrates Wildavsky's (1975) missing category, the combination of richness and uncertainty—and it was not surprising that such a position resulted in a surplus. But the interest of using Ulston as an empirical illustration is that the budget process was in fact a fairly standard one. It included roles similar to those indicated in budget theory, and the people occupying these roles faced situations that are common to many organizations. We can now examine some of these common characteristics to provide the background necessary to our discussion of the role of responsibility-allocation in decision-making.

Roles: Guardians, Champions and Hoarders

Budgeting theory (Wildavsky 1974) describes the budget as a process of bargaining between actors pursuing different interests and occupying different roles. This was indubitably the case in Ulston, where we found advocates or champions of the various operations as well as guardians of the cash box.

We cannot expect actors playing the role of champions to bother themselves about the balance-sheet total, or about whether their precious projects might mean an increase in taxes. That is the guardians' job. Thus, if Ulston was to keep its present tax rate, the guardians would have had to be strong and there should preferably have been many of them. However, as in most organizations, the guardians in Ulston were few in number. The role of the guardian is traditionally played mainly by the top management, while the various departments assume the champion role.

In Ulston the politicians on the executive committee who belonged to the non-Socialist majority assumed the guardian role. The members of the opposition, on the other hand, were committed champions. An opposition does not have the same necessity to urge thrift, since their budget proposals are not expected to be implemented. In this case the opposition also thought taxes should be increased, so they saw plenty of scope for both current and future operations. They had even more scope than could be exploited, according to the most optimistic plans of the various departments. In this way the executive committee in its guardian role was substantially weakened when it came to battling with the champions in the various branches of the administration.

The situation was not improved by the role that the members of the various special committees chose to play. The politicians on these committees can be envisaged, at least in principle, as playing either the guardian or the champion role. They can either see themselves as representing the executive committee and the council, checking that the administrators keep within the prescribed limits and so on, or they can see themselves as representatives of the schools, the roads or whatever it may be, seeing it as their task to provide for the relevant interests in the best possible way.

In Ulston almost all the politicians on the various committees chose to be champions. They sought to ensure that their own departments received a larger portion—or at least not a smaller one—of the available resources. Their choice of role naturally made saving even more difficult, since it meant that the champions appeared not only in the opposition parties but also in the ruling coalition. It was not uncommon to hear people referring to the 'schools party', the 'roads party' etc., i.e. the clash of interests between the members of different committees was often stronger than the conflict between the regular political parties.

There was always a majority in favour of growth: champions always far outnumbered guardians, both as a whole and in the respective parties. Nor were the champions trying to promote their own demands against the demands of other departments. On the contrary, in this context there was a marked sense of loyalty and consideration for one another. Even in interviews no one was prepared to say which departments they thought had received too much money. So it was left entirely to the guardians to strike the balance between the different departments, and they were unable to exploit the knowledge and arguments that the various committee members certainly possessed about one another's operations. Such loyalty could of course hamper the arguments of any individual department in favour of expanding its own operations, but disloyalty might jeopardize the expansion of the whole administration.

For many reasons it is natural for committee members to assume the champion role. For instance, people are generally recruited on to committees because they already have an interest in, say, schools or roads, and they could easily get arguments for their cause from the relevant department. It must have been particularly easy to assume the role of champion in a period of stagnation:

if an operation seems likely to face a cutback, it is all the more important to defend it. Another reason for adopting the champion role in this case was the flexibility of the cash limits set by the the the council for the various committees. However much the guardians declared the limits could not be changed, everyone thought of preparing the budget process as a chance not only for adjusting costs to cash limits, but also for influencing the limits themselves. It thus seemed natural to committee members to try to increase the limits set for their own particular sphere of interest, which then made it impossible for them to act as guardians *vis-à-vis* the administration.

But champions and guardians were not the only roles that were played. Naturally the officials in the finance office did not play the champion role. Nor, however, did they really act as guardians. They were certainly trying to get the departments to save and to restrict their demands, i.e. they aimed to hold back costs. But they worked just as hard to get revenues increased, mainly by increasing taxes. The aim was a budget surplus. Their goal thus resembles the one generally assigned by economists to entrepreneurs: namely to maximize profit. They were playing the role of the hoarder. They wanted to produce a capacious budget; a budget that should if possible yield a surplus, and certainly one that would avoid a deficit. A capacious budget leaves room for manoeuvres now, and provides resources for an uncertain future.

In Ulston there were naturally good reasons for adopting a hoarder role, not least the large debts which had been accumulated and which now represented a heavy burden. The finance office was in a strong position, particularly when it came to discussing revenue requirements. These were the officers who analysed changes in the economic situation of the municipality and forecast how they would affect costs and revenues. The hoarders employed two main instruments: one for restraining costs and one for increasing revenues. On the cost-containing front this meant recommending concrete expedients for saving. On the revenue side they talked a lot about tax levels, seeking to establish certain expectations of future tax increases in people's minds. They did this in the five-year plan, which they had produced and which had been accepted by the council; it showed an awkward 'imbalance' in the future. And they also did it in their budget guidelines for the next year, which threw cold water on any hope of keeping taxes at the present rate.

The hoarders were successful when it came to protecting revenues, but this immediately complicated their other goal, namely to hold back costs: the expectation that taxes were anyway going to be increased provided the champions with arguments and filled them with optimism.

Actors—Their Values, Knowledge, Expectations and Organization

The politicians' view of their role is important to an understanding of the budget process described here. Almost all the politicians drew a line between 'politics' and 'saving'. By politics they meant inventing and deciding new activities. Given this definition, there was deplorably little scope for politics when saving was the order of the day. Saving was perceived as a really tough option. Some decisions to save were almost impossible to make. 'I don't want to be remembered as the one who stopped the new museum,' as one leading politician put it.

Some people knew much more than others about municipal operations and the possibility of effecting savings. Naturally the heads of departments knew a great deal more about such things than the central politicians and officials. It was far more difficult for the central units to see where cuts could or should be made, than it had been previously for them to see where increases could or should be allowed. The departments could always help them in their search for growth areas. The guardians suspected that there must be ways of improving efficiency in the departments, but they were not knowledgeable enough themselves to hit upon any appropriate measures. Committee members had a little more knowledge, but this did not help the guardians, as these politicians had assumed the champion role.

The different levels of knowledge as between guardians and champions is a typical aspect of budget processes. The guardians are all too likely to have just the amount of knowledge that makes savings difficult: if you know nothing about an operation, you can easily convince yourself that there must be plenty of scope for saving, and if you know a lot about it you have a good chance of seeing concrete opportunities for saving; but if you just know a little bit, it is more difficult to see how savings can be made.

Budgeting is a planning process in which expectations of the future are of central importance. They include expectations about the results of the budget process itself and about economic conditions during the budget year. In Ulston all the leading actors had firmly expected a tax increase to be necessary, despite the non-Socialist majority's express ambition to avoid this. As we have already seen, this expectation was confirmed by the finance office, not least in their five-year plan. The effects of this plan on expectations were very considerable. In the five-year plan the necessity for a 0.75 percentage point increase in the taxes for 1981 had been put on record. When the tax rate was contained at 0.5 percentage point many people perceived this as a 0.25 percentage point reduction! To them the plan was more real than the facts of life. Moreover this provided an excellent argument for the majority coalition to counter any charges that they had failed to keep their election promise.

Expectations engendered by the plan became so firmly rooted that people seem to have found it difficult or uninteresting to distinguish plans from reality. It took three interviews with various financial officers before I discovered that what some people were referring to as estimated cost savings were actually reductions compared with the (expansive) plan, but not compared with present costs! In order to discover whether there was any real reduction, further complicated calculations were required. Very few of the others interviewed were able to say how the 'cost savings' had been calculated.

Despite the powerful impact of the long-term plan on expectations, and consequently on the results of the budget process, the politicians showed comparatively little interest in the revision of the plan, which they were supposed to undertake each year. They concentrated instead on the immediate year's budget. After all, they thought, a decision in the long-term plan was not 'binding'.

The hoarders also benefited from the great uncertainty that prevailed. People were uncertain about various factors which were outside the municipality's control. Above all there was great uncertainty about what measures the national government would impose to enforce saving. Several government proposals were put forward during the budget process, and more were expected. It was difficult to predict exactly what measures would be imposed, and what their impact on the municipal economy might be. As a result of this uncertainty many people felt it would be safest to allow for margins in the budget; and at any rate the uncertainty provided the hoarders with good arguments. Even at the municipal departmental level the uncertainty could be used as an argument for seeking more money; the real estate department, for instance, could plead caution in cutting back their allotment, in view of the unpredictability of future oil prices.

THE ALLOCATION OF RESPONSIBILITY

The guardians' main instrument for controlling the budget was their right—and their duty—to make budget decisions. One major reason why it was difficult for them to acquire any real influence by exploiting this tool was the significant role of responsibility in the budget process: like other decisions, the budget is a question not only of distributing money but also of allocating responsibility.

During times of growth it is often quite easy to assume responsibility for various municipal activities, particularly in the budget process which is geared to future plans; dissatisfaction and criticism do not generally arise until some activity is actually being carried out. The sort of questions that are usually discussed, particularly in expansive budgets, are concerned with marginal increases in resources, i.e. new undertakings, or perhaps improvements in some currently criticized operation. In periods of stagnation, on the other hand, responsibility can easily become a heavy and unwanted burden. It can hardly ever be pleasant to bear the responsibility for cutting allowances, terminating activities, or making substantial cutbacks in budget applications.

There are two ways of avoiding this pain. One is not to take any cost-cutting action; the other is to avoid any responsibility for it. The disadvantage of the first method is that the overall budget is likely to be too generous; to the guardians the second method must therefore be preferable. For the champions, however, it is much better to let the guardians bear the responsibility for the cutbacks, thus reducing the risk that they will ever take place. The guardians would not have the courage to assume responsibility for them. The struggle between guardians and champions thus becomes essentially a question of the distribution of responsibility.

Responsibility is something assigned to us by other people, and it is connected with the blame or credit for some particular action or happening that is supposed to accrue to us. We are responsible for an action if we are regarded as having caused it to happen, for instance if we made the decision that it should take place. The extent of our responsibility depends ultimately on two factors: the importance ascribed to our own part in the particular context, and the conspicuousness of the relation between ourselves and the action concerned. If we want to play down our responsibility, we can point out that we share it with several others. Alternatively we can point out that we did not cause the action, for instance because we did not make any decision about it.

Since responsibility is something we possess in the eyes of other people, the responsibility for a particular action can only be ascribed to us in so far as the action is seen to have taken place. So a third way of avoiding responsibility is to try to make the action less obvious or visible.

The guardians in Ulston employed two main strategies, one involving the rejection of responsibility and one involving its assumption. The first was to call for savings and to threaten cuts in grants without involving themselves in the specifics of the administration's handling of the situation. Thus they attacked the administration on the grants side, hoping to avoid responsibility for the individual cutbacks. They were then accused by the departmental heads of having an unprofessional approach, for not caring whether things worked out or not. Committee members provided a suitable channel for the transmission of such messages since they knew just about enough, and yet did not know too much, to see that the cutbacks were unworkable.

Because of the difficulties involved in the first strategy the guardians turned to the second, which meant attacking the administration on the operational side. The idea was to compensate for the assumption of considerable responsibility by acquiring more knowledge. The guardians would make the decisions about cutbacks and thus assume responsibility for them, but they would also try to find the cuts for which it would be least painful to bear the responsibility or, better still, to look for ways of improving efficiency, since having responsibility for efficiency was no bad thing. They scrutinized every item of the budget in their discussions with the individual departments during the final budget negotiations. Some cost-cutting was achieved by discontinuing certain operations or investment projects. This approach left even less scope for improving efficiency than the first method. And it was also difficult to include any really radical cutbacks. Once again 'practice took over from politics', as one politician put it. 'Practice' meant looking at operations through the eyes of the administrators, and recognizing just how difficult or impossible it was to save. Consequently, some of the departments adopted a policy of willingly giving the guardians information about details, as a way of avoiding cutbacks.

Proposals and Arguments as Strategies

The chief response of the champions to the cash limits proposed by the guardians was not only to invoke the difficulty or impossibility of saving, but also to counter with some special proposals of their own. They declared that if savings must be made they should be substantial and concentrated to a single area. It was better to discontinue one operation altogether than to reduce standards across the board. Such discontinuations—the closing of a leisure centre for example—are highly visible to the world at large, and the formal decisions are taken by the politicians in the executive committee and the council. So the central politicians, i.e. the guardians, bear a heavy burden of responsibility.

The guardians' proposals were different. They preferred the idea of saving by making minor cuts over the whole range of operations. Their favoured proposal was what they called 'the little axe', i.e. that all departments should save roughly the same amount, e.g. 3% per year, but without saying how it should be done. Such a slight lowering of standards would be perceived as the responsibility of the departments; if holes in the road are not repaired people do not ring the top politicians to complain, they call the highways department. Moreover the guardians suspected that efficiency could probably be improved in most areas, and this would make any lowering of standards, and certainly any closures, unnecessary.

Thus the champions threatened the guardians, declaring that if they did not get enough money, closures would be necessary, and the closures or cancellations they suggested were often extremely visible and sure to be unpopular; in previous years the education department had suggested stopping school milk. Now it was being suggested that the recreation committee should cancel the grants to certain associations. Such grants were made direct from the finance office after a council decision. There was no risk of the administration or the committees being ascribed the responsibility for such a measure.

The champions' threats were largely effective. The only major closure decision concerned an unprofitable minor service facility. But even this met with violent protests from the opposition, which made a big political issue of the shutdown. In other words it was made very clear where the responsibility lay.

Responsibility is concerned not only with *what* people believe others are doing, but also *why* they think they are doing it. For example more responsibility is ascribed to someone who is assumed to have carried out (or decided upon) an action of his 'own free will', than to someone who has been 'compelled' to do it. It is important to note that the actor's own motives for his action are uninteresting in this context; it is the motives which others ascribe to him which matter. These ascribed motives can be affected by argument, i.e. presenting explanations of actions and decisions which can be used in the process of allocating responsibility. An actor can use such explanations to soften the link between himself and his action, or to present the action in a positive light so that it becomes a good thing to be held responsible for it. In Ulston the actors tried to steer the distribution of responsibility not only by proposing what actions were to be taken but also by arguing their case.

For instance the actors would deliberate on the savings theme: was it a good thing or a bad thing to save, and why did they want to save? On the first of these points the champions would talk about the importance of various municipal activities, not only to demonstrate the negative aspect of cutbacks and retrenchments but also in terms of the much needed jobs that these same activities provided. The guardians meanwhile talked about the negative aspects of a tax increase. And on the second point they referred to the poor economy of the country as a whole as well as in the municipality, and generally tried to spread a sense of 'crisis'. It was not their fault that costs would have to be cut. As a result of the proposed across-the-board cuts, they were simply transferring the savings inflicted by environmental conditions to the departments, without really making any decisions themselves. But when the opposition (and even the hoarders) pointed out that it would be possible to increase taxes, then it became difficult for the guardians to claim that they 'had' to make cuts: if they had decided *not* to increase taxes, they would also have been held largely responsible for the cutbacks which would then have become necessary.

To cut down in a general way in order to prevent tax increases seemed at least to some actors to be a positive thing, i.e. they did not mind being held responsible for it. But to cut back, or refuse to increase an allocation in some specific case, was not pleasant. Thus the guardians found it very difficult to counter the arguments of the individual departments. Their own argument about the country's generally poor economy was not much help. The champions simply claimed that even if the economy as a whole was in a poor way there was still no need to save in their particular field. It was not impossible to increase taxes or charges or the borrowing debt (particularly by the little bit necessary in order to avoid one particular cutback). And in any case it was always possible to make a cut somewhere else. And when the guardians claimed that the same saving was being made everywhere else, they were still talking about a decision of their own. In other words, if a cut was made in a particular sphere of operations, it was the guardians who had freely chosen to make it and they must bear the responsibility.

The champions also argued that they were not responsible for the fact that no cuts would be made in their department. They referred to a series of conditions out of their control, such as laws forcing them to produce certain services or general price increases making their operations more expensive. The champions also argued that there were close links between money and service— less money would always result in proportionately less service. In other words, they excluded the possibility of increased efficiency, thereby emphasizing the only negative element in the proposed cutbacks.

Generally speaking the champions had the best arguments, in

that it was easier for them to demonstrate that the negatively charged responsibility belonged to the other party, namely the guardians. The guardians did not have much to set against these arguments. It is difficult to prove that an operation is not necessary, or that outside circumstances make some specific cutback unavoidable, and it is very hard to show that the champions are responsible—particularly if the guardians make the formal decisions on individual cuts.

As it turned out, the guardians later found it quite easy to justify why they finally decided to increase taxes. They pointed out that they were still keeping within the limits recommended by the national government. They felt they had done a good job at saving, for a first attempt; it is difficult to change everything in one year, nor is it possible to make an abrupt break with everything the administration has planned. In other words the result was not so bad, and in any case they were not fully responsible for it.

'Division of Labour' for Expansion

In many ways the budget process in Ulston was determined by two factors: the ease with which the guardians could be held responsible, and the champions' superior knowledge. All ways of saving (closures or cancellations, lowering of standards or improvements in efficiency) were blocked by a kind of division of labour between guardians, champions and hoarders.

Guardians can most easily be held responsible for closures or cancellations. These are the most visible of all savings, and those which are most obviously the result of central political decisions. The guardians in Ulston were often unable to cope with the heavy responsibility that such measures involve, and therefore tried as far as possible to prevent them from occurring. This left the lowering of standards, or improvements in efficiency. But the champions were very good at pointing out the impossibility of any acceptable reduction in standards or improvements in efficiency, safe in the knowledge that the guardians did not know enough about the complicated issues. Thus the champions ensured that there would be no lowering of standards and no improvements in efficiency. Whereas the guardians' role was to prevent closures or cancellations, and the champions' to prevent a lowering of standards or improvements in efficiency, the role of the hoarders seems to have been to promote this 'division of labour' by encouraging expansion. If ample resources are made available, the necessity for any cutbacks immediately becomes less urgent. The hoarders found it almost as difficult as the guardians to push through cutbacks, but it was quite easy for them to see that more resources were made available. This was because they held the purse strings, they handled the financial reporting, and they made the budget estimates—in short they were the experts on the municipal economy, and when they claimed that money was lacking and a financial crisis was pending no one had the knowledge to argue against them. The hoarders also had a lot of good arguments showing the advantages of capacious budgeting. 'In these uncertain and difficult times, it is important that the municipal economy should be strong and resistant.'

The result of the budget process was that expansion and tax increases both continued, which meant that at the end of the budget year there was a large cash surplus. The threat of a 'poor' economy had resulted in a surplus. The champions had succeeded in getting so much money that they had been unable to spend it all. Both champions and hoarders had done well.

The budget process in Ulston illustrates clearly how difficult it can be for decision-makers to exert influence just because they must make the formal decisions. The guardians certainly had little influence on the design of the budget; and the major impediment to their influence was the very fact of their right and duty to make decisions! The responsibility generated by their decision-making impeded any influence they might otherwise have had.

CONTROL—SUPPLY AND DEMAND

The budget process in Ulston shows how the responsibility attaching to decisions can have paradoxical effects on control in organizations. When the guardians became aware of economic problems, they were no longer interested in the kind of decoupling of decisions and actions which had been typical of the expansion period, and which involved them in decisions rather than action. Now, instead, they wanted to use the budget to limit the amount of action and consequently also the cost, in other words to link decision and action together.

Paradoxically, however, this ambition on the part of the guardians resulted in bargaining strategies aimed at loosening the link between decisions and actions. The guardians were trying to avoid deciding exactly what actions should be carried out. They preferred to indicate general economic cash limits to the departments, without saying how these should be achieved. They tried to get the champions to make the decisions about what specific actions the money should be used for. In order to tackle the economy as a whole, they tried to abstain from controlling individual actions. The supply of control was clearly limited.

But the demand for control was all the more marked. The champions tried to get the guardians to say exactly what cutbacks they were to make, hoping that if the guardians were forced into a control situation they would not be able to achieve much in the way of cutbacks (perhaps none at all). This proved to be an accurate assessment of the situation; the guardians turned out to be almost wholly incapable of controlling cutbacks; all they could control was expansion.

Thus there was a shortage of control: the demand was greater than the supply. It was the very people who would be controlled who were demanding control, while those who would exert the control were trying to avoid it. We appear to have a situation here that contradicts most theories of control and power: it is generally assumed that there is an ample supply of control but little demand for it, that there will always be at least some people who want to exert control and who strive to acquire it, while those who are exposed to their strivings for control will try to evade it. The seeming paradox in this case can be explained by the fact that guardians and champions were both fully aware that control over specific actions would mean less control over the economy as a whole—either the municipal economy in the case of the guardians or the department economy in the case of the champions.

The champions won the battle to force others to assume control, and the guardians finally decided on a number of expansive measures. Thus decision and action were mutually consistent; decisions were coupled to actions, but, as in the case of Greaton, not in such a way as to put the decision-makers in control of the actions. Rather, those who were directly involved in the actions steered the decision-makers towards the decisions they wanted. As a result of these decisions, the actions acquired the financial and other kinds of support needed for their implementation from the central politicians and administrators.

The explanation of all these effects is that decisions generate responsibility. In periods of expansion the budget decision granted responsibility but little influence; the departments were allowed considerable freedom, and there was often little consistency between specific decisions in the budget and in the actions actually performed. Even when budget and action agreed, the process normally inclined to yield more responsibility than influence: the budget decision may refer to the whole operation, but in designing the budget the discussions generally revolve around minor changes in grants compared with the previous year (so-called incrementalism). During the period of stagnation the relation between responsibility and influence became more crucial to the guardians: they wanted to avoid responsibility for cutbacks while also wanting to influence the content of the budget so that reasonably appropriate cutbacks would in fact be achieved. But responsibility inevitably attached to them, because it was after all their duty to make budget decisions, and this impeded their influence. Because of the negative effects of bearing responsibility for cutbacks, the guardians no longer either wanted or dared to make any decisions on the subject.

In Chapter 4 we saw how difficult it was to use decisions as a way of acquiring influence, but also how easy it was to acquire responsibility in this way. Now we have also found that responsibility can directly influence the content of a decision, i.e. the choice which the organization makes. By putting most of the responsibility on the decision-makers, the champions were able to influence not only the decision-makers' choices but also what the guardians said they wanted to achieve. Even preferences appear to have been affected by the burden of responsibility. Thus, once again, it was not simply an implementation problem, caused by actors refusing to obey the decisions of the decision-makers.

What is more, the decisions of the guardians about continuing or expanding operations were not binding on the champions. If they wanted to make some cutback of their own during the budget year, they were free to do so. The guardians would be only too grateful, even if the champions had declared those very cutbacks to be impossible during the budget process. Moreover, as in the expansive period, the budget process generated a surplus of money both centrally and in the departments—money which was used or which could have been used for further operations.

Presumably the influence of the guardians would have been greater if they had not been lured into trying to control the content of the budget by their decisions. If they had actually succeeded in restricting their decisions to indicating cash limits for the different departments, and had not included the content of the operations in their decisions, they would have had a better chance of achieving at least one of their goals: to limit expenditure and thus also the tax rate. More influence can be acquired by avoiding the decision-maker role than by shouldering it; responsibility can impede influence.

Thus the budget process was concerned with control, even if the control did not proceed in the same direction as is suggested in normative budget literature. The top was controlled by the bottom. The budget became a question of financing—not a process in which the central level allocated money to the local level according to its preferences, but a process whereby the local level ensured that its operations would be financed.

One of the main reasons why responsibility was so important in the budget was that the relevant talk and decisions were being played before external as well as internal audiences. They not only affected internal affairs; they also constituted organizational outputs to be observed by the world outside. The decision-makers were not only responsible in the eyes of the organization's own members but also in the eyes of the public which was to enjoy the services and pay the taxes. Budget processes are also concerned with an organization's relations with its environment. This aspect of the process will be discussed in the next subsection.

BUDGETING AS AN INSTRUMENT FOR FINANCING

As was noted in the introduction to this chapter, budget processes provide suitable instruments for the production of hypocrisy. In one sense the Ulston budget process produced less hypocrisy than organizations in periods of expansion are capable of. The link between budget decisions and subsequent actions in Ulston became much firmer than it had been, in that a greater number of the budget decisions were actually carried out. As we have seen, this was because both guardians and champions perceived resources as scarce; consequently the guardians tried to limit the number of decisions about expenditure, and the champions tried to ensure that financing really was available for the actions they wanted to realize.

But in another sense the process produced more hypocrisy. The external demands on the organization, as perceived by its members, were inconsistent: the organization was under pressure to reduce taxes, or at least to hold them at the current level, while it was also being asked to provide more and better services. The budget processes reflected both these demands. A lot of talk about cost reductions was produced but in practice services actually continued to expand. This was typical behaviour in Sweden at the time: there was a great deal of talk about efficiency and savings on all kinds of occasions devoted to this topic, but virtually no improvements in efficiency were ever actually made (Rombach 1986) and expansion continued.

Høgheim *et al.* (1989) reported similar results in Norwegian municipalities. One major difference, however, was that budgets were being used there as proof of saving. The decisions in the budget implied continual reductions in total operations, while actual developments as reported in the accounting records revealed uninterrupted growth. This hypocrisy was produced by fixing attention on the future, so that both the actors themselves and external observers in the media and the state organizations stuck to the budget figures in comparing different years.

External Financing

The budget process is thus well suited to the job of maintaining legitimacy in inconsistent environments; but it can also have other more direct effects: it can operate as a financing instrument not only internally but even externally as well.

The model of the budget process which I have described here can be used not only for describing the struggle between organizational levels but also for describing the organization's relations with its environment. In terms of this model the relations between public organizations and taxpayers can be conceived as relations between different roles in the budget process. The organizations can be seen as champions and hoarders, as against the general public acting as guardians. Like the organization's own guardians, the public cannot easily acquire information about the various operations or learn fully to understand them, and this makes it difficult for the public to say no. In their champion role organizations employ a number of classical tricks: they claim that 'activity' is identical to 'money' (if health care is not granted more money, there will simply be less health care); they threaten to discontinue whole operations; they conceal opportunities for improving efficiency; they describe in lurid detail the effects of any reduction of their grants, and they are careful to ensure that they have no competitors, who might be able to show that the same operation could be run more cheaply. As hoarders, the organizations obscure their resources in incomprehensible accounting systems and explain that there is no money, or at least that there will be no money soon when the crisis they have all been talking about actually appears (normally in two years' time).

Financing calls for different strategies, depending on whether it is based on taxes or borrowing, for example. When a company or any other organization wants to borrow money from a bank or to acquire capital by issuing shares, it first has to show that it is solvent. In its share prospectus the company and its future prospects are described in glowing terms. In order to protect creditors or shareholders, various laws and accounting norms are designed to prevent companies and others from exaggerating their economic status. In tax-based financing the reverse strategy obtains: in order to emphasize the need for money it is necessary to describe the organization's economic status in gloomy terms, to claim a present or future shortage of money, to point to threatening crisis. Nor are there generally the same strict legal rules obstructing organizations from understating their economic status.

The internal struggle for money between guardians, champions and hoarders makes a strong impact outside the organization, as the whole budget process gets a lot of attention in the media. A typical budget process opens with the guardians telling the champions about the great shortage of money, and the hoarders talking about a threatening financial crisis. The champions are told they must lower their sights. The attentive taxpayer is thus clearly given to understand that the money he has previously paid is now finished and more is needed. A few months later the champions respond, showing just how impossible it would be to save as much as the guardians want without very seriously or even fatally affecting operations. Newspaper headlines shout about all the programmes, so dear to the people, that are going to be abolished. Staff and public are moved to protest, lists of names are collected, demonstrations held. The public recognizes that the only chance of rescuing the particular programme they want most is to give more money to the organization. Some months later it becomes increasingly obvious that taxes or charges must be increased, or at most that they cannot be cut. By the time the final budget decision is reached, most people probably accept it as perfectly sensible and right.

Thus the budget process does not only help the champions to win acceptance from the guardians for the expenditure they crave, but it also helps the organization as a whole to win the understanding of those who will ultimately pay the additional costs. Again the budget process is more successful as an instrument of control from 'the bottom up' than from 'the top down', as a financing instrument rather than a means of control by the leaders, since it can alter the way the external contributors perceive the supply of money and the need for it. Thus once again the budget process can be described not only as a process which shows in a very general way how the organization responds to a variety of demands; it is also a process directly linked to financing.

In Ulston the financing process was very successful: the organization was able to procure much more money than it could spend, a result that Ulston shared with many municipalities in a similar situation. At the same time the budget process was useful in concealing or legitimizing this excess of liquidity since it focused attention on the future, not the present. And in the future today's figures are irrelevant, and money is always in short supply.

Internal Decisions and External Effects

Decisions have been the subject of this and the previous chapter. Decision processes offer a natural way of coupling politics to action in organizations. But our discussion has also shown that decisions tend to endow the decision-makers with responsibility rather than influence. We have also seen how responsibility can promote both implementation and financing; in both cases the decisions help to convince the outside world of the rightness of the organization's actions. Thus the decisions help to create consistent views in the environment's demands, and it is easier to achieve action once these inconsistencies have been reduced.

The decision processes described here have thus been largely determined by intentions and deliberations concerned with internal conditions; but they have also had external consequences. In the next two chapters I shall describe how politics in an organization can have a more direct effect on its external relations. And once again the concept of responsibility will be important to our understanding of organizational behaviour.

6
The Responsible Organization

On an organization's ability to confront and reflect external demands much of its legitimacy rests. Success in reflecting a large number of inconsistent demands benefits the organization, which thus actively needs such demands to be made. But it is also important to the organization to be able, up to a point, to determine the way in which the demands are reflected.

Many organizations also encounter external demands that ultimately refer to circumstances outside the organization; these demands imply that the organization should influence events in the common environment which it shares with those making the demands. The organization becomes responsible for part of its environment. This is typical of the demands made by governments, for instance, but the same kind of thing is also spreading to other large organizations. Such organizations are seen as instruments for the satisfaction of the demand-maker's interests, but if the organizations are to be able to exert a powerful controlling impact on their environment, they need to coordinate their talk, decisions and products and point them in a particular direction. But this kind of coordination makes it difficult or impossible to reflect a diversity of interests.

Organizations with pronounced political characteristics can easily be perceived as 'generally benevolent', geared to other people's well-being rather than to their own, and as manipulative, geared to changing the world around them. But in practice there is a conflict between the ability to reflect a lot of inconsistent demands, and the possibility of satisfying all these demands as they are actually formulated. Not all demands can be satisfied by the organization's products or by its assumption of control. Some must be handled by talk and decisions instead. The organization must be able to avoid production, or the assumption of control, without at the same time abandoning the idea of presenting itself as engaged in both. This will be the subject of this chapter and the following one.

First I shall examine ways in which organizations operating under the controller's flag can avoid exerting control in practice. In both chapters my examples will be culled from national and local governments and their relations with industry. In the present chapter I shall be looking at national industrial policy.

SOCIETY AS HIERARCHY

In the popular political debate the state is often perceived as a controlling force. It is assumed that the state controls or at least strives to control large sections of societal development. Society is often perceived as a hierarchy, in which the state occupies the controlling leadership position. This is the same image as the one generally employed to describe the state's own vast apparatus, which is also assumed to be hierarchic in that it is headed by parliament and government, which control the work of the departments or ministries, which in turn control the various public agencies. Order and meaning are created in terms of a vertical concept of society. The role of the state in society is thus often discussed in terms derived from theories of organizational management. It is assumed that the state and its 'management', consisting of elective politicians, possess both the will and the ability to change the behaviour of other subordinate actors in light of their own 'goals', and that these goals are concerned with the development of society as a whole. The politicians' decisions are then 'implemented', thus leading to the fulfilment of the political goals. But many obstacles can appear along the way: a complex and often contrary administration, or the resistance and unwillingness of other groups in society. An area of research known as 'implementation research' is concerned about the problem why so many weighty decisions fail to generate the relevant action or to produce the effects of which the decision-makers spoke.

One area to which the hierarchy metaphor is commonly applied is the area of industrial policy. It is assumed that the purpose of industrial policy is to steer the structure and development of business companies in such a way as to align them more closely with the preferences of the politicians, perhaps as regards employment, growth, level of technological development or export sales. Such ambitions require not only that the political leadership actively moves to control the development of the industrial companies, but also that it solves certain difficult problems; it is by no means clear, after all, how the desired goals should be achieved. Industrial policy in Western countries has given rise to a wide-ranging normative debate, in which the conduct of the various policies has been sharply criticized and many possible alternative approaches have been suggested (Wolff 1986).

According to the hierarchy metaphor industrial policy is initiated and carried through by the political system. If we abandon this image, however, we can see more clearly that industrial policy requires the participation of at least two parties, namely industry and politicians. Industrial policy can be defined as the interaction between these two. It is not self-evident which party has the greatest interest in industrial policy, which is most active, or which takes the most initiative. The balance will vary from one situation and one case to another. Industry and politicians both conduct industrial policy. Industrial companies often have powerful reasons for associating themselves with the state politicians: the state has money, and it is a source of financing which can often be tapped when other sources have dried up. States have also shown a capacity for survival that far outstrips that of almost any business company. Thus the interest of the business world in industrial policy is not difficult to understand. The fact that politicians associate themselves with business companies seems more difficult to explain. The hierarchical notion that the role of the politicians is to control and organize offers a possible explanation, but a highly dubious one.

IMPLEMENTATION OR LEGITIMATION

The hierarchy metaphor gives expression to an idea of implementation: that the state seeks to control its environment. Against this can be set an idea of legitimation: that the task of the state is rather to create legitimacy for its own situation and that of society. I shall now examine these two interpretive modes a little more closely.

Implementation is generally taken to mean the way in which ideas, as expressed in decisions for instance, can generate the corresponding action. The implication is that some person or persons tries to produce certain concrete results, without having full control over the processes that lead to the results. In particular it is generally assumed that control over those parts of the process that consist of action is weaker than the control over the parts that concern ideology. Anyone who wants to implement something has to try to influence the actions of others. We can speak of different 'degrees' of implementation.

The most extreme form would consist of *problem-solving*: the organization tries to solve problems in its environment, i.e. it is not only equipped with powerful intentions (which identify major problems and possible solutions), but it also commands activities geared to discovering the best possible action to take, or at least some action that will be acceptable. These actions are then carried out by others.

In a less extreme variant the organization aims not at problem-solving but at *control*. Even if the organization does not initiate action with a view to solving the problems of others, it may still want to be party to determining the action that others could take. The organization wants to control what happens, and is an active initiator.

In the mildest form of implementation the organization still expects to ensure that certain actions are undertaken, but it does not actively concern itself in determining what they are. The organization *supports* certain actions. The actions need not be controlled by the organization; even less need they represent solutions to problems which the organization itself has posed.

Thus we have three different kinds of implementation: problem-solving, control and support. In all of them influence is to be brought to bear on the behaviour of the environment, but the link between the organization and this behaviour will vary in strength.

In the implementation perspective, national industrial policy means that the leading political bodies such as parliament and government try to bring influence to bear on the industrial system. The politicians may solve the problems experienced or generated by the industrial system, they may steer industrial development, or at least they support developments already under way in the industrial system.

In a legitimation perspective, on the other hand, neither actions nor the behaviour of the environment have any importance as results of the organization's undertakings. Here, the behaviour of the environment is not a goal but, at most, a means. Now the essential result is legitimacy. The main strategy whereby an organization can create legitimacy consists of reflecting in its own structure and processes and products a variety of norms, values and interests that obtain in the environment. This strategy provides a *direct* means of legitimation.

But legitimacy can also be created indirectly, via the legitimacy of the environment; the indirect approach brings us to the question of *responsibility*, to the question of how far the organization is regarded as having caused external events to happen. Responsibility for external conditions can be ascribed to the organization either because it is believed to have actively influenced the environment through its actions or because it is thought to be in a position to exert such influence whether or not it has actually chosen to do so. This responsibility links the organization to the environment, and its own legitimacy becomes dependent on the legitimacy of the external circumstances. If the external circumstances for which the organization is held responsible are of a negative kind, the organization can maintain its own legitimacy in either of two diametrically opposite ways: by trying to dispossess itself of any responsibility for the external situation, or by assuming responsibility for it but endowing it with greater legitimacy.

If the organization adopts the second of these strategies, i.e. it assumes responsibility, it can increase its legitimacy by trying to show the external situation in a positive light. Theoretically this can be done by taking action of a kind likely to affect people's views of the situation—in other words implementation by problem-solving, with all the difficulties this can involve. But perceptions of the external situation can also be influenced without making any material change in the situation itself. Exerting influence exclusively on perceptions can be called *situational legitimation*. In this type of legitimation not only is the organization legitimated, but its environment is also influenced—but with a different kind of influence than the implementation strategy implies.

Thus legitimation can be produced in three ways: by direct means, by influencing responsibility, or by situational legitimation. In the case of national industrial policy 'responsibility' means that the state and the political leadership are responsible for conditions in the industrial system in the sense that they are regarded as being able to steer industrial development. If the industrial system exhibits negative qualities and its legitimacy is consequently low, this responsibility will be a negative property.

If the state renounces this responsibility, it decouples itself from the industrial system. We could call this responsibility-avoidance the destabilization strategy; if it is adopted on a wide front it means the state leadership distancing itself from significant aspects of societal development, and this in turn can lead to conflict and instability in the industrial system and perhaps in the long run even in the state leadership itself. Correspondingly the assumption of responsibility can be called the stabilization strategy, and it is this strategy which has generally speaking been the main strategy of the governments of many industrialized countries since the Second World War. It has also led to what is sometimes referred to as government overload, i.e. governments have assumed responsibility for almost everything from the global business cycle and industrial development to the youth problem and the technology of housing construction.

Instruments

There are three instruments for creating legitimacy: talk, decisions and production. Talk is an important tool; it is through talk that we can describe situations as positive or negative, or describe our own roles, influence our own responsibility or present arguments about decisions, actions and situations. Decisions allocate responsibility and the decision process can be designed so as to reinforce or to weaken legitimacy. Different types of production, depending perhaps on where it is initiated, can also affect legitimation in different ways.

Talk, decisions and products are also tools which organizations employ in implementation contexts. An organization can try to change the behaviour of others by arguing, by making forceful decisions and by taking action itself.

AN ILLUSTRATION

To illustrate this discussion of implementation and legitimation I shall briefly describe and analyse a case of state industrial policy. It concerns a government proposal for saving jobs in a town suffering from severe unemployment.

Stanby

Stanby is a town with high unemployment. It is dominated by a large state-owned industrial company and is a major recipient of industrial aid from the state. On several occasions hopes of a more favourable situation for industry and more jobs have been dashed. In the middle of the 1980s the government presented a special bill for the town, including various decisions and expedients which were to improve its situation. It was estimated that the cost of these various measures would run into several hundred million pounds. The idea was to restructure the main state-owned company in the town, which would lead to more unemployment, while at the same time launching an aid package and new investment by the state, which would help to improve the employment situation. The bill was presented as the government's way of solving Stanby's problems. Thus the government was claiming that it was engaged in the most extreme form of implementation, namely problem-solving. How had the government arrived at this comprehensive bill, incorporating decisions about so many measures that would cost so much money?

The story had begun several years earlier. First the trade unions in the town had produced a union programme of action. A little later local members of parliament also raised the question with the government party and persuaded the national party organization to declare its stand on tackling unemployment in the area. The local members then presented the party's national executive with further demands for action. The national executive decided that a plan of action should be drawn up.

A working group was appointed, including central and local party members. The central politicians were anxious that any proposals should be firmly rooted in the community, where the people best knew their own difficulties, and the local politicians were anxious that 'the people from outside' should really face up to the problems and needs of the town. Thus common goals underpinned the way things were organized: the working group talked to various leading actors in Stanby and in the unions, thereby collecting virtually all the suggestions that were being made by every kind of local interest.

It was then a question of deciding which proposals to include in the plan, and how they should be presented. The plan was to include only promises which would be kept. Where the technical problems connected with a proposal appeared insoluble, or the decision base was inadequate in some other way, or opinions were divided in the town, then a cautious approach was adopted; it might be suggested that a proposal be 'investigated further', or it might be recognized as 'important' without any promise being made about definite action. It was often suggested that something 'ought' to be done rather than that it 'would' be done. A great many concrete and often minor proposals were included in an appendix, which—it was felt—implied no promises.

A provisional plan was then circulated for comment by all those involved in the proposals. As a result a great many instances of 'ought to be' were altered to 'must be'. After this the plan was approved by the local party branch, thus providing the basis for the party's election manifesto.

The plan then formed the grounds on which a government bill could be based. The practicability, the costs and the possible employment effects of the various proposals in the plan had been thoroughly investigated, but a bare month was then allowed for a last round of deliberations and negotiations between the ministry of finance and various other departments. The state-owned enterprise and other organizations in Stanby were given another opportunity to submit their demands. A further round of comments from the various state departments generated several new suggestions about the arguments which could be used.

The final bill included a little more than half the proposals (about 30) originally included in the plan. Most of the other proposals were not mentioned at all or it was suggested that they should be considered by other on-going investigations. Only a few were explicitly rejected.

When the bill was presented three points were emphasized: that the various measures were intended to deal with the problems both now and in the longer run; that the costs amounted to hundreds of millions—this was the main point in a five-line summary of the bill on its first page; and that the bill was based on the plan. In interviews in the media the prime minister emphasized the 'democratic' background to the bill: the proposals had been worked out by the people of Stanby themselves. Subsequent developments would depend on the people there, and not on centralized decisions in the capital city.

STANBY—IMPLEMENTATION OR LEGITIMATION?

How can we interpret the activities described above? To what extent can they be understood in terms of the model presented here: how far can they be interpreted as different kinds of implementation or legitimation?

Problem-solving

There is nothing to suggest that the work on the Stanby bill had a problem-solving function. Problem-solving would have presupposed an analysis, in which the causes of the problems—in this case long-term unemployment—would have been investigated. The actions to be taken would then have emerged from the analysis. Such an analysis was almost demonstratively avoided; information-gathering rather than analysis was the method adopted for generating solutions. Furthermore, ideas were sought in the town, i.e. among those who had demonstrably *not* succeeded in solving the problems themselves. If a start had been made by analysing the problems, there would have been a risk of producing problems without solutions; now, instead, solutions were produced without problems. Nor did the time allowed really permit of any problem-solving: a month was spent on the plan, while the bill was designed in a couple of months and actually written in a few days.

Nor were the criteria for eliciting the proposals based on any analysis of the problems. Suggestions were rejected or changed because they were costly, because they did not fit into the present aid system, because they lacked energetic backers, because they came within the brief of other investigations already under way, because they would compete too much with other towns, or because they were unrealistic (e.g. industrial projects which were obviously not profitable). Estimates of how much money was needed for the various subprogrammes and their employment effects were produced in a slapdash manner.

Nor did any of the leading politicians interviewed claim to know how the town's problems could be solved. They did not believe they would be solved and doubted that they were at all possible to solve. Unemployment would remain high. Above all they did not think the bill would help. The problems were formulated in the foggiest of terms; in the bill the emphasis was on the long-term employment effects while the proposals were geared to short-term results. And when the actors discussed the results of the bill they were more inclined to talk of 'a new spirit' in the town or of better profitability in the state-owned enterprise.

Control

The whole process leading up to the bill seems incomprehensible if we assume that its function was to solve problems. It is also difficult to interpret it in terms of control, or even as attempted control. In presenting the bill the politicians emphasized that it was the town's own recommendations they were supporting, not their own. And this was of course quite correct, although in fact the recommendations came from two sources: most of the proposals stemmed from the plan, but the recommended cutbacks in the state-owned company came from the company itself. And the declared policy regarding this company was that the political system should *not* exert control: the company was intent on improving its profitability, and the way this goal was attained was not a political question; it was something to be decided by the board and corporate management.

The central politicians intentionally assumed the role of defensive scrutineers in relation to the proposals of the local politicians and trade unions and the local administrators in Stanby. Instead of taking the initiative themselves, they waited for proposals which they then examined and assessed. It was not the central politicians but the people in Stanby who initiated the idea of the development plan. The central politicians made no suggestions; they simply listened to proposals from the grassroots. They let themselves be controlled. On this basis they put their names to a bill containing promises of future action and future financial contributions.

The defensive scrutineer presupposes the existence of suggestion-makers, and many such had indeed been mobilized. All the ideas that were being talked about in the local party or the trade unions were swept together into one glorious heap. The plan did not contain a single original thought, as one opposition politician declared. But no one had intended that it should.

'Control' in this case consisted largely of the government letting it be known that proposals would be welcome; unemployment was after all a problem they knew they had to tackle. This was the purpose of the plan, and of other plans that the state-owned company in the area had been asked to submit.

Thus the government was letting itself be controlled. The central politicians exposed themselves to the influence of their own civil servants and of the local actors. They limited their own role to saying 'yes' or 'no' to proposals initiated and worked out by local politicians or administrators. Even the selection of proposals to be included in the bill was made in collaboration with the proposers; and, as we have seen, it was based mainly on criteria which had nothing to do with any political will. The central politicians had no need to consider proposals that lacked impassioned backers; they were not included in the bill.

Support

Thus the bill-generating process had nothing to do with problem-solving and very little with control by any political leaders. And yet it could still have possessed an element of implementation in that it lent support to certain actions which—although not qualifying as problem-solving or having very much to do with any political initiative or will—were nonetheless intended to be carried out.

However, in the Stanby case there was little need for support for action. Most of the measures had been suggested by various interested parties on the spot and thus enjoyed strong support from the start.

Moreover, the politicians' support for many of the measures was rather vague. Most of the proposals were worded so cautiously that it was not clear whether they were really to be implemented or not: they 'ought to be implemented', they were 'urgent', or they should be 'investigated further'. Some proposals referred not to any concrete actions but to some sort of 'goal'. Other proposals were non-operational, e.g. it was difficult to know exactly what was meant by 'encouraging' or 'supporting' some particular development. Finally, of course, a whole series of proposals was simply lodged in the appendix to the plan. In only a few instances was any definite promise made.

The only measures for which it was difficult to gain acceptance in the town, and which thus needed support if they were to be realized, were the cutbacks in the state-owned company. These commanded support, but not in the plan. Support and justification were to be found instead in the company's own plans. The main argument was that like other state-owned companies this one must be run on businesslike lines and must aim to be profitable. Any negative effects should be specially handled. The cutbacks were to be complemented by other more positive expedients. It is even possible to see the whole bill as a way of compensating—and thus supporting—the reduction in the workforce in the state-owned company.

Direct Legitimation

Thus there is little to suggest that the preparation of the bill was particularly concerned about implementation. There is much more to suggest that its essential function was directly or indirectly to provide legitimation for the political leadership. Let us look first at direct means of legitimation, whereby an organization reflects in itself the interests and values of its environment. We have discussed three instruments of reflection—talk, decisions and products—and in working on this bill the government employed all of them.

The work was organized in three stages, corresponding to the three instruments. The plan represented the talk level: no decisions were made at that stage. Most of the text of the plan was devoted to enumerating the problems of the town and expressing a general wish that various measures should be looked into, or considered, or that some action should be taken. Every proposal which had some degree of support in the town was given positive treatment in the development plan. In some cases concrete and binding pledges were made. All the proposals mentioned were of course already familiar and nobody expected the group to reject them. Thus the function of the text was not to support physical production. Nor, however, did it support non-action; on the contrary the seriousness of the problems and the necessity of doing something about them was emphasized. Thus the function of this part of the process can be regarded as a legitimation of the political leadership, by reflecting in talk the perceptions and values of the relevant environment. The politicians did not reject the proposals; instead they associated themselves with them, but without committing themselves to realizing them.

In the bill, which represents the decision level, the number of proposals had to be reduced: in a decision context any inconsistency between different proposals becomes more obvious and the link with implementation stronger. The proposals had to be weeded out more severely; any that were weakly supported in the town or about which opinions differed were dropped. No negative decisions were made unnecessarily, and most of the proposals that were not adopted were simply not mentioned at all. However, the number adopted was still very high, and some were counted twice. A great many proposals were postponed for decision at a later date after further investigation.

Many but not all the remaining proposals were subsequently realized. Because of the time lag between plan and bill, between talking and deciding, it was possible to defend any lack of consistency. And in any case it was never intended that everything in the plan should be decided or implemented. This applied particularly to the proposals which came under the 'ought to happen' heading.

The government itself stressed the legitimizing function of the bill. The Prime Minister claimed that the process had been 'democratic'. He emphasized the massive battery of measures: it was obvious that the government cared and was tackling the problems. And the high costs were much emphasized. From a problem-solving point of view, costs should be kept as low as possible, but when it is a question of legitimation the reverse may be true.

The effect of all these legitimizing actions is naturally difficult to pinpoint. But many politicians felt they provided a high degree of legitimacy: for example, that they contributed to the party's continuing election successes.

Responsibility

The main point of the bill was to give expression to the responsibility of the local and central political systems for developments in Stanby. And all the work that went into preparing the bill was in itself further evidence of this responsibility. However, the preparation of the bill was also accompanied by a series of declarations to the effect that the responsibility of the central politicians and the departments was limited, particularly in terms of the future: the proposals which were now being decided had emanated from the town and not from the government; this was the last time the central politicians would take action; from now on the town was to manage on its own and the bill was making it possible for them to do so; just because such vast sums of money were being invested now, the government would not be responsible for the future; the large state-owned company had been provided with the conditions needed to improve its profitability—fulfilling the goals would be the responsibility of its own management, not of the government.

In one case the government did decide to assume responsibility even for the future, namely when it came to maintaining one other profitable state-owned company in the area. If this company had been sold to local interests, the need for further subsidies would have disappeared altogether. But that proposal had been rejected before the plan was ever written. Perhaps this town and its problems provided the government with an important arena for politics, which the politicians did not want to lose altogether.

Legitimation of the Situation

According to the politicians some aspects of this process were also useful in making the town feel more satisfied with its situation. The bill undeniably demonstrated that despite the severity of the problems the government was doing everything it possibly could. No suggestions that could be regarded as technically possible or that enjoyed widespread support in the town were ever actually rejected. Somebody cared, somebody wanted to help. This was supposed to give the impression that things would be better in the future, that the problems might perhaps be solved. This publicly expressed belief in the future appears particularly striking in view of the fact that the politicians themselves did not believe the problems could ever be solved.

Most of the politicians emphasized the importance of the bill in legitimizing the situation. When they were asked about the possible future effects of the bill, they said that the effects had already appeared. They felt that the bill had altered people's way of perceiving and confronting their situation, although no concrete action had yet been taken. The great importance of the plan and the bill was that a 'new spirit' was abroad in the town; people looked forward to the future with optimism, courage, self-confidence and determination. The depression and pessimism which had formerly prevailed had been the main reason for designing the plan and the bill in the first place.

Endowing the prevailing situation with legitimacy must have been an important function of the process, just because the politicians were pessimistic and did not believe that the concrete problems of the town would be resolved, despite the measures which were to be adopted. If the impact on the mood of the town was really as great as the politicians claimed, it represented a remarkable achievement. Just when this change of heart was apparently taking place, unemployment in the area was actually increasing as a result of the cutbacks in the failing state-owned company.

Summary

The result of this analysis is not particularly surprising. The process is incomprehensible if we assume that its function was implementation in the sense of problem-solving or control. What actually happened has little in common with the picture conjured up by the traditional implementation model, whereby an organization attempts to impose its ideas on a refractory environment. The whole thing becomes comprehensible only if we assume that support and legitimation were the prime goals. That the work on the bill had no problem-solving function is not surprising, since nobody involved had any idea how the problems could be solved, and did not even believe that they were solvable at all. Perhaps it was just because the problem really was insoluble that the politicians felt they must intervene. And since it was not possible to devote themselves to solving the problems, they naturally had little interest in exerting control either; instead they restricted themselves mainly to what was feasible and desirable, namely supporting the 'necessary' cutbacks in the state-owned company and legitimizing the political system and the situation in the town.

The main function of the work on the bill was legitimation. And this also seems to have been what was intended. Nothing suggests that the actors were being forced into anything against their will, and they seem to have regarded their own actions as perfectly appropriate.

THE ROLE OF POLITICS

The Stanby case illustrates the role of the state as legitimator, legitimizing both itself and its environment. Naturally the case does not suggest that legitimation is the state's sole function. But it serves to show that the state cannot always be assumed to be aiming at implementation—at solving problems, exerting control, or transforming decisions into action. The hierarchy metaphor is as misleading in the case of external control as it is in connection with internal control of the type discussed in Chapters 4 and 5. Organizations of strong political intent find it difficult to control their environments; nor is their interest limited to their environments but includes also their own position. And relations with the environment need not necessarily involve control; instead they can be aimed at legitimation.

All the interest devoted to implementation, and all the talk about highly political organizations solving problems and exerting control, does not necessarily have much to do with things as they are. Rather, these attitudes reflect myths about organizations—myths which are in fact extremely useful and effective. Paradoxically, organizations which try to establish their legitimacy by producing politics often proclaim their interest in action and the problems of others, and disclaiming any interest in their own legitimacy.

Industrial policy seems to be an area in which implementation is very difficult, and as far as possible sensible governments can be expected to avoid it. Too little is known about identifying the problems, about their interconnections, their causes, and their possible solutions, for it to be possible to provide any basis for rational (as opposed to superstitious) problem-solving. It is difficult to say what kind of industrial development is appropriate. How, for example, should we balance an interest in job opportunities against an interest in advanced technological development? Nobody knows what causes industrial development, and we know even less about how political systems can stimulate it. Controlling industrial companies and steering their development is no easy matter. And this being so, it does not seem particularly sensible to put the main emphasis of industrial policy on problem-solving and control. Rather, we should expect industrial policy to include a significant element of legitimation. A policy geared to making people 'happier', to 'increasing their welfare' or to 'promoting their interests', for example, can be expected to contain a large measure of legitimation strategy.

Attempts on the part of a government to steer the industrial system in a particular direction can substantially reduce the same government's ability to reflect a broad range of interests and values and thus to create legitimacy. Legitimacy then has to be based on products instead, i.e. on implementing actions that satisfy diverse interests and views. But if there is doubt about the efficacy of the products, then legitimation by talk and decisions will suit the political leaders better. Perhaps it is also better for the industrial system and the people at large?

Perhaps the role in society of politicians and other leaders often involves something far more important than controlling and redistributing material resources. Their task may instead be to create well-being and happiness, in other words to exert an influence on ideology. If so, it is not always necessary to go the long way round, by controlling material resources. This was the idea in the Stanby case, for example when the local politicians felt that the major effects arose from their own talk and decisions, not from any actions undertaken by the state.

A given situation can be legitimized by affecting the way people think about it. But it can also be legitimized by the assumption of responsibility. Man has a strong desire to explain events, both good and bad (Geertz 1973). In a secularized culture such as our own, it is important to be able to explain things by reference to people: if people rather than God, chance, natural forces or social laws have caused an event, this also means that the event can be controlled. An illusion of explanation and control can help to reduce existential anxiety (van Gunsteren 1976). To assume responsibility is to establish that one has caused something, for instance by having made decisions.

Political leaders set great store by decisions, and politicians often claim openly to have influenced decisions. Furthermore they can make decisions about almost anything, not only the government's actions but also those of the people or of business firms. Politicians readily assume responsibility or have it assigned to them. For the people around them it is perhaps particularly important that politicians assume responsibility for situations perceived as troublesome or tough. In this light our constant carping at politicians, and our criticism of the state and its institutions in times of economic decline, are quite natural and even serve a necessary function. Politics and politicians are more important to our culture than the hierarchy metaphor implies.

Assuming responsibility and creating legitimacy are important tasks for leaders in highly political organizations. The means adopted are decisions and the claim to control. But we should not unreflectingly mistake the means for the goal.

7
Projects and Organizations

Politics makes organizations vulnerable to the demands and norms of its environment. An organization in which politics is important gives away much control to its environment; it is the environment that formulates the demands which the organization shall reflect. And the organization cannot necessarily choose for itself which demands to reflect: it generally has little chance to select some and reject others. The very methods by which it reflects external demands make it difficult for the organization to ignore certain pressures, even if many of its leaders would like to. For instance, if its leaders include representatives of diverse interests, any external demand has a good chance of finding at least some internal champions.

By openly displaying its internal processes, the organization makes it easy for those outside to articulate their demands at the right moments. If an organization is highly generalized, this will mean that its area of responsibility will be a broad one. If general opinion assumes that certain demands come within the organization's area of responsibility, even ignoring the demands may not do the organization much good: people can still assume that it has *chosen* to ignore them, and is thus still responsible.

The state is an example of an extremely open organization. Almost any kind of demand can be addressed to a government or a parliament. These institutions deal with a great many of the demands, and their attempts to ignore others are often regarded as a conscious act of rejection. And so they can be held responsible when things go well or badly, in almost all spheres from the national to the personal.

But companies have also become more open. As a result of a greater concentration in the corporate world many formerly independent companies are now included in large conglomerates, and companies which belong to groups are more open to one another's view than companies simply linked by contact on the market. Various external interests such as the state or the employees acquire representatives inside a business organization. Interests inside and outside the company—employees, local authorities, national authorities and so on—are all stepping up their demands for information about present and future operations. The state in particular has been able to make tougher demands as a result of its extensive financial aid programmes and other involvements in industry.

Openness is an important basis for the legitimacy of organizations but it can also be a threat, at least if the external demands concern production. An organization cannot produce in accordance with too many inconsistent demands. Even if the organization has little control over which demands to reflect, it must at least be able to choose to some extent how it reflects them; it must sometimes be able to choose talk and decision as its instruments rather than products.

Handling external demands in other ways than by products is particularly important since politics does not only create openness but also difficulty in producing organizational action and thereby products, especially new actions. In order to produce new actions and products it may be necessary to create new organizations. Large organizations today often work through 'project organizations', i.e. they establish special units within the main organization to undertake new activities, such as developing new products. Such projects can be organized on action principles; they can focus on effective action, since the parent organization can take care of the politics. Action is facilitated by action rationality rather than decision rationality (see Chapter 2): people are strongly committed to an action, convinced that it is worthwhile and that it will really take place. Project groups can often kindle the kind of enthusiasm for a project that is often necessary to its success.

The trouble is that project groups can become over-enthusiastic. It is unlikely that a group acting in accordance with action rationality will ever entertain doubts or think of stopping a project, even if the external conditions for its successful conclusion are no longer present. Projects of this kind can thus acquire a life of their own. If at some point the original leadership wants to stop a project, enthusiasts in the project management will have plenty of opportunities for associating their project with other organizations which might be persuaded to supply the necessary resources. If the organization in which a project is being conducted is very open, external groups are more likely to hear of threatened cancellations and to have an opportunity to take a project over. Or projects may be launched outside any established organization, and then easily become associated with an open organization later.

Thus as a result of the increasing politicization of organizations, new activities are often conducted in the shape of major projects embarking on a life of their own outside the established organizations. Such projects can transfer themselves at any time to another organization that appears to offer better support, and they may therefore be very difficult to halt. The established organizations lose some of their former control over activities and over the general direction of developments. Politics and openness in established organizations thus easily leads to a world of organizations and projects, in which the projects answer for the action and the organizations for legitimation and financing; a world in which projects stand for action rationality and organizations for decision rationality.

Local authorities and state institutions are particularly exposed to demands to support a variety of projects, often involving major investment in areas such as industry, transportation, and so on. The handling of such demands is often referred to as 'industrial policy'. In Chapter 6 I examined the way in which industrial policy can be presented by the political bodies as an example of their own initiative, but it is fairly obvious that in many if not most cases the initiative comes from industry. Individual companies or projects exert pressure on the state and local government for financial subsidies of various kinds.

Industrial policy provides state and local authorities with an opportunity to reflect conflicts and problems in society. But it can also put dangerous pressure on them to make financial contributions. In this chapter I shall be discussing how organizations can handle this dilemma. Whereas in the previous chapter we asked whether strongly political organizations *want* to control others, we can now ask ourselves whether they *can*. We will start by looking at two industrial projects, both of which put great pressure on companies, the state and local authorities to provide financial support. In both cases leading actors in the organizations whose help was· being sought were negative towards the projects, which did not seem to them to meet reasonable requirements as regards profitability, employment effects, etc. In one case it was not possible to avoid making any financial contributions, in the second case it was. I shall now briefly describe the way the two projects were handled.

TWO PROJECTS

Product B

This is the story of a major investment in the chemical industry. It involved starting a factory for the production of B, a product which had previously always been imported. Production requires very large plants with high fixed costs and big production volumes. The idea was that most of the output should be sold on the export market.

The industry concerned was previously regarded as an industry with a future, and many companies were naturally interested in entering it. Among these was a company owned by the state, which we can call CON. In 1976 CON therefore acquired Stolo, a small company in the same industry whose management had long been dreaming of investing in product B. Its previous group management had not allowed any money for such an investment, but the new owner promised to do so. Stolo now began to look into the whole question of investing in B. The findings were presented successively to the board, which was accordingly persuaded to make step-by-step decisions to continue the investigation, and eventually to put money into planning, land purchase, licence purchase and so on.

The champions of the project had three main arguments. First, they emphasized the absurdity of the present situation: they were buying B from foreign companies to make products which then competed on the market with the products of these other companies. Secondly, it was impossible to discontinue production of these products, since they accounted for more than half the company's turnover. Thirdly, a comprehensive investment calculus seemed to show that the investment in production plant would be profitable.

The foremost critics were CON's representatives on Stolo's board. To begin with the critics did not question the investment calculus as such, but they wondered whether the product area as a whole was profitable, whether it really was an area with a big future. The critics also questioned the sales forecasts and wondered whether it would be possible to find a market for the products.

By 1978 the project had been so thoroughly analysed that the time had come to make a decision, and at this point the criticism grew more vociferous. CON's representatives ordered an independent investigation from a foreign consultant, who was regarded as an expert on the industry in question. The consultant criticized the forecasts of the global production capacity for B as well as Stolo's alleged cost advantages. The B project group found it easy to counter these arguments; they even found some obvious errors in the consultant's estimates. Nor had they much patience with the argument that the product area in itself was slightly dubious. Some of them felt that CON was simply out to stop the project, without producing any cogent arguments against it. These discussions resulted in a joint memorandum to CON, complete with estimates and comments on several uncertain factors. Stolo's board decided to proceed with the project, provided CON would supply the financial resources required.

The people running the project at Stolo now made direct contact with CON's owner, the ministry for industry. They pointed out that the ministry had been calling for investment in the industry, and here was a project representing just such an investment. It was in fact the only major project that had been suggested.

The ministry agreed that the project suited its strategy, and declared in favour of pursuing it. At a CON board meeting early in 1979, however, CON's managing director succeeded in getting another decision passed, namely that the project was to keep within the original financial limits. Since current cost estimates suggested that the project was going to cost more than these limits allowed, this seemed like a major setback.

Thus Stolo had now arranged some financial support for its project, but had not yet decided to go on with it. At a board meeting about a month later Stolo's managing director presented a new estimate, showing that the project could be carried out more cheaply and thus without exceeding the original limits. The opposition from CON's representatives was fierce: they demanded that the decision should at least be postponed. However, the meeting ended in a board decision that work on the project should continue, but that it should be reviewed again in six months time 'before any major financial commitment had been made'. CON's managing director went along with the decision, but the other CON representative recorded a reservation against it.

Towards the end of 1979 Stolo's finances deteriorated further. At the same time it became clear that the project would be more costly than had been estimated at the time of the decision. But its promoters were still claiming that it might yet be profitable, and that in any case it would be expensive to discontinue it. The board decided to ask for full financial support for the investment from CON. But CON decided to proceed to the next level: they submitted a request for aid to the ministry for industry. They pointed out that jobs would be lost if the project were stopped, and asked for support in the shape of a loan or grant from the state. Only if they were given this aid could CON consider going on with the plans.

The ministry obviously felt that the project belonged to an industry with a future; up to now they seemed to have been giving all their aid to industries with their futures behind them. At the beginning of 1980 the government decided to approve a relocation loan amounting to almost the whole sum required.

Stolo's shaky finances deteriorated further, and there was no sign that the price of their products was recovering. During the summer of 1980 it became obvious even to some members of the project group that the price forecast, and thus the entire estimate, was completely unrealistic. New estimates were made and a board meeting was held. It was now quite clear that the project would never be profitable. In September the board decided to write a memorandum to CON, explaining that Stolo was not prepared to make a decision for or against the project: that decision belonged to CON. Included in the memo was an estimate of the cost of discontinuing the project.

CON in turn submitted an estimate to the ministry. They explained that it would cost just about the same to go on with the project as it would to stop it. But if the project continued, there would at least be a chance of recovering the costs. The government decided to recommend parliament to give CON the additional capital requested. During the spring of 1981 parliament voted in favour of the government's proposal. Two years later, in 1983, the investment was complete, and had now cost more than £100 million, far more than the amount originally planned. There was absolutely no chance of finding a market for the production capacity that had been built up. Nor was there any hope of recovering the investment cost. Despite immediate depreciation, the factory had been running at a loss ever since it started. A few years later the factory was sold to another company, still without any hope of recovering the investment cost.

The end result was thus a huge industrial investment that proved to have no economic value. None of the actors involved had of course desired such a result. For at least the last five years it cannot have been difficult to predict this outcome. And for an even longer time critical voices had been raised and considerable doubts expressed. Leading actors in the ministry for industry had long regarded the project as economically crazy. They were quite certain it would make a loss. They saw no advantage in it. And yet they had not been able to reject it.

The Transport Project

This case concerns plans for a major investment in a regional transport network, in order to promote the transport of goods in and out of the region. Again, the estimated cost was very high, more than £100 million. The chief argument in favour of the project was that it would reduce industrial transport costs, thus creating industrial growth and employment in the region concerned. The idea had been promoted by a project group consisting of various local interests.

The idea was first launched in 1968, when the project group sought support from municipal and state bodies at the regional and central levels in the shape of an investigation and money for development. The project dragged on for almost twenty years and the results were meagre. No investigation of the kind requested by the project group was ever made.

The champions of the project employed the following strategies in trying to associate themselves with highly political organizations. In 1969 they tackled the county council, and persuaded some councillors to propose that the question be investigated. The county council sounded out reactions to their proposal in several industrial organizations and received a negative response; in the subsequent debate the authors of the proposal found it difficult to defend themselves against the critics. In particular their suggestion was compared with various alternative transport arrangements. The proposal was turned down, although even its opponents said a few appreciative words about the good job that had been done, with the best interests of the region at heart.

Over the next few years the project's promoters tried to persuade individual municipalities in the region to put some money into investigating the project. They did eventually succeed, but the sums were so tiny that they could only pay for a mini-study. Nonetheless, on a basis of this study, the promotors approached the county administration in 1977. The officials were definitely against the project, but the politicians were less sure and less unanimous. The county administration decided to put the issue before the national government, without making any recommendation of their own.

In 1978 the issue was dealt with at government level, but despite the protests of the project promoters—by the ministry of transport rather than the ministry for industry which takes care of industrial and regional development. A rough estimate of profitability was made and the investment was found to be unprofitable. It was also found that support for the project in the region was weak. The government therefore decided not to approve the proposal.

In 1979 several individual members of parliament from the region proposed motions on the issue in parliament. The motions were discussed in the traffic committee and rejected—nothing else was to be expected, as almost all private members' motions are rejected in parliament. However, it was felt that the committee's comments were not too discouraging. In 1980 the motions were brought up again, and this time parliament referred them to a special committee which had just been appointed to deal more generally with transport questions. Two years later the special committee presented its findings: it found the investment unprofitable and recommended that it be rejected. The project was not handled again at the central level, but it was not abandoned. Its promoters continued to work on it.

STRATEGIES FOR MEETING EXTERNAL DEMANDS—DELEGATION, RATIONALITY AND IDEOLOGY

These stories show the awkward position of the highly political organizations: they could not ignore the projects. And since they had to deal with them, they were going to be held responsible whether they said yes or no. And either acceptance or rejection would have to be justified to the environment. But access to arguments is often tipped one way: arguments in favour of accepting demands are generally supplied by those who are making them, while counter-arguments generally have to be worked out by the organizations themselves. If they know much less about the subject than the proposers do, they are at a considerable disadvantage.

What counter-strategies are available? Here we have organizations which are open to external pressures and which want to remain so, but which must find some way of withstanding these pressures, that is to say to making up their own minds how they should react to them. The cases illustrate three possible counter-strategies, but they also indicate several related problems. The strategies were delegation, rationality and the production of ideology.

Delegation

The fundamental problem is that organizations of a strongly political bent have to deal with projects which are powerfully action-oriented. Several factors weaken their bargaining position: their greater openness, their high level of conflict, and the generalized nature of their interests. An immediately obvious counter-strategy is to try to put the organizations and the projects on a more equal footing in these respects. The state has applied this strategy *vis-à-vis* industry; it has supported the politicization of companies, for instance by way of legislation on union co-determination, and has thereby strengthened its bargaining position.

But the politicization of companies is also one of the reasons for the appearance of many major projects, which then in turn seem to be more difficult to politicize. It might be simpler for highly political organizations to try instead to be less political. Some organizations do sometimes manage to close themselves to external claims or to handle them by consensus. But this is not always possible for organizations whose main activity is the handling of external demands. For instance, to make industrial policy a non-political issue would be exceedingly difficult for a national government, not least for internal reasons: it is difficult to envisage any demand for which the support of at least a few members of parliament could not be won.

A more feasible strategy may be to delegate questions of external support to administrative units which are on a more equal footing with those making the demands, since they are less political. Thus for once the administrative units would be serving as buffers between the top management and the environment; by claiming that the issues have been delegated to the administration, top management can avoid dealing with them. The product B case illustrates this strategy but it also reveals some of the problems that can arise.

The idea was that CON would cope with most of the concrete industrial policy. They had the expertise on industry, industrial development and economics. But CON was not entirely disas-

sociated from the ministry. At the start the ministry had established a simple strategy which CON was to follow, namely to
expand and to invest in certain industries. Exactly how this should
be done was left to CON itself, as was the task of running its
companies profitably. This type of strategy clearly corresponds to
a common model, whereby top management is supposed to be
responsible for the overall ideas and the administration for the
details. But this case shows how difficult it can be in practice to
distinguish between strategy and specifics. At first it was difficult
for CON to say that the project should not be carried out; at that
stage there were no very clear indications that it would be unprofitable. Against the evident truth that the project fitted the
strategy were mere speculations about its possibly unprofitable
nature. The champions could adapt the project to the strategy, and
when it came to details they were more expert than CON's staff
and more skilful in argument. This strategy launched the project
on its path to the ministry and parliament. In other words it
provided the bridge from CON to the ministry, over which the
project could make its way. And the ministry was unable to
withstand the arguments of the project promoters.

In other words the strategy did not provide a good instrument
with which its inventors could exert control. It could be utilized
by the project's supporters to exploit the relative ignorance of
the ministry about industry in general and this industry in
particular. Instead the strategy provided a link between the
political and administrative units, which was used to steer the
political bodies.

At a later stage the ministry had acquired some knowledge at
least: they now knew that the project was unprofitable. But there
were still reasons, albeit different ones, for not being able to turn
it down. In the interim CON had become increasingly committed
to the project; it had made decisions in its favour on several
occasions; a good deal of money had been invested in it, and a
whole lot of physical preparations had been made. These commitments were so strong that the ministry felt unable to say no, and
instead invested more money in the project. So here too CON
failed to act as a buffer. On the contrary, it was CON which
generated the commitments that trapped the ministry. At the
same time CON's involvement made it easier for the ministry to
decide to invest in something which they knew was wrong: after

all, they were not the only ones responsible for promoting the project. CON could also take a good deal of the responsibility. And by putting the issue before parliament, which was thus the final authority that decided to accept the project, the ministry succeeded in diluting the responsibility even more. Similarly, it had been relatively easy for CON to generate commitment to the project because they would be sharing the responsibility with the ministry.

Thus in this case the administrative unit, CON, did not act as a buffer for the top units. In making important decisions about the project, the ministry was greatly influenced by the project itself. Top management and administration had not been kept completely apart; instead there were bridges between them consisting of the strategy adopted and CON's opportunities for seeking more money from the ministry. Both these bridges were skilfully exploited by the project's promotors in order to associate themselves with the ministry and to steer it in the way they wanted it to go. The strategy bridge was used to exploit the ministry's relative ignorance of both the industry and the project; the aid-seeking bridge was used to exploit the heavy commitments which had already been made.

Rationality

In both these projects the champions exhibited a high level of irrationality: they saw no possible alternatives to their projects; they firmly believed in their positive outcome and did not perceive strong signals to the contrary, and they adapted goals to projects rather than the other way round. This irrationality kept uncertainty at bay and generated a vast amount of energy. The promoters were thus working under the norms of action rationality rather than decision rationality. Action rationality is appropriate to the coordination and promotion of difficult organizational activities. But if it is necessary to stop some action, then rationality in the traditional sense—decision rationality—can be an effective means. By establishing goals that are independent of the action concerned, by producing alternatives to it, and by emphasizing its negative consequences, it is possible to spread uncertainty and to shake people's faith in the undertaking. This kind of rationality can thus provide a strategy with which to counter the type of project we have been discussing here. By using decision rationality it may be possible to find arguments which will be acceptable to other people as a legitimate reason for rejecting the project. Decision rationality can be used to increase the uncertainty to such a degree that it appears impossible to make a decision; in this way commitment to the project can be avoided. Rationality can also be used to prevent people within the organization from becoming convinced that the project is a good one, or expecting it to materialize. Finally, rationality may even succeed in shaking the confidence of the project group, thus reducing its energy and drive.

Decision rationality represented an important counter-strategy in both the cases reported here, but it was not without its attendant problems. The ministry had laid down guidelines for possible investments and, as we have seen, it was easy to present the product B project as agreeing with these. Since projects of this kind only exist in the abstract at first, they can often be adapted quite easily to almost any goal (itself equally abstract), so goals are not going to provide much protection at this vital launching stage. The promoters can anyway exploit the existence of contradictory goals in highly political organizations: if they cannot adapt their project to one goal, they may be able to link it up with another. This method was used by the product B promoters; once it had become obvious that the project would be an economic catastrophe, they referred to its value, to the balance of trade, to employment and to local development—goals which they knew were important to the ministry and even more so to parliament.

The product B supporters also managed to avoid attempts to compare their project with more acceptable alternatives. When CON tried to find alternative products in Stolo, the product B people pointed out that investments had already been made in them all. The only alternative that could compete with the product B project would be to close down most of Stolo. At the ministry product B thus appeared as the only growth alternative, at a time when all their other major cases were concerned with industrial closures.

When an organization has to find alternatives or to point out the negative consequences of external proposals, it needs to command knowledge equal to or greater than that of those promoting the idea. In the product B case not even CON's knowledge was sufficient; the project promoters were the country's leading experts in this area. Other experts belonged to rival companies, and were therefore hardly to be relied on. The unsuccessful attempt to let foreign expertise supply the counter-arguments shows that the promoters possessed superior knowledge about their project, which was not altogether surprising.

In the transport case the rationality strategy was more successful. The ministry took the decisive step of redefining the project. While the project promoters were claiming it was connected with industrial development in the region, the organization defined it as a question of communications. In this way they altered the whole situation as regards possible goals and alternatives, as well as the relevance of the various consequences. Thus in this case the project's own promoters were not able to choose its goals. In the field of communications it was a long-held principle that every individual solution should be economically viable—a principle not generally applied in the area of regional and industrial development. Profitability was not at any rate among the promoters' original arguments. Given this redefinition, the alternatives also changed: once it became a question of organizing transport, there were several obvious alternatives (investment in other means of transport), while there had been no one who could suggest any alternative ways of encouraging industrial development in the region. By redefining the project, the promoters' constant demand that alternative methods for industrial development should be suggested could be disregarded. In a communications perspective it was easy to point out negative features in the project, in particular its weak profitability. In this case the distribution of knowledge among those involved also favoured the organizations. If it had been a matter of discussing industrial development, the project promoters could have coped reasonably well, since no generally accepted expertise in the field was available. When it came to discussing the profitability of investment in transport, they were amateurs.

Moreover the organizations mobilized opposing interests, in particular in nature conservation circles. By seeking the opinion of experts in nature conservation they acquired counter-arguments which were powerful and which also functioned in a different value context.

Production of Ideology

These projects both involved attempts to persuade the organizations concerned to provide material resources. The project promotors were eager to get the various organizations to grant money for a planned investment which meant they were interested in the *product* aspect of the organizations' output. An organization facing such a situation can adopt a third counter-strategy, namely to produce talk and decisions referring to the project in positive terms, instead of producing money or action. The organization can try to compensate for its lack of product aid by expressing supportive ideology.

The transport case provides an example of the ideology strategy. The various organizations produced a good deal of benevolent talk and sympathetic decisions about the project, all of which actually helped them to hinder rather than promote its realization. Several organizations avoided negative talk and negative decisions which would have been difficult for them to legitimate, in view of their lack of arguments and alternatives on the subject of regional development. The proposal was formally and openly discussed in the organizations approached. Altogether it was being investigated for about twenty years and always received sympathetic treatment: the project was 'interesting and innovative', and it 'showed that its authors cared personally about the region'. Many decisions were also relatively positive; several were taken further. Only parliament finally said no, and even this was not regarded as too negative a result.

But none of the positive decisions created any commitment to the project; on the contrary, the decisions were more in the nature of attempts to avoid commitment. The whole project was passed up the system without being given any financial support from the organizations involved. Nor did the decisions lead to any real expectation of the project materializing (except in the hearts of its most enthusiastic champions).

In the product B case, the project was fortunate in that the organizations never had a chance to accept or reject it in its entirety; it was presented bit by bit, and these small bits were more difficult to reject. In the transport case, too, any necessity to judge the whole problem at one go would have meant rejecting it, but in this case it was the organizations which were most anxious to avoid a definite rejection—they had no call to assume the responsibility for saying no. Instead they succeeded in producing talk and decisions couched in the most positive terms possible, while at the same time making sure that the chances of the project being realized were minimized. The result was that the project was neither realized nor stopped; one reason why it stayed alive for at least twenty years was that it never faced a definite rejection. Thus the organizations were able to handle the project over and over again. By their continued handling of the project the organizations could show that they were taking an interest in regional policy, without running much risk of having to pay for it. Thus from the point of view of these organizations the transport case was reasonably successful.

Different Results

These two cases have been used to illustrate some of the different strategies which organizations can use in order to defend themselves against external demands, although we cannot of course base any conclusions about the strategies most likely to be effective in different situations on such a narrow sample. The organizations' failure in the product B case, and their success in the transport case, may well have depended on other factors besides their strategies. There was also a big difference in the level of knowledge possessed by the project promotors in the two cases; in the product B project they were the leading experts in the country; in the transport case the promotors were enlightened members of the public. The strategies also differed in their exploitation of the profitability argument: during the important early stages of the product B project its promoters claimed that it would be profitable, while the transport scheme supporters tried to avoid any discussion of profitability at all. The profitability argument is of course particularly powerful because it begs the whole question: if the project is profitable, the organizations will get their money back and so will not have made any sacrifice.

From most points of view the fact that the organizations could not stop the product B project must be counted as a negative result. The case shows that even poor and expensive projects can be realized, if there is a combination of powerful irrationality in the project group and weakness in the organizations with which the group seeks to associate itself. Many countries can quote similar examples of unsuccessful projects (Persson 1977), which can be regarded as a result of the unwieldy nature of modern industrial societies: once a project has started it becomes very difficult to stop it, even if the original conditions and motivations have changed.

But projects can also be regarded as major sources of renewal. Innovations may find it difficult to take root in large, highly political organizations. Big projects can provide such organizations or innovative people in large organizations with a chance to develop their projects, while using the resources of these organizations. At best, the irrationality and drive of the project-promoting groups can be balanced by the rationality of the organizations. But this presupposes that the organizations can exert some control.

The difficulties that dog an organizational leadership that is skilful at politics when it has to try to control action have been a major theme of the last four chapters. In Chapter 4 we saw how the leaders were associated with action largely by assuming responsibility, which meant that their chief function was to promote the realization of the action rather than to control its content. They could choose whether or not to accept responsibility for the action, even if it was easier to accept it than not to. This was essentially the same role as that played by the organizations discussed in the present chapter. The examples illustrated in Chapters 5 and 6 showed that responsibility—regardless of whether it was being avoided or assumed—was more important to the organizational leaders than the content of the actions. Actions may have an indirect effect on leaders' position; responsibility has a direct effect.

In all cases decisions were important when it came to associating the leadership with action. The decisions were concerned more with responsibility and legitimacy than with choice or the control of activities. This is not the role assigned to decisions in traditional decision theory. One theme in the next chapter will be the theory of organizational decision-making to which our discussion of politics has led us.

8
Ideas, Decisions and Actions in Organizations

In the previous four chapters I have discussed the relation between politics and action in organizations. Both are easier to
achieve if they are kept apart, something which speaks for decoupling leaders and the led in an organization. But this is not always
possible, and there may well be powerful groups inside or outside
the organization which seek to link the leaders with the led. I have
argued that it is easier to link the two by letting the led control the
leaders rather than the other way round; also, this solution
provides more scope for action, politics and hypocrisy as well as
for legitimizing the organization. The concept of responsibility
has played a significant part in my explanations. Responsibility is
important to the legitimation of action, of organizations and of
environmental situations.

In these two final chapters I shall sum up and develop some
aspects of these arguments further. The concept of responsibility
contains an element of hypocrisy, since it is based on the perception and often the illusion of control. But responsibility is only one
example of what I will call hypocrisy of the second degree, that is
to say the kind that organizations tend to employ in relating the
way they present their manner of functioning to their actual
behaviour. This type of hypocrisy will be one of the main topics
addressed in Chapter 9.

The argument in this book questions some common assumptions about organizations. The commom assumptions concerning the relation between leaders and led will be further examined, but this time in a normative perspective, in Chapter 9. Other assumptions concern rationality and the role of decision-making in organizations. These assumptions will be discussed in the present chapter. I will start with a brief summary of the position to which our discussion has led us thus far, as regards the wider issue of the relation between ideas and action in organizations.

IDEAS AND ACTION

In the four preceding chapters two different systems have been identified in organizations: a system of thought or ideas and a system of action. The ideas system defines what is handled in mental and communicative processes, and the action system what is handled in material processes. Membership of an organization may have a standardizing effect on the cognitions of that organization's members, thus creating what can be called organizational ideologies. Organizational ideas are often expressed in talk aimed at other organizational members or at external listeners. In the action system members coordinate their individual actions in order to act together, and these actions result in products in the form of goods or services.

Once having made this distinction, we can also examine different ways in which ideas and action are related. In this book I have discussed four possible relationships—or absence of relationships—between them: the ideas and action systems may be unrelated, i.e. independent of one another; ideas can control action; action can control ideas; ideas and action can compensate for one another.

Since a distinction has been made between ideas and action, an obvious assumption would be that the two are unrelated. Certainly this dichotomy belongs to a persistent Western philosophical tradition, in which spirit is contrasted with matter, soul with body. This tradition has many tentacles; researchers are not the only ones to describe organizations in such terms; the members of organizations do the same. They envisage one system for management and leadership, and another for production: management analyses, plans, commands, decides, and presents the organization both to itself and to the outside world, while others manufacture, service, repair, sell and distribute. A common distinction is also made between strategic tasks primarily concerned with analysis and formulation, and operational tasks geared mainly to everyday activities.

This distinction seems a natural one in view of the very different conditions surrounding ideas and action. Ideas can range widely in time and space; ideas may be about the past, the future, or things that are far away; action happens in the here and now. Ideas about the future in particular need not be confused or constrained by action. Thought is not subject to the same powerful restrictions as action; we can easily think or talk about actions which we cannot actually perform. Against this freedom of thought we have the constraints and limitations of action. Ideas can be inconsistent—there is nothing to stop us thinking about contradictory conditions; but it is generally much more difficult to produce contradictory actions.

If the conditions for ideas and action are really so different, and if different people in organizations are involved in each of them, it seems reasonable to assume that the links between ideas and action will often be fairly loose, i.e. that the ideologies of the ideologists will have little effect on the actions of the actors, and vice versa. And if there is no relationship between the two, any agreement between them will be a matter of chance. Examples of the loose links between ideas and action systems are well documented; organizations collect information which they do not use in their actions (Feldman and March 1981); they invest huge resources in investigations and analyses which have no effect on their actions (Wildavsky 1972), they design strategic plans for certain events, which are never applied when the events actually occur (Ansoff *et al.* 1976), and their way of describing and analysing their own histories can deviate markedly from other people's descriptions of the same events (March and Olsen 1975).

And yet such a picture, assuming the loosest of links between ideas and action, is not the most common one. Many theories of organizations make the opposite assumption: that there is a strong link between ideas and action. This applies in particular to normative theories, and to the theories which practitioners often adopt in presenting their organizations to themselves and others.

In such contexts great importance is attributed to management: analysis is crucial to action.

Ideas as Control

A particularly common view is that thought controls action. First we think, then we act. This is in line with a tradition that puts spirit before matter, soul before body. This hierarchy reappears in the organizational chart, where management is placed at the top— like the head on the body—and is assumed to be controlling the actions of the other members.

If thought is to control action, the two will have to be congruent. This means that freedom of thought will have to be circumscribed: the ideas must be practical and feasible; the ideology and the talk must adjust to the practicable; the fantastic, the grandiose and the beautiful generally have to surrender. If ideas are really to be in control, it is no good losing ourselves in abstractions; we must provide concrete instructions, and the inconsistencies must be removed.

In an organizational context this aspect is particularly important. Organized action implies the coordination of the acts of several people. Moreover, the usual intention is that management's ideas should be injected into the actions of others. This coordination may be produced by talk, by management issuing decrees and being obeyed; and so the decrees must also be clear and concrete. The actors have to be persuaded that the actions are seriously intended. The persuaders will emphasize the advantages of what they propose, they will avoid creating uncertainty and will suppress any alternatives which could threaten their own proposal. Finally, coordination can be achieved because the actors think in the same way, i.e. they have a common ideology. As noted in Chapter 2, if an ideology is to produce effective coordination, it will have to be consistent, conclusive and complex—all qualities which represent evident restrictions on freedom of thought.

If ideas and actions cannot be made to agree, there is a control problem. Or, to put it another way, there are problems of implementation; the ideas cannot be realized in action. This may simply be because those who do the acting refuse to pay sufficient attention to management's ideas, i.e. their action is not adapted to the ideas. But it may also be because the ideas are not suitable for translation into action, that they are not clear-cut and precise enough. For instance, the directives may be the result of a compromise based on contradictory ideas and expressed in vague terms.

Ideas as Explanation

Another possible relationship between ideas and action is that action controls ideas: ideology and talk are used to describe, understand, interpret, evaluate and explain the actions which the organization has already performed. The ideas succeed the action. The action is the point of departure for the ideas, rather than the other way round. Descriptions and explanations of this kind can be used to get the organization's actions accepted by the environment. This relationship, too, means that ideas must be adapted to action; not all ideas suit all actions. Typical explanations are used for purposes of legitimation, to link concrete action to accepted general norms. When ideas are to control action, they have to be reduced to the concrete level of action; but when they are to explain action, they can distance themselves from the concrete and become abstract and more inconsistent. In the case of control, the direction was from the abstract to the concrete; here it is from the concrete to the abstract. Explanation can liberate thought; control blocks it. Paradoxically, action's control over ideas is thus less inhibiting than the control exerted by ideas over action. The maintenance of some distance between actors and management can be a good thing for management: the less it actually knows about the organization's actions, the more freedom it has to describe and explain them.

The notions that ideas control or explain action seems natural, if it is assumed that organizations win the support of their environments solely by their products. Actions are the immediate source of products and are therefore of primary importance. Ideas are important only indirectly as a possible determinant or explanation of the content of the action. Organizational leaders who define their task in terms of maintaining external support for the organization may want to imbue its actions with a content which they expect the environment to accept and value. An important instrument for achieving this goal may be talk.

Hypocrisy

In the case of both control and explanation there has to be some congruence between ideas and action. In a fourth case, there is no such congruence, but there is a relationship. This is the case when ideas and action compensate for one another, i.e. they systematically contradict one another. Organizational talk is adapted to some norms, and action to others. This is hypocrisy. Hypocrisy can be useful if the organizational output includes not only products but also talk. Hypocrisy may be the answer to the problem of the inconsistent norms which face the organization. Hypocrisy means that ideas and action do not directly support one another. On the other hand we could say that the action is being protected, in that management satisfies by talk the demands which the action does not meet. It then becomes easier to act since the action does not have to satisfy inconsistent norms. Unlike the control and explanation relationships, hypocrisy allows for reasonable freedom of thought, albeit less is possible when thought and action are not related at all.

Hypocrisy benefits from some kind of distance—physical or chronological—between ideas and action. If the talkers are far enough removed from the actions to make any influence over them seem impossible, then there is less likelihood of talk or action being adapted to one another. Abstaining from control in this way need not to be a great sacrifice to leaders if the organizational action is anyhow difficult to control, as it often is. And it is easier to avoid letting action influence and restrict ideas and talk, if the talk is concerned with action in the past or the fairly distant future.

In particular, hypocrisy benefits from the 'futures approach'. By definition, speaking of the future means speaking of something which does not exist. If present actions satisfy some demands but not others, then we can always talk about some future actions which will meet the unsatisfied demands. To promise improvements is one way of handling inconsistencies.

Decisions: A Link Between Ideas and Action

If ideas and action are to be linked together, we need a coupling mechanism. The decision is such a mechanism. In standard decision theory decisions are discussed as a method of determining action. According to current normative decision theory, the decision is seen as a way of reducing the variety that characterizes ideas to the unity required for action. According to normative theory, the decision process consists of reducing a number of possible action alternatives to one, by comparing the alternatives with consistent preferences and by applying a choice rule which ultimately yields a single option. The same result can be achieved with the help of rules that limit the search for alternatives, for instance by satisficing.

Thus decisions can be said to occur between ideas and action. How close the decisions are to the respective categories will depend on the emphasis in the particular context. The decision process has two parts: on the one hand the search for alternatives, preferences and consequences, and on the other the decision itself and the indication of a single option. If we emphasize the search aspect of the process, then the decision is more in the nature of free thought; it becomes a form of talk. The decision process itself can provide a good way of discovering and demonstrating different views, at least so long as choices are avoided. But if we emphasize the second subprocess, the indication of a single option, then the decision is more in the nature of action.

The Dream of Rationality

It is difficult to combine ideas and action, or the freedom of thought with the concreteness of action. But there is a dream of handling these difficulties, and of doing it with the help of decisions; this is the dream of rationality. According to the rational model, action is guided by reason. Ideas rank above action, while action is also their ultimate goal. In the rational model, all alternatives and consequences are known and analysed; all goals or preferences are known, stated and ranked; finally, a decision is made as the result of a choice to which the optimizing rule of choice has been applied. Thus everything is accounted for; all the confusion is reduced to the unity of action through the agency of the decision. Ideas can control action, without themselves being affected by it.

The rational model is not attractive only as a dream of a better state of affairs; it also provides an ideal type. It refines and clarifies certain fundamental logical conditions. It has also been launched as a normative model, and constitutes an important source of inspiration and an ingredient in normative concepts—all of which exhort us to be more rational. The rational model has also been used as a descriptive model, and as a means to an understanding of human thought and action in the real world.

The argument so far has questioned three assumptions of the rational model, two concerning the irrelevance of the decision process and the decision, and one concerning causality between decisions and actions. First, the rational model assumes that the decision process has no value of its own; it is just a way of arriving at a decision. Even the decision itself is ultimately irrelevant; it represents a choice between alternatives, and the subsequent action is what will later be judged and evaluated. Decisions are simply instruments for achieving action. My argument has been that, on the contrary, decision processes and decisions both possess an immediate relevance as organizational outputs.

Secondly, the rational model also assumes that the decision process is irrelevant to action; action follows decision regardless of the process by which the decision was arrived at. The decision isolates the action from analysis. The diverse preferences, alternatives and consequences, and the uncertainty that these produce, do not disturb the action. I have argued that this may be too strong an assumption. Decision processes that follow the exact norms which are specified in the rational model—starting from preferences, analysing many alternatives and their consequences—may certainly make explicit a great variety of opinion, but they also tend to lower the chances of mobilizing organizational action.

Thirdly, the rational model assumes a causal link between ideas and action, which is supplemented by assumptions of consistency and sequentiality. Consistency is assumed between decision process, decision, and action: the action is described in the decision and the decision process includes arguments in favour of the action. And according to the assumption of sequentiality the decision process precedes the decision, and the decision precedes the action. In this way the decision process and the decision cause the action; the symbolical and ideological activities control the practical and concrete. In other words, there is a control hierarchy between thought, decisions and actions. Those who think and decide control those who act. I have argued that these assumptions do not necessarily coincide with practice, particularly not in organizations with a strong political element. Ideas and decisions may be inconsistent with action; they may succeed action rather than the other way round, and they may be controlled by action.

Thus decision processes and decisions are important to organizational norms and to organizational practice, but norm and practice do not agree very well. The rest of this chapter will be devoted to a more detailed discussion of decision-making in organizations, to the way in which it is related more or less firmly to talk or action, and to the possible impact of this on rationality.

ALTERNATIVE INTERPRETATIONS OF ORGANIZATIONAL DECISION-MAKING

Decision-making has been an important theme in this book. It has also long been an important area of organizational research in general. Perhaps partly because of this, decisions are also an important organizational activity. As has been demonstrated here and elsewhere, people in organizations often talk about 'making decisions' and sometimes behave roughly in accordance with what is described in decision theory, i.e. they look for alternative actions, predict consequences, compare consequences with preferences, and then declare that they have 'decided'.

In many decision and organizational theories, decisions and decision-making are not treated as phenomena on their own. Instead they are considered to be inextricably linked to action; they are assumed to be a sort of necessary prerequisite of action: if somebody has acted in a particular way it is assumed to be because he has decided to do so. At the same time decisions are assumed to be geared towards action: action is assumed to be the purpose and normal result of decisions. In this book, decisions have been analysed as independent activities, separate from action: they may or may not influence actions, and actions may or may not be produced by decisions. It has even been argued that organizations sometimes make decisions in order to avoid action, that decisions may relieve people of the burden of acting, and that decisions may obstruct action. We would certainly do well to ask ourselves why organizations or people sometimes make decisions before acting instead of simply acting, or why they may decide on something and then do it, instead of simply deciding and stopping at that.

Decision theories tend to vary in content, depending on whether they are prescriptive or descriptive; descriptive theories generally describe real-world decision processes as being less rational than the prescriptive theories would recommend. But standard decision theories, whether prescriptive or descriptive, are based on a common assumption: that decision-making and decisions are concerned with *choice*. Decisions have been described as choices, and organizational choice has been analysed in terms of decisions. Other descriptive studies have questioned the general validity of this assumption, and have suggested another role which organizational decisions sometimes play. This role is concerned with *mobilizing organizational action*, and it is a role requiring less rationality than the choice role. But organizational decision-making and decisions go beyond even the roles of choice and mobilization. In this book I have argued that two further roles can be posited. Decisions can assign *responsibility* and can *legitimate* decision-makers and organizations. These different roles can explain a great deal about the design of decisions, about the extent to which the decision processes follow rational norms, and about the frequency of organizational decisions.

Decisions as Choices and Mobilizers

On the standard assumption that the purpose and main result of decision-making is choice rests the whole notion of the decision-maker's potential or real control over action. Since the decision-makers make the choices, they and their preferences determine future events.

The choice assumption consists of a series of minor suppositions. It is assumed that the decision-makers are looking for the best among several alternative actions. Decision-making can be described as problem-solving, where the problem consists of the existence of more than one alternative. The basic uncertainty is thus connected with the alternatives. Normative decision theory tells us how this problem should be solved by following the rules of rational decision-making: by establishing a preference function, listing all possible options, describing all relevant consequences and comparing these with the preference function.

In practice the problem is generally more difficult than this, since the decision-makers may be uncertain, or they may lack information about the relative qualities of the options or even about what options there are, or they may lack information about consequences or preferences. These uncertainties constitute one of the main reasons why decision-makers in practice may lack much of the influence they are assumed to possess. As was shown in Chapters 4 and 5, the actors may have more information about preferences, alternatives and consequences than the decision-makers, and may thus be less uncertain about them; the actors may then see in the decision process a useful vehicle for bringing certain preferences, alternatives and consequences to the attention of the decision-makers and thereby influencing the content of the decisions subsequently made.

The fact that the uncertainty is often more comprehensive than is assumed in the rational model may also explain the decision-makers' reluctance to follow the norms of rationality. Most decision-makers lack the capacity or the competence to perform the complicated information-processing activities that rational decision-making requires (March and Simon 1958, Huysmans 1970, Kahneman and Tversky 1973, Nisbett and Ross 1980). Or decision-makers, problems, solutions and choice opportunities may interact randomly, producing a certain randomness in the choice of alternatives (Cohen et al. 1972).

All these explanations of deviations from the rational norms suggest that even though deviations are common they do not undermine the norms themselves. If the purpose of decision-making is to choose the best alternative, there is no reason why the decision-maker should not try to stick to the rational norms—even though it is not always possible to succeed. Deviations have no positive function.

But there are other theories which see decisions as ways of discovering preferences or consequences, i.e. the prerequisites of choice, rather than the other way round. Decisions may precede the recognition of preferences or consequences; we may make decisions in order to discover or develop our preferences (March 1976), or we may make and implement a decision to find out what consequences attach to a particular alternative. Thus instead of waiting for uncertainty to be resolved before making the decision, decisions can be used for resolving the uncertainty. Sometimes, however, decisions may not be connected with choice or the prerequisites of choice at all.

Organizations have other problems besides choice. One such fundamental organizational problem concerns the achievement of coordinated collective action. Decision-making and decisions are sometimes used for solving this problem, and this in turn affects the design of the decision process. In order to mobilize organizational action, it is important to secure the commitment of the presumptive actors. Commitment attaches the actor to the action in advance. It represents a kind of promise of personal support for an action; actors thus committed can be expected to contribute to the organizational action. Decision-making may be used both directly and indirectly as a way of engendering commitment. Decision processes can be the means whereby the participants express their commitment to the action decided. Decision processes can also be used to create motivation and expectations strong enough to make actors willing to commit themselves to the action concerned.

Decision processes geared to arousing commitment are directed at uncertainty about actors rather than uncertainty about alternatives. This has implications for the design of the decision process. The generation of commitment is facilitated by decision processes that systematically fail to follow the norms of rational decision-making. Decision processes which handle one or a small number of alternatives and a biased set of positive consequences for one alternative express the decision-makers' commitment to the alternative concerned. And it is easier to limit the process to dealing with one or a small number of alternatives and to a biased set of consequences, if preferences are adapted to alternatives rather than the other way round. The last step in the decision process, the formal designation of a single alternative, is also important as an expression of the commitment of the participants. Thus the involvement of the actors in a decision process geared to norms of irrationality is one means of expressing commitment. Decision processes geared to the rational norms, whereby the decision-makers describe several alternatives and the pros and cons of each one, can easily be used as a way of avoiding commitment to any one of them.

Irrational decision processes can also arouse in the presumptive actors a willingness to commit themselves, regardless of whether or not they are involved in the decision process. It has been argued elsewhere (Brunsson 1985) that the commitment of the actors depends on their motivation and expectations. If actors believe that an action is a good one, and if they expect it to be performed by the organization, they will be more apt to commit themselves to it than if such motivation and expectations are lacking. Strong motivation and expectations attaching to a specific action are promoted by irrational decision processes, which give a positive picture of the action and clearly designate it as something which will materialize.

Both the interpretations of decisions illustrated above—decision as choice or as mobilization—give the decision-makers an attractive part to play. It is assumed that they influence decisions or subsequent actions but they are not themselves affected in any way. In many cases this suggests too rosy a picture of the role of decision-makers, as the next section will show.

DECISION-MAKING AND THE ALLOCATION OF RESPONSIBILITY

Uncertainty does not stop at alternatives and actors; there may be uncertainty about the decision-makers themselves. Decision processes are sometimes used in dealing with this uncertainty, to show clearly who the decision-makers are. This is the case when decision processes are used for the allocation of responsibility.

Responsibility describes a perceived relation between human

beings and actions (Edwards 1969, Spiro 1969). One of its connotations refers to the attribution of causes. If someone is perceived as the cause of an event, he is regarded as being
responsible for it. This definition of responsibility is fundamental in law, where it is closely linked to the concept of 'culpa',
blame and guilt, and is the basis for notions of punishment (Ross
1975, French 1984). The causal definition of responsibility is also
important in moral philosophy, and can be regarded as the basis
of other connotations, such as the connotation of duty or obligation (Helkama 1981). In Western law and in Western moral
philosophy since Aristotle, responsibility has been assumed to
be dependent on the existence of voluntary action: only a person
who wills an action can be said to be causing it; if he is being
compelled by other people or other things, or if his actions occur
by chance, he is not their cause and is not therefore responsible.
The question of voluntary action was defined as early as by
Aristotle in terms of choice. Actions at least appear voluntary if
'at the time they are performed they are the result of a deliberate
choice between alternatives' (Aristotle, Book 3, Ch. 1). The basic
association of willed action and choice with responsibility has
remained a commonplace of philosophical debate into our own
time (Edwards 1969).

Psychological experiments in the field of attribution theory
have revealed no dramatic differences between the basic rules of
the moral philosophers and the rules that ordinary people apply
in judging whether certain individuals are causing actions (Kelley
1972). Causation has been identified with responsibility in that
most empirical studies make no distinction between the attribution of cause and the attribution of responsibility. But the findings
also suggest that, like philosophers and law experts, laymen tend
to associate causation with responsibility (Fincham and Jaspers
1980). It seems safe to assume that causal attribution is an important condition of responsibility-allocation in practice, although it
may not always be sufficient.

In classical administration theory, too, the right or ability to
cause events was assumed to generate responsibility; the connection between power or authority on the one hand and responsibility on the other was a strong one: 'Wheresoever authority is
exercised responsibility arises' (Fayol 1916). Authority at high

hierarchical levels is a means whereby individuals at lower levels can reduce their responsibility for their own actions (Barnard 1938, p. 170). And the authority of higher levels is accepted just because it generates responsibility (Simon 1947 (1965), Ch. 7).

Thus according to all these theories responsibility is ascribed to people who are seen (by themselves or by others) to have influenced events by some action (or inaction) freely chosen from among several possible actions and then carried out. People are held to be responsible if others see them as having made decisions that influence events, and if these decisions are regarded as choices. But not everyone necessarily sees things the same way: the influence on events as perceived by the decision-makers may not correspond to the influence as perceived by the observers. Experimental research on attribution suggests that there may even be some systematic perceptual differences here (Jones and Nisbett 1972). And a person can actively influence the way others perceive his responsibility by dramatizing his choices. By making decisions which look like choices and displaying them ostentatiously to other people, individual actors or groups can acquire responsibility in the eyes of the world; by avoiding such decisions they can avoid responsibility.

Standard decision theory plays an important part here. By describing decision-making in terms of making choices, the standard theory assigns responsibility to the decision-makers: since they have made a choice, they must have had several alternative actions to choose from; by choosing one of these, they have established themselves as at least one of its major causes. Thus, whenever the standard choice-based conception of decision-making is used to define real-world decision-making, it tends to allocate responsibility to the decision-makers. And the very spread of the ideas and ideals attaching to standard decision theory means that decisions produce responsibility.

There is thus a paradoxical relationship between the 'choice' and the 'responsibility' interpretations of decision-making: decision-making can operate as a way of allocating responsibility only if observers perceive it as dealing with choice. This paradox may help to explain why the choice interpretation of decision-making is so popular: it is useful both for indicating choice and for allocating responsibility.

Responsibility via Decisions

The responsibility-allocating role has implications for the design of the decision process. If the decision process is to designate the human cause of an action, it obviously has to point at some particular person or persons. This means that the decision-makers and the decision process itself must both be clearly visible. The visibility of the final decision, designating the action to be carried out, is particularly important. Organizations often employ special procedures to ensure visibility at this stage, such as formal meetings with minutes announcing what decisions have been made and by whom. Votes can be held not only to find out which alternative is preferred by most decision-makers, but also to demonstrate exactly who is making the decision. The recording of reservations serves the same purpose. The visibility of formal decisions is in sharp contrast to that of decision-making geared to choice only. These decisions can be very difficult to observe; the discussion of alternatives sometimes slips over into action without any formal decision being taken or any statement made (Danielsson and Malmberg 1979).

If the decision process is to operate as a way of allocating responsibility, it must also clearly establish the causal role of the decision-makers. It must ensure that people perceive the decision-makers as making a choice between two or more alternatives, as making this choice themselves, and as being personally and strongly associated with the alternative that is carried out. Thus the decision process must give the impression that a choice has been made, but the procedure may well look irrational: the decision-makers' personal association with the action increases as they stress their preference for it. This can be done by focusing exclusively on positive consequences or, as described in Chapter 4, by adapting preferences to alternatives rather than the other way round.

Responsibility can also be established by argument. Decision-makers can claim not only that they were party to a decision but also that they helped to influence what was decided, that they actually made a choice. Their responsibility can also be reinforced by argument, stressing that it is the decision-makers' own values, beliefs and perceptions that determine the decision, and that these determining values, beliefs and perceptions are not objective or automatic or controlled by others. All these methods can be used in reverse by decision-makers who want to avoid responsibility. They can follow rational decision procedures which easily produce uncertainty, and which can be used at the same time to display that uncertainty publicly; in this way the decision-makers can demonstrate their lack of any strong attachment to the chosen alternative, and can show that the choice of a particular alternative is the result of logical and therefore objective and impersonal reasoning based on certain shared goals and values. If it can be claimed that these goals and values are shared by many people, the decision-makers' attachment is even further diluted. In the extreme case the decision-makers may reduce their responsibility almost entirely by substituting formal models and computer programs for their own reasoning, thus indicating that the choice was made not by them but by the model or the computer (Brunsson and Malmer 1978).

Decision-makers can also evade responsibility by making the decision or their own role as decision-makers less visible, perhaps by abstaining from a formal decision ritual. Or they may try to show that they had no choice, that only one alternative was possible. Even without using impersonal rationalistic models they can argue that they did not influence the decision, that they were compelled by outside forces. Decision-makers can also evade responsibility by claiming that they were not party to the decision: they formed a minority, they voted against the decision, or they registered reservations.

The amount of responsibility vested in the individual decision-maker can also be affected by the size of the deciding body as a whole. The greater the number of people responsible for an action, the smaller the responsibility of any one of them. A single decision-maker has to bear all the responsibility. But if everyone is responsible, then no one is. In general referenda, to take an extreme example, the vote of any single individual does not normally alter the majority decision. Thus no individual is responsible, only some abstract entity such as 'the majority' or 'the electorate'. Responsibility can also be diluted over time: by splitting a major decision into a series of minor ones, the burden of responsibility attaching to each separate decision is greatly reduced.

The product B project described in the previous chapter is an example of responsibility dilution on a grand scale, among several organizations and over long periods of time. The product B project was passed up and down the line between one company board, one group board, the national government and parliament; the decision was also broken down into a series of subdecisions, each one calling for further investigation or investment involving relatively minor costs; some of the subdivisions were made conditional (such as 'we accept if others do'). Responsibility for each such minor decision was easier to accept than responsibility for a decision on the whole investment. There was never any single decision stating that the investment should be made. This meant that the decision could in fact be made, despite the fact that almost all the decision-makers were very sceptical or even opposed to it. When the decision proved to have been an economic disaster, no one was able to point the finger at anyone else as bearing the chief responsibility.

Implications for Decision-makers

In the choice and action perspectives the decision-makers are allotted the attractive role of affecting future actions without being affected themselves. The widespread propagation of the choice perspective can be assumed to have increased the popularity of decision-making positions and processes. But in light of the fact that decisions also tend to affect the decision-makers by making them responsible, their role appears less attractive. When the success of a proposed action is uncertain, responsibility may be perceived as a negative feature of decision-making.

If decision-makers perceive the balance between influence and responsibility as unfair to themselves, they may try to change the balance, or they may abandon their decision-making role. The perception of undue or unwanted responsibility explains why individuals or groups sometimes abstain from participation in decision-making. But many organizations are unable to avoid making decisions; they are expected to make them, and are thus easily held responsible.

To top management the responsibility factor may be more important than the choice factor. This could be seen in the budgeting case in Chapter 5, for example, where responsibility was avoided by altering the contents of the budget. And there are many indications that responsibility rather than choice was the normal result of the decisions made by the organizational leaders described in this book. Most of their decisions were rendered highly visible with the help of various techniques: the decision-makers made it clear that they were making decisions, and they demonstrated the content of these decisions: minutes were prepared in which the decisions were recorded, or in the government cases information about decisions was publicized in minutes, at meetings open to the public, and in various other ways. By voting or recording reservations it was clearly shown who was making the decisions. Decisions were preceded by processes—the discussion of problems, preferences, alternatives and consequences—all of which gave the decisions the appearance of choices. External observers such as the press, or various people affected by the decisions, described the decision-makers as implying influence: it was assumed that the decision-makers—at least those belonging to the ruling majority—had influenced the content of the decisions. But the top managements studied were concerned almost exclusively with the final decision; other parts of the decision process were delegated. Experts, administrators or special committees first investigated preferences, alternatives and consequences; later they, or other groups, were supposed to implement management's decisions. The important choices were normally made before the issue ever reached the decision-makers.

The observations reported in this book are not unique. Many other studies have shown that boards and councils making formal decisions often have little influence over the content of these decisions, which have been largely determined by experts preparing the decision base (van Gunsteren 1976, Hanf and Scharpf 1978). It has also been shown that decisions in managements or in boards and councils can still be followed by choices; the decision can have been so vaguely formulated, for instance, that a wide range of subsequent action is still possible (Baier *et al.* 1986). Yet in spite of all this, the members of boards and councils seldom complain officially that they lack influence. In the organizations studied here no decision-makers tried to alter the public image of themselves as influence-wielders, even though some of them complained of their lack of influence in private discussion with the author.

Thus, even if decisions do not have much influence on the choice of alternatives, they are publicly presented as being concerned with and resulting in choices. A glance at any textbook on management or political science confirms that the top management of an organization is expected to make choices and exert influence. This discrepancy between presentation and actual behaviour can be explained by the responsibility paradox: if you claim influence, you will be held responsible. Decision-makers or decision-making units which are anxious to accept responsibility must claim to have influenced the choice. Those who claim lack of influence are actually saying that they did not cause the action and thus have no responsibility for it. Whatever real influence they may have, decision-makers must be regarded as influential if they are to be held responsible. Participation in decision-making processes is supposed to endow the participant with influence. Thus if an organization is given the power to make decisions, it is also being given the ability to absorb responsibility. The purpose of union participation in management decisions, or the role of elected representatives in government decisions, is often described in terms of the assumed influence on the choice of actions. In view of the element of responsibility in decision-making, such arrangements can equally well be interpreted as an attempt to assign responsibility to the groups concerned.

By getting some organizations or groups or individuals to absorb responsibility, it is possible to reduce or void the responsibility of others. And the decision-makers become the potential scapegoats or heroes. Decisions can thus serve as instruments of control; they indicate who should be rewarded or punished—something which in turn can be used to influence people's decisions. The notion of a fair balance between responsibility and influence is also important in a control perspective. If decision-makers do not wield influence, then there is no point in having control over them; and if influence-wielders are not decision-makers and thus not responsible, they may be difficult to control.

Implications for Action

Responsibility provides a link between actions and decision-makers. It affects not only decision-maker but also actions. Actions may be affected by being granted legitimacy: by making decisions and accepting responsibility, decision-makers who possess a high degree of personal or role legitimacy can also endow an action with legitimacy. For example, organizational leaders such as top politicians decide many of the actions undertaken by administrative subunits, thus giving these actions social legitimacy. Such legitimation is important if it is to be possible to complete certain highly controversial actions. As was shown in Chapter 4, the leaders can protect the administration and its actions from turbulence in the environment, by making decisions and sticking to them in spite of external criticism and protests. This is particularly important in the case of long-term actions that are difficult to alter once they have been set in motion.

Decisions may also endow events with meaning. By allocating responsibility, decisions answer a human need to know why things happen. And decisions suggest that certain people, rather than natural forces, chance or God, have influenced events. This may explain why decisions are sometimes made about things which the decision-makers cannot possibly control. Governments, for instance, make decisions about insoluble problems. In traditional African societies witchcraft and 'witch-detectives' serve to exaggerate the responsibility of certain people for disastrous events (Gluckman 1972). In Western society politics, leaders, top managers and politicians may fulfil a similar function.

The responsibility effects of decisions can be used to link the organization to certain parts of its environment. Organizations may make decisions about events and actions in the environment, thereby accepting responsibility for them. During this century Western national governments have been addressing a growing number of societal issues. Their main way of dealing with these issues is to make decisions—about money payments, about resource allocation to public utilities, about legislation. As a result of these decisions they may become responsible not only for the actions of the public sector but also for the results of these actions, and thus for what happens in society at large. If an organization makes decisions for some area that is generally regarded in a positive light—or that comes to appear positive due to the organization's actions—the organization may acquire legitimacy; a government that spends money on prosperous industries demonstrates its responsibility for this success. If an organization make decisions for an area perceived in a negative light, despite the actions proposed, it may transfer some of its own legitimacy to the area in question, as was described in Chapter 6.

DECISIONS AS LEGITIMATION

A factor common to the three aspects of decisions discussed above is that in different ways they link decisions to actions. Actions are chosen, action is mobilized, or responsibility for actions is allocated, through the agency of decision-making and decisions. But sometimes decision-making may have no connection with action at all. There are plenty of examples of decisions that are not followed by action, or of actions that do not accord with preceding decisions. This is often explained as a problem of implementation: the decision-makers have been unable to get other people to act as decided, with problems for both decision-makers and organization as a result (Pressman and Wildavsky 1973, Mayntz 1976). But it has been argued in the present book that the decoupling of decision and action does not necessarily have to be regarded as a problem; it can also be interpreted as a solution—when decisions are counted as organizational outputs.

If decisions reflect external norms, they can also serve as independent instruments for external legitimation and support. Many organizations or parts of organizations such as parliaments, governments, councils or boards even specialize in producing decisions while refraining from producing any organizational action at all.

In this book I have described how organizations can deal with inconsistent norms by acting according to certain norms and making their decisions according to others, thus reflecting a wide range of external norms. This behaviour creates inconsistency between decisions and actions, but the inconsistency is a solution rather than a problem: a solution to the problem of winning and maintaining external legitimacy and support in an environment where inconsistent norms obtain. The uncertainty handled by decisions of this kind is associated with organizational legitimacy rather than with alternatives, actions or decision-makers. Many implementation studies refer to the frequent inconsistency between the decisions made by leaders at various levels, and the actions taken by units lower down the organization. This may be due to one of the strategies for dealing with inconsistent norms, namely letting some units specialize in decision-making and others in action. Decisions can then reflect some norms and actions others. Decisions can compensate for action.

When formal decisions are used as legitimating devices, they have to be clearly visible to the environment. An organization using decisions in this way can be expected to be eager to publicize its decisions.

Decisions may be inconsistent not only with products but also with the talk which the organization directs at its environment. But decisions may also constitute a rationale for producing talk; in talk they can be described and explained. Under inconsistent norms it is possible for different descriptions of a single decision to be inconsistent; and explanations of the decisions to the public may be inconsistent with the content of the decisions as described in minutes and other records. In such situations it is quite obvious that a decision has been made, but it is not at all clear what exactly it consists of. The decision is both evident and equivocal.

Talk can also be produced in the process preceding the decision, which is one reason why organizations should publicize not only their decisions but also their decision processes. The norm-reflecting function of the organization may influence the design of its decision process. Different norms are consistent with different preferences, alternatives and consequences. Rational decision processes in which many preferences, alternatives and consequences are considered therefore provide a better instrument for reflecting inconsistent norms than more irrational processes could do.

FOUR ROLES OF DECISIONS

Organizational decision-making and decisions can thus be interpreted in four ways (Figure 1). Decision-making may fulfil a role not only in choice and the mobilization of organizational action but also in the allocation of responsibility and the provision of organizational legitimacy. Decision-making can reduce the uncertainty associated with alternatives, commitment, decision-makers or legitimacy. Decision-makers may adapt the design of the decision-making processes to these different roles, each one of which requires a different design. If decisions are highly formal and visible, it seems likely that they are concerned with more than choice alone, and possibly not even with choice at all. How far a decision process will follow the rational norms of standard decision theory can be expected to vary according to its role. A high degree of rationality can be interpreted as an attempt to solve the problems of choice, to prevent or stop organizational action, to evade responsibility, or to legitimate the organization in an environment in which inconsistent norms are an important element. Rationality puts some 'distance' between decision and action: rational decision-making is geared to choice rather than mobilization; it decouples decision-makers from actions, and it provides legitimacy in situations where some inconsistency between decision and action is beneficial.

Role:	*Choice*	*Mobilization*	*Responsibility*	*Legitimation*
Handle uncertainty as to	alternatives	commitment	decision-makers	organizational legitimacy
Connection to actions	connected	connected	connected	disconnected
Design	rationality	irrationality	irrationality for responsibility acceptance	rationality in environments of inconsistent norms

Figure 1 *Four roles of decisions*

A high degree of irrationality does not necessarily mean that the decision-makers have failed to make a rational choice; it can also be interpreted as an attempt at creating strong commitment, accepting heavy responsibility, or legitimizing the organization in relation to a group of consistent norms. Irrationality creates a strong link between decisions and actions; it mobilizes action, it links decision-maker and action, and it is useful as a means of legitimation when the prevailing norms are consistent and consistency between decisions and actions is therefore important.

Naturally neither the level of rationality nor the effects of the decisions are necessarily the result of the decision-makers' intentions. Both may be affected by other circumstances, some of which are outside the decision-makers' control. If the decision-makers are the representatives of diverse interests, or if they are exposed to the varied claims of several interest groups, the decision process tends to be more rational and to include more preferences, alternatives and consequences. If the decision-makers possess a strong common ideology, they may not be able to produce much decision rationality. A high level of rationality may also be the result of explicit rationality norms which the decision-makers may consider important to display, or in which they believe. Such norms may stem from current teaching at business-schools, thus gaining wide acceptance; they will then make a considerable impact on the design of decision processes in organizations and thus on the effects of decisions made there.

Decision-makers may also find it difficult to mobilize the actions they want by making decisions; or they may find they have initiated some action as a result of their decisions, which they cannot stop even if they want to. They may hope that external observers will judge them by their actions rather than by their talk and decisions, but the hope may be a vain one. Or talk and decisions intended for internal use may have important external effects: internal budget processes, for instance, may have important effects on external financing as explained in Chapter 5. Or decision-makers may be ascribed more responsibility than they want or less than they would like.

In practice decision processes may of course play more than one of the roles described here; sometimes they may play all four. Several decision-makers—or even one—may want to use a decision process for different purposes, or decision-makers may be aware that regardless of their own intentions observers are interpreting the decision process in a variety of ways. A decision process may involve a struggle between several groups, trying to establish the process in one or other of its roles. Such processes can become very complicated, and are likely to appear extremely fuzzy both to their own participants and to external observers; it is simply not possible to understand them in terms of a single interpretation.

The four roles affect not only the design of decisions but also their number. They suggest not only four different benefits that can be gained from decisions; they also indicate four possible costs. Potential decision-makers may avoid decision-making because they expect it to lead to the choice of an alternative which they do not want, or to a mobilization or demobilization of action stronger or weaker than they want, or to responsibility being ascribed to the wrong people, or to a loss of organizational legitimacy; and they may avoid decision-making because they realize there are other ways of making choices, or mobilizing action, or allocating responsibility, or providing legitimacy. It is not always necessary to make decisions; nor is the capacity for making them always available.

Choices can be made by rules rather than decisions. A great many organizational actions are chosen according to rules of varying degrees of abstraction, ranging from assembly lines to organizational ideologies. An organization that is subject to many strict rules is less dependent on decision-making as a way of making choices. Organizations that breed strong ideologies are able to make choices without decisions, even in unfamiliar situations. Rules also provide a way of mobilizing organizational action; they can supply so much motivation and arouse so many expectations, that decisions and commitment are evoked without any need for decision processes. Hierarchy can have the same effect: if orders direct from the top are imbued with great legitimacy, decision processes are less necessary as a way of mobilizing action.

Rules can also affect the number of decisions that will be made in an organization by restricting the opportunities for benefiting from them. Strict rules make it difficult to exploit decisions as a means to choice or the acceptance of responsibility, or the acquisition of legitimacy; the rules control the choices, and rules rather than decision-makers will be coupled to the action.

Similarly the need for decisions as legitimating devices depends on the ability or opportunity available for using other instruments of legitimation. Organizations that find it difficult to generate or maintain legitimacy by their products or talk become more dependent on decisions as legitimating devices. For instance, many decision-oriented organizations do not produce any products, and it could be difficult to get people to listen to their talk if they did not even produce decisions either (Rombach 1986).

Responsibility, whether desired or not, can be acquired without the help of decisions, as much current debate on corporate responsibility reveals; some organizations occupy positions in society such that responsibility attaches to them without their having made any active decisions (Epstein and Votaw 1978).

Organizations which possess a capacity for decision-making may find it advisable or necessary to use it: an organization that is perceived as able to make decisions in specific areas, for example, may be held responsible for events even though it has made no decisions about them; so perhaps by making decisions the organization might have a better chance of influencing whatever it is being held responsible for. A government which is held responsible for the economic situation of a country may be better off making some positively perceived decisions about it.

The variety of roles that decision-making can play has implications for both descriptive and normative research. The roles can help us towards a better understanding of decision processes, and even towards a better understanding of the roles and behaviour of decision-oriented organizations. It is generally assumed that top management, boards, parliaments and governments are a very important factor in their organizations; they are important also to other people or organizations, and even to society as a whole. If this assumption is correct, then a deeper understanding of the decision-making of society's large and varied leadership corps is vital to an understanding also of the larger systems concerned.

The usual interpretation of decision-making in terms of choice has led to recommendations of rationality. But the other interpretations of decision-making suggest that irrationality would sometimes be more appropriate. Organizations would often be well advised not to adopt rational decision models. Because of the focus on choice, people intending to influence action have also been recommended to launch decision-making processes prior to action, and to ensure their own involvement in these processes. But the other interpretations suggest that decision-making procedures may not be a useful way of acquiring influence, or that they may cost too much in the way of responsibility to be worthwhile. People seeking influence are not always well advised to profile themselves as decision-makers, particularly if they are not prepared to accept the related responsibility.

Descriptive and normative research should not only investigate decision process designs that promote choice but also designs that promote the other roles of decisions. It is also important to explore other possible ways of producing choice, mobilization, responsibility and legitimation apart from using decisions.

9
The Dynamics of Hypocrisy

The distinction that I have made between talk, decisions and actions provides a basis for dealing with hypocrisy, i.e. with inconsistencies between these three factors. In this final chapter a further aspect of hypocrisy will be examined, one that arises from the interaction between the action and political models of organizations. I shall also discuss the spread of politics and hypocrisy in the world of organizations, and will conclude with some advice to organizational stakeholders about ways of handling politics in organizations.

THE PARADOXES OF PRESENTATION AND RESULT

In this book I have compared two models for describing organizations: one action-oriented and one political. In the action model external effects are in focus: the organization makes something happen, it solves some important problem, or it changes its environment. To be able to do this, it must be an independent unit using instruments appropriate to producing coordinated action; it collects resources, produces consistent goals or ideologies and builds structures and processes which favour agreement, control and consistency. The organization specializes in fulfilling the demands of a specific part of its environment. Management produces talk and decisions in order to encourage and inspire its members to act, and to control the contents of their actions. This model agrees with the way in which most organizational theories define and present organizations.

The political model is in essential ways the opposite of the action model. Instead of independence, the organization's dependence on its environment is emphasized. And instead of having clear boundaries with the environment its borders are vague, or so general as not to distinguish the organization from the environment at all. The organization is part of the very environment which is going to judge it. This, and not because the organization produces action for its environment, is why it can appear valuable. The organization thrives on generalization rather than specialization; instead of building upon the enthusiasm of a few, it builds on the tolerance of many. Instead of being involved in action, problem-solving and change, the organization handles important issues and addresses difficult or insoluble problems; the organization is involved in administration rather than change. The organization does not influence its environment, but accepts responsibility for it. Goals are important and valuable in themselves, regardless of where they lead; it is the good intentions of the organization that are important. Similarly, control is important not in order to influence action but in order to show that the right people are in power. Both goals and control can be dramatized in talk and decisions. With the help of these instruments, the organization can convince its environment that it is meeting the environment's norms; it can also demonstrate that its management is busily engaged in organizational activities.

The contents of the action model and the political model contradict one another. They can be used for describing different organizational behaviours. The behaviour of most large organizations is difficult to understand if we do not allow for both models.

This does not mean that both models are equally applicable in all cases. Some organizations, such as those described in the previous chapters, for example, may exhibit a good deal of behaviour which can be described and explained as political, while other organizations are more action-oriented. Or the models may be less appropriate to certain parts of an organization than to others. Organizations may have reason to separate politics and action chronologically, situationally, or intra-organizationally as described in Chapter 2. The empirical descriptions in the previous chapters have focused on the behaviour of organizational managements, and the relationship between leaders and led. The task of organizational managements is often to deal with external contacts, such as financers, the media and others who represent norms for organizational structures, processes and ideologies. It is thus natural that politics, which concerns this kind of environment, will be more important to management than it is to the individual production departments.

But the two models can do more than explain the different behaviour of various actors. I shall argue below that, despite the contradiction between them, they can also be used to explain a single behaviour. The two models are even mutually dependent, in the sense that each makes possible the existence of the other. If the action model is valid, then its contradictory fellow, the political model, is also valid. How can these paradoxes be explained?

In the case studies, the action model emerged as the descriptive model of the organization which the actors were able and willing to present both to themselves and to other people. They were anxious to describe their own behaviour as geared to implementation, to producing action, to getting agreement between talk, decisions and action, and to acquiring control over the organization's activities. In several cases, as in Runtown for example, it was also obvious that the actors themselves really were striving for action, for consistency and for influence. The action model appears to provide a legitimate way of describing the ambitions and intentions of organizations. It can thus also provide an important explanation of the behaviour of individual actors. It describes either their intentions or the intentions they claim in order to motivate their actions to the outside world, or both. In both cases the model is able to influence or restrict their behaviour.

The political model did not lend itself in the same way to outward display. It was not as good at describing intentions: the actors themselves did not describe their intentions in its terms, and presumably it did little to reflect their innermost intentions. On the contrary, several important qualities of the political model would not be easy to present consciously and openly as intentions, for example inconsistencies between talk, decisions and action, or talk and decisions as independent organizational outputs. The political model explains results rather than intentions. The efforts of the actors did not generate consistency, action and influence;

rather, they produced inconsistencies, talk and responsibility. The political model explains how these results can arise, and why they do not threaten the existence of the organization but can even provide it with legitimacy and support. Thus the explanations are concerned with the behaviour of the organization rather than the behaviour of individual actors.

The action model can be called a presentation model and the political model a results model. The difference between presentation and results explains how two contradictory models can be simultaneously valid: they describe different aspects of the same behaviour. For the purposes both of organizational analysis and of organizations themselves, the models complement rather than compete with one another. The organizational analyst is helped by the action model towards an understanding of the behaviour of individual actors in the organization, and by the political model towards an understanding of why organizations which fail to achieve what the action model prescribes can yet be counted successful.

From the organization's point of view, the action model can even be described as a condition for the effective functioning of the political model. The models complement one another because of the different roles they play regarding intentions and results. Although the political model expressed in terms of results asserts the legitimacy of the organization in face of inconsistent external demands, the same model expressed in terms of intentions appears to have the opposite effect. I have argued that if the action model is expressed in terms of results it will not be good at generating legitimacy or external support, but it can avoid this negative effect if it is expressed in terms of intentions. Indeed, the way the action model is used as a model of intent suggests that it agrees with most people's ideas about acceptable intentions. Thus in a world of inconsistent demands results must be provided with other intentions, and intentions with other results. The two models of presentation and results become one another's necessary complement.

Same Instruments—Different Meanings

The action and political models also complement one another in that they refer to many of the same behaviours. Ways of behaving prescribed as meaningful in the action model are also meaningful and important to the production of political results, although the meanings invoked are different in the two models. For instance, according to the action model control is important as a way of coordinating action; in the political model control is linked to responsibility: by displaying and dramatizing the leaders' influence or control, responsibility is engendered. Organizational structures and processes, as well as talk and decisions, are useful instruments for acquiring control and coordination; at the same time they serve to demonstrate the organization's conformity with external values. Decisions are presented as control tools, but much of their importance for results lies in the distribution of responsibility which they beget.

Organizational ideologies are often presented in terms of disinterest: the organization has no self-interest, it is simply an agent for the interests of others. Its results can only be registered in relation to its environment, to the way its actions are valued there. In the political model the important results of an organization's activities are its own legitimacy and survival; but the notion of organizational altruism projected by the action model tends to create legitimacy. In other words it is important to present the myth of altruism only if is not true; just because the organization has to worry about its own position and its legitimacy, it will benefit from presenting an altruistic ideology which may help to enhance legitimacy, i.e. to promote self-interest.

Rationality as Illusion

Rationality is a useful attribute of presentation models. As was described in the previous chapter, the rational model contains a number of specific assumptions about the relationship between ideas and action. These assumptions are particularly suited to using the action model as the presentation model while producing political results. One assumption concerns instrumentality: the idea that management's talk and decisions exist only to influence action. This idea makes it possible for management to produce talk and decisions and yet to proclaim themselves as action-oriented, and to be seen as such by others.

The rational assumption of hierarchy and control—that decisions and decision-makers control actions and actors—is also important. The assumption of control combined with the assumption of instrumentality links management's talk and decisions to the organization's actions. In this way the legitimacy which management enjoys can be projected on to these actions. There are three conditions which make it particularly important to assert the myth of control when presenting the organization to the outside world: first, when it is difficult to gain external acceptance for actions, and their legitimacy thus needs reinforcing; second, when management enjoys greater legitimacy than the suborganization carrying out the action, so that a stronger link between management and action increases the legitimacy of the action; third, when management's control over an action is not obvious to an outside observer, as may often be the case if management's talk and decisions frequently contradict organizational action. These three conditions are typical of any organization that faces inconsistent norms and which deals with them by conducting politics.

Conversely, the link between management and action that the rational model provides, can do much to enhance management's legitimacy. In an environment that sets great store by material products and concrete action, it is difficult to gain a hearing for talk and decisions as such; it is the assumption that they are connected with action which makes them worth listening to.

The rational notion that goals should be formulated is useful to the political model in which goals are also important. Reference to goals occurs in both models, but in the presentation model goals are described as instruments for guiding action, while in the result model they compensate for action.

The assumption in the rational presentation model that decisions generate control means that in the result model they generate responsibility. Making decisions thus becomes a handy way for management to acquire responsibility. Management's responsibility need not refer exclusively to its own or the organization's actions; it can be extended to the situation over which it is assumed to have exercised, or to be able to exercise, control. By affecting perceptions of control, e.g. by the selective use of the decision instrument, an organization can influence the extent of the responsibility ascribed to it. Decisions can thus be used for generalizing the organization: by making decisions affecting some new area, the organization appears to be exerting control, i.e. it becomes responsible for this area. The range of its real influence, however, need not have grown.

Last, but not least, the rational dream that the free-ranging complexity of thought can be easily reduced to the unity of action is fundamental to the credibility of the action model in organizations exposed to powerful inconsistencies. The rational dream conceals the contrast between politics and action. Instead it proclaims the possibility and indeed the appropriateness of letting action follow the consideration of conflicting goals and different alternatives and of the positive or negative consequences of them all—something which any organization with a strong political streak will be particularly good at. Were the opposite view to dominate, i.e. that ideological tolerance can seriously impede organizational action, it would naturally be difficult to assert that the main purpose of a politically oriented organization was to produce action.

In the preceding chapter the rational model was described as unrealistic in the sense that it did not mirror the organizational conditions for either action or politics especially well. But, as we have seen, this does not mean that the rational model is useless. On the contrary it provides an extremely useful and beneficial way for organizations to present themselves.

Strategy for Failure—Hypocrisy Again

There are thus big differences between the action model and the political model, between presented intentions and results. Whenever the action model is being used to describe intentions while results would best be described by the political model, the organization is bound to appear to have failed in various important ways. The political model is a kind of failure in the categories of the action model. The consistency between talk, decisions and actions which the organization claims to desire is not being achieved; management's influence is circumscribed and the organization has little ability to act. The discrepancy between presentation and results may explain why people are often discontented with the way the organization and its leadership works, even in organizations which are successful in terms of profitability and prosperity.

As a presentation category, influence differs from action and consistency. Even if organizational leaders succeed in convincing their environment that they are striving for action and consistency, they may find it extremely difficult to convince others that they are actually achieving these things; both categories can be too readily observed from outside. And if the political model is to work, the leaders must not succeed. Influence, on the other hand, cannot be directly observed; it refers to an intricate conception of relations, into which the actors possess more insight than observers. This makes it relatively easy to claim influence in situations where there is none. And the claims will be all the more convincing if it is possible to demonstrate a set of observable procedures which are commonly believed to generate influence. There is less likelihood that the organization will be thought to have failed in the influence dimension than in the case of action and consistency. Organization leaders can thus easily appear responsible, but will find it more difficult to appear successful.

When the inconsistencies between decisions and actions are obvious and unmistakable, it may be possible for organizational leaders to proclaim their lack of influence, which would also mean they were not responsible. The problem here, however, is that the strategy cannot be used on any permanent basis. In the long run it would threaten management's legitimacy and thus indirectly the organization's as well—if management is not responsible for the organization's actions, then what is its *raison d'être*, and what do its talk and decisions matter? This is one reason why organizational leaders often let themselves become responsible for bad results in terms of their own declared intentions; they become responsible for failure.

The discrepancies between the model of presentation and the model of results confront organizations with yet another inconsistency, this time at a higher level; an inconsistency that arises when organizations handle inconsistencies. This is a second type of hypocrisy, of claiming one thing while achieving another.

The inconsistency also expresses failure—the organization has striven for consistency and vigorous action, but has achieved the opposite. There is an obvious risk here. Neither the environment nor the organization's own members are likely to be happy about failure, or likely to tolerate it, even though the survival of organizations with attributes such as I have described suggests that a fair amount of such tolerance nonetheless exists. The methods for handling this inconsistency of the second degree are somewhat similar to those which we have already analysed above. Certain features of the politically oriented organizations can also increase the tolerance of failure. The main strategy is to meet the failure by 'more of the same', by acting as before but more so.

To begin with, the failure must not look planned; nor should it seem inevitable. It must have some appearance of being temporary, a difficulty which could be overcome in the future. Consequently a firm fundamental belief in the rational action model is needed, a belief that conflicting ideologies about action can be combined, that the organization's structures and processes really are suited to generating influence and action. Thus, paradoxically, the failure makes it even more important to cite the action model and its rational specification.

The production of more political behaviour can also help to reinforce the tolerance of failure. For one thing, management can invoke its own good intentions and its goals, while blaming the failure on problems in implementation—on practical obstacles and perhaps an unwieldy or intractable organization, or on the difficulty of getting the support of oppositional groups outside the organization. The politicians in Greaton accepted responsibility for the decisions, but disclaimed responsibility for any failure at the implementation stage. The public presentation of good intentions also directs attention towards the group which has these intentions (management), and away from practical action.

The organization can also associate itself with external critics. Obvious weaknesses may be made the subject of conflict and debate within the organization, which thus demonstrates its concern for the particular problem. Various internal groups in the organization can point the finger at present shortcomings and explain how much better everything would be if the decision were in their hands. One day in the future all will be well: 'we will be in the majority', 'an intelligent evaluator will show that we are right'. Organizations that are strong in politics are unsuccessful but full of promise.

Finally, external criticism may be slightly softened by the recognition that up to a point the organization is having to tackle insoluble problems. In such cases there is unlikely to be any competition: it would be difficult to find any other organization that had solved the problems. In comparison with others, the organization probably does not look too bad.

So the strategies for handling a failure stemming from the discrepancy between presentation and results tend to produce more of this very discrepancy. The rational action model is stressed more than ever in presenting the organization, while the political elements of behaviour—intentions, compensatory actions, debate, emphasis on the future and a focus on problems— are all being reinforced. In other words, the reaction to hypocrisy of the second degree is to produce yet more hypocrisy of the same degree; to display the action model while behaving politically.

Organizational Reform

The failure that is produced by the discrepancy between presentation and results also encourages explicit promises to do penance. A common answer to criticism is to promise organizational reform. It is natural for leaders convinced of their own good intentions to blame poor results on organizational structures and processes, which they therefore seek to improve. Many organizations live in an almost continual state of reform intended to improve their way of working; and many new organizational managements proclaim their interest in reform. But reform often fails to lead to any great change in the way an organization works; nor is management always interested in its doing so. March and Olsen (1984) pointed out that every new American president since the war has introduced reforms of the administrative apparatus, but the results have been modest and there has never been much real interest in the subject. But by promising reform, by promising to improve in the future, an organization can inspire a little hope even among critics of the present situation: at least the signposts are pointing in the right direction. The reforming zeal results in talk and decisions which compensate for present actions.

Organizational reform is often aimed at improving one aspect of an organization's multifaceted life. If an organization is examined from a single angle, many of its structures and processes may appear incomprehensible or superfluous, inviting attempts at abolition or reform. Action has provided a popular angle from which to criticize organizations and suggest reforms. Researchers and practitioners, supported by numerous organizational theories, are both inclined to look at organizations as though they were, and ought to be, systems geared solely to organized action. Structures and processes which do not promote efficient action must be abolished; the organization must be trimmed and rationalized! Reforms under the action flag may seem particularly appropriate when action is intended but politics results. In such a case the intentions are clearly right, but the organization in which the intentions are to be fulfilled is obviously wrong in some way. Reforms geared to the action model spring from a conviction that the structures, processes and ideologies prescribed in this model do actually make it easier for organizations to act. People may not be able to agree on the actions that should be undertaken, but at least they can agree that action in general is a good thing and should be encouraged.

There is another reason as well why reform may seem desirable in organizations which intend action but achieve politics instead. We have seen that in such organizations the leaders easily become distanced from the action. Action is often delegated to other parts of the organization, in other words to the led; the links between the leaders' talk and decisions and these organizational actions will be weak or non-existent. The leaders will find it difficult to influence the action, and if they do achieve any success in their attempts then the organization's ability to act may easily be undermined. In such a situation it must be very frustrating to believe in the action model, and leaders may start looking for actions in which they can really participate and which they can control. Reforms can provide just the right opportunity for the leaders to engage themselves directly in what seems to be an important action. Here their knowledge comes into its own; it is not necessary to delegate reform activities to lower organizational levels; at such levels people have no need to know much—and often do not know much—about reforms.

The greatest risk attaching to action reforms as a strategy for handling failure is that the reforms succeed; it then becomes difficult to introduce new reforms. But in highly political organizations the danger is slight. The reason why it is so difficult to implement the action model in practice is that the environmental norms are inconsistent, that the leaders are in conflict with one another and embrace different ideologies, that the organization has to handle insoluble problems, and so on. Furthermore, in such a situation a real change in organizational structures, processes and ideologies, bringing them closer to the action model, would imply a serious threat to the survival of the organization. Thus action reforms in such situations rarely move much beyond the planning stage or the decision to reorganize, where they have little impact on everyday activities; they typically fail, thus providing new grounds for initiating new reforms.

Thus inconsistency of the second degree gives rise to what appear to be new paradoxes: in order to succeed you have to fail; good intentions are followed by bad results. And to deal successfully with failure you have to fail; you produce more politics while emphasizing your intended adherence to the action model; and action-oriented reforms must not succeed if the organization is to be able to continue to reflect inconsistencies. Hypocrisy—inconsistency between talk and action, presentation and results—is the source of these paradoxes as well as their solution. Organizations may present themselves as simple instruments for coordinated action, but they tend to behave in a much more complicated way. In the next section I will argue that these complications in organizational life are becoming an increasingly important facet of modern societies.

PUBLIC ORGANIZATIONS AND THE PUBLICNESS OF ORGANIZATIONS

Most of the empirical cases described in this book refer to organizations belonging to the so-called public sector, i.e. they are associated with local authorities or the state. To these organizations both action and politics are important. They are involved in the production of extensive goods and services, and the quality and efficiency of their production determine the support which the organizations can command. Thus to some extent they must be organized for efficient action. But they also systematically exploit inconsistent ideas in their environments, and exhibit strongly political features. They seek support from 'the public', and not only from special groups with special demands. They incorporate conflicts existing in the public into their own structures, by including in their management representatives of various demands, so that the public has some chance, albeit generally fairly small, of influencing the composition of the group of leaders. The organizations are open to inspection in various ways. For instance there are public debates and hearings, and there is often a right-of-access principle which states that many of the documents produced or handled by the organizations should be available to all. The processes thus exposed also reflect a broad spectrum of demands. In particular, decision processes exhibiting high levels of rationality will be displayed. It is usual, for example, for issues to be diligently explored in multi-interest committees, which handle several goals and options and provide relatively balanced descriptions of the consequences of the alternatives. There are strong tendencies to isolate politics and action from one another in several ways, as described in Chapter 2, and 'poor coordination' between politics and action makes it easy to maintain inconsistency between talk, decision and products.

Many organizations in the public sector possess a powerfully intellectual streak: they cultivate many varying ideologies, they use relatively rational decision processes, and they handle problems that are generally regarded as important but very difficult to solve. Many problems handled by public organizations are essentially insoluble, or have defied solution for thousands of years. Members of the organization are very likely to acknowledge that errors have been made in the analysis of a problem or in the way it has been tackled, since the organization cultivates criticism and maintains an internal opposition whose task is to point out its faults continuously. At the same time it is difficult for the organization to change its production, since there would be conflict about what changes to make. Intellectuality and depression are equally common in the public sector.

The rationality myth is also important to public organizations. Constitutions, which usually express the most authoritative picture which the public organizations have of themselves, often proclaim the idea that the organizations are 'controlled' by politicians, who in turn are appointed by the environment ('the people'). The organizations are presented as instruments for realizing in action the will of the people. Even when this control does not function in practice, it still means that responsibility for the organization and its actions lies ultimately with the people themselves, i.e. with the environment on whose support the organization depends. If this myth is believed, the organization becomes legitimate by definition.

To describe public organizations in terms of legitimacy may seem strange, since they have direct access to the state's coercive system. They can use force to generate resources in the form of taxes from the environment, and could well appear to be independent of any need for legitimacy. But we could also say that legitimacy is essential to them, so that they do not in fact have to resort to force; and in view of the enormous resources they need in modern societies, their legitimacy becomes even more vital. That politics is important to their legitimacy is natural, since most of their resources are derived from taxes, i.e. payments which by definition are not directly associated with the result of particular actions, with the supply of any particular good or service. It is not enough for citizens to pay for the products that they personally want. Traditionally the public organizations operate in areas where they command a monopoly, and the acknowledged fact that it has proved difficult for various reasons to create competition in such areas as telecommunications, postal services and railways provides an argument in favour of using public organizations. But since it is difficult for monopolistic organizations to insist that their products are as good as they can be, and as efficiently produced, it will be natural for them to base their legitimacy on political qualities instead.

The Politicization of Organizations

Even if most examples in this book have been taken from what are known as public organizations, it is not the public ownership itself that has been of interest. Rather, the theme of this book has been the 'publicness' of organizations: how, by opening their structures, processes and ideologies to inspection, organizations can seek the support of a wider public.

In Western European countries problems have traditionally been considered the task of the public sector and solutions of the private sector. Such a division of labour implies that public-sector organizations are good at politics, able and willing to take on the difficult or insoluble problems, and more skilled in talk and decisions than in action. In the private sector action is generally more important; these organizations can concentrate on solutions and be well prepared to act. According to this view, researchers looking at problems will be found at state-subsidized universities, but once the researchers come up with a solution they start a private company: the technological researcher becomes a computer manufacturer, the organization researcher becomes a consultant. When industrial companies come up against problems which they cannot solve, they demand public subsidies or ask to be taken over by the state.

But this view of the division of labour between the public and private sectors has never been more than approximately correct. Many publicly owned organizations have a strong action orientation, and many private ones are highly politicized. The borderline between public and private is also becoming increasingly blurred, as the state becomes more active in industry and business seeks support from the state. Over the last few decades the politicization of manufacturing and service companies appears to have increased in most Western industrial countries.

Developments point towards an economy in which the interdependence and interactions between state authorities, local authorities, special-interest organizations and private companies will be increasingly important. In this kind of economy organizations are exposed to a growing number of inconsistent demands. In modern economies it is not enough for industrial companies to produce industrial products as efficiently as they can; they must also conform to a series of other norms as described in Chapter 1. Demands for efficiency are often easier to avoid than norms for structures and processes (Meyer and Rowan 1977). Companies are becoming relatively less dependent on market sales and increasingly dependent on special-interest groups and on the state, which typically communicates conflicting norms. Institutional environments favour institutionalized organizations.

Thus in modern economies politics and action often become mixed; they are no longer organizationally separate. Many organizations have to work hard at both tasks. They become responsible, being perceived by themselves or others as being able to influence many things and therefore compelled to consider a wide range of values and norms over and above the efficient production of some specialized physical product or service. When private-sector organizations become better at reflecting inconsistencies, the role of the public sector becomes blurred. This may help to explain current calls for privatization and for greater efficiency and action-orientation in the public sector.

Politicization even occurs in special-interest organizations such as trade unions or industrial associations. Such organizations are supposed to represent the particular interests of their members and could therefore be expected to be concerned with consistent demands. However, in highly corporative societies such as those in Western Europe a fairly small number of large special-interest organizations tend to acquire most of the bargaining power in negotiations with their main opposite members or with the political system (Micheletti 1987). The strength of these organizations lies in their size in terms of number of members; but because of their size they are also very likely to include groups whose interests are mutually conflicting. In certain respects the conflicts within an organization may be even greater than the conflicts between the organization as a whole and its opposite numbers. Such an organization will find it difficult to represent a special interest *vis-à-vis* the environment, and on this count it will lose a lot of its strength as a negotiator. On the other hand it will be strong in the sense that it can have many members. Organizations which in this way become 'general' or 'public', tend to find themselves facing conflicting demands. To generalize is one way of growing, but the growth leaves the organizations weaker in both acting and bargaining.

If organizations were always subject to their original narrow goals, they would never be able to reflect inconsistencies. It is when an organization's survival and growth acquire a value of their own that it becomes desirable or necessary to deal with inconsistent demands. Political behaviour is most important to those concerned with organizational well-being; it is less important to those interested only in what an organization can do for them.

In a study of what they called 'permanently failing organizations', Meyer and Zucker (1989) showed that the ability of such organizations to reflect the interests of diverse groups also brought them continuing support and ensured their survival, even though in a more traditional sense their results were poor, with a low level of efficiency or weak profitability. Peters and Waterman (1982) reported that what they called 'excellent companies' showed evidence of fragmentation and internal rivalries. On the basis of their study of successful organizations they also advocated various management practices which may appear inconsistent and paradoxical, such as favouring smallness in order to become big or diversifying by 'sticking to one's knitting' (Peters and Waterman 1982, van der Ven 1983).

Inconsistent demands can also arise when an organization is heavily dependent on several other organizations which embrace mutually conflicting norms and rules. Gustafsson and Seeman (1985) described a new social organization with fresh ideas about the care of children in trouble, and its difficulties with the reactions and demands of various bureaucratic organizations such as schools, the social services, etc., which had their own ideas about how to handle these children and their families. Lipman-Blumen and Schram (1984) described the problems of the American agricultural research community, which was exposed to continuously changing demands from various interest groups and commissions at different levels in the federal and state hierarchies. As in the cases reported in the present book, the conflicting demands in the one case on the social organization and in the other case on the research community generated a great deal of criticism. The research units found themselves in the paradoxical situation of being heavily criticized while very successful in the sense that they were producing a lot of research which according to several accepted criteria was certainly good. Judged purely on the quality of the work the research should have had a high status; but because of all the criticism its status was instead very low.

Even if the members of organizations like these have set their sights on action, regarding the organization simply as an instrument for the action that interests them, they can still be forced to produce politics in order to ensure that their instrument, i.e. their organization, can survive at all, or that their actions will not suffer too much disturbance from external groups and external demands.

The organizations of the agricultural research community created a number of separate committees composed of researchers and various external interests, who collaborated in the discussion of research priorities. The committees produced a lot of collaboration but their deliberations made little impact on the research itself. The organizational structure also became increasingly decentralized, i.e. individual units were only loosely linked to one another and to the central level. The decentralization helped to isolate the leader's talk directed at the environment from the organization's actual operations; at the same time the various units could work relatively independently of one another in pursuance of their own goals. Although this created a good deal of double work, and made it more difficult to achieve efficient coordination, the decentralization was nonetheless useful in protecting the research from the leader's talk.

The introduction of co-determination in private-sector companies in some countries is another example of growing politicization. Structural arrangements are made, for instance that the unions should be represented on company boards, or rules are established whereby joint consultation is made mandatory before management makes its decisions. These arrangements resemble the structures and processes commonly employed in public organizations. Conflict is being incorporated into the management body; the union is included on the board because it is assumed to represent different interests from those of the other board members. Decisions are made and different points of view are expressed during the decision process. With or without co-determination, companies are being increasingly called upon to motivate their actions to a critical environment, which means in turn that rationality is needed. The production of ideologies becomes even more essential; for example, beautiful goals, at least in areas where it is difficult to satisfy external interests by the production of action, are an important accessory.

It may seem surprising to find that organizations which have previously been regarded as predominantly geared to action are now exhibiting obvious political characteristics. Some of the political attributes—the handling of difficult problems, the unwieldiness, and the emphasis on criticism and conflict—must seem pretty unattractive to many of the members of these organizations, particularly their leaders. Frustrated municipal administrators should surely provide a warning example! Moreover, it is an irksome business, having to cope with demands for both politics and action in one and the same organization.

Organizations could therefore be expected to be drawn towards one or other of the extreme forms: seeking to avoid politics if they originally had a strong action orientation, and avoiding action if they are good at politics.

But politicization does have one advantage: it seems to provide a better chance of survival. And therefore the desire to survive can act as a powerful impetus to politicization. The organizations which have survived the longest are universities, churches, and nation states—all of which are good at reflecting inconsistencies in structures, processes and ideologies. On the other hand, organizations whose most important basis for legitimation is action, such as small production or service businesses, have a strikingly short average life (Starbuck and Nystrom 1981). It is not difficult to see why.

Highly political organizations are by definition more open than acting organizations: they reflect their own surroundings within themselves. Since the members of these organizations include representatives of various interests in the environment, the organizations actually constitute part of this environment and cannot simply be abandoned. The organizations reflect many values upheld by external groups, so these groups are likely to work hard for the survival of the organization (Meyer and Zucker 1989). Open organizations are also more adaptable (von Bertalanffy 1968). Organizations that concentrate on action have to avoid excessive influence from without in order to facilitate internal mobilization directed towards specific actions. A certain amount of independence is a necessary quality of action-oriented organizations. Their action involves fewer values; they invest a great deal in their particular niches. Specialization can yield high profits, but it also makes for vulnerability (Hannan and Freeman 1977). Niches can disappear and rapid adjustment may be called for. As a method of expansion, generalization offers more security. Solutions normally last for a much shorter time than insoluble problems. Politics also provides an organization with more instruments suited to adaptation. It is often both cheaper and quicker to adjust ideologies to changes in the environment than to adapt products in the same way.

Highly political organizations may provide a depressive setting for their members and are apt to be accused of inefficiency, but because of their good chances of survival they can also offer great

security. More action-oriented organizations supply a more enthusiastic setting but less security.

But politicization in organizations does not necessarily depend
exclusively on inconsistent demands from a given environment.
Politicization may equally well be due to the mutual reinforce-
ment of inconsistent external norms, organizational structures,
processes and outputs (Figure 2). In other words the political
characteristics arise as effects of one another. One political attribute may stem direct from some external or internal event in
the organization, while others may be secondary effects of this
primary attribute. Politicization could thus start from any of the
ellipses in Figure 2. Exactly how this works is an empirical question, but it is still possible to discuss a few hypotheses.

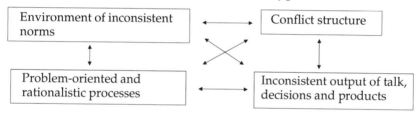

Figure 2 *Interaction between political attributes of the organization*

The inconsistent environment need not only cause the other
characteristics; it can also result from them. Organizations with
the three other political characteristics may seek environments
with inconsistent norms, since they are good at reflecting such
environments. But such organizations may also create and reinforce environmental inconsistencies. The highly political organization propagates the notion, both actively and indirectly by
its behaviour, that its way of perceiving and structuring inconsistencies is the norm. If other organizations and individuals regard
this organization as an important one, it may seem sensible and
reasonable to them to adapt to its particular structural differentiation and to the issues that it handles. Sometimes this may even be
the only possible way of proceeding. For instance, anyone who
wishes to wield any influence in British politics, would be wise to
associate themselves with one of the two main parties. Similarly,
it is generally wise to define any issue in which one wants to have
a say, in the same categories that the organizations apply to their
own areas of internal conflict; if an organization reflects the con-

cept of environmental protection in its structure, processes and ideologies, it is sensible to define a pet issue as an environmental one. Such classifications often acquire a dynamism of their own, so that claims and norms evolve in established areas, which makes the organizations even more important to their environment, etc. Organizational environments therefore tend to reflect organizational structures with astonishing accuracy.

In some organizations, we can assume that the conflict structure will compel continued politicization. This was the case in Runtown, as we saw in Chapter 3. According to national constitutions, national and political assemblies should be composed of representatives of 'the people', which has traditionally meant different parties with their own ideologies. The conflict structure provokes the organization to reflect and create inconsistent demands in its environment, to handle difficult or insoluble problems in rationalistic processes, and to produce inconsistent ideology.

But this does not mean that, once upon a time, the conflict structure in national and local government emerged independently of any of the other political attributes. The democratic reforms introduced in several countries around the turn of the century may have been the result of more obvious and more sharply conflicting demands in society, as well as the result of the other political aspects. For instance, another hypothesis is that the politicization of governments is due to their problem orientation; these organizations have little control over their agenda (Kingdon 1984) and therefore acquire a series of insoluble problems which can only be reflected by ideological outputs and conflict structures.

Similarly, the launching of various forms of industrial democracy and co-determination in Western Europe over the last few decades may be explained in several ways. The conflict structures that these reforms imply may have been initiated or accepted by companies which had faced extremely inconsistent demands within their own environments, perhaps because they had themselves come to define their environment in broader terms (including, for instance, the health and working conditions of their workers). Business and industry may also have been facing insoluble problems, for example simultaneous demands for profitability and the maintenance of jobs and higher wages, while at the same time the demand for their products was declining. Or hypocritical outputs can generate or reinforce inconsistent claims on the organization; they may produce a demand for the representation of various interests in the organizational leadership; and they can give rise to the expectation that the organization will solve difficult problems. Whether or not the conflict structures were introduced for these reasons, once they were established they probably created more inconsistent environments as well as reinforcing both the incentive and the capability for dealing with conflict-ridden environments and difficult problems, and for producing ideological and hypocritical outputs.

Although it can be assumed that the different aspects of politics in organizations are closely related, there is nothing automatic about this. Some organizations with discordant characteristics exist; organizations may resist the forces of politicization. For instance, even in contact with the state, organizations can join a segment of society in which politicians, public administrators and business enterprises support each other, arguing and acting together in their relations with other segments. For the members of such an 'iron triangle' (Hernes 1978) it may be possible to maintain the necessary links with the state without too much politicization.

Organizations may also make inconsistencies seem more consistent by producing ambiguity—by letting talk, decisions and products become vague enough not to conflict with any external norm; although it is hard to see that this strategy is very often likely to offer a better way of getting support than actively reflecting different values. The organization may also be able to influence the external norms through its own propaganda, which demonstrates that only certain norms are reasonable, or by negotiating with those making the demands. Finally political behaviour can be avoided in spite of inconsistencies by using force as a way of getting resources for the organization—this is the strategy of the one-party state.

The Societal Significance of Politics

Lastly, we can assume that the simultaneous reflection of both action and inconsistency in organizations is affected by the importance of these two categories in society as a whole. Modern society is highly dependent on actions that only organizations can realize. The reflection of inconsistencies may fulfil the important function of producing symbols (Olsen 1983; March and Olsen 1984). By reflecting inconsistencies organizations dramatize people's inconsistent values, thus perhaps reducing tension within and between individuals and groups in much the same way as legal proceedings or myths (Arnold 1935; Martin *et al.* 1983).

Organizations which specialize in reflecting inconsistencies, and organizations which specialize in organizational action, may complement one another by providing each other with support and legitimacy. Powerfully political organizations such as parliaments handle problems that cannot be solved by their somewhat more action-oriented fellows, such as industrial organizations; they give meaning to what happens in their environment (Olsen 1983), i.e. to events which are often produced by the interaction of acting organizations, and they accept the responsibility for them.

Organizations in modern societies are public not only in the sense that their structures, processes and ideologies are open to observation, but also in their ultimate dependence on public acceptance, i.e. of positioning themselves in relation to the perceptions and policies of society at large. Organizations in modern societies base their legitimacy on society's perception of their contribution to the public good; they are part of the 'modern project of justice and progress' (Jepperson and Meyer 1989). The public good is of course a conception infused with inconsistent norms and demands, calling for a wide range of action as well as talk. Politics as described in these pages is the way in which some of these inconsistencies can be explicitly incorporated into the individual organization.

It could then be expected that the extent to which organizations display politics in a society will depend on the theories the society embraces about the division of tasks between different organizations. There may be a strongly held theory that the public good is best attained by cooperation or competition between groups of organizations, each working in its own way; organizations can then specialize in reflecting one set of values and yet remain part of the 'project'. Under this heading we find all those economic theories which claim that the striving of organizations and individuals for their own welfare will lead to the welfare of all, or the theory that different interests should be the concern of specialized interest groups which elaborate and reinforce specific demands. The specialization allowed by these theories permits a relatively high degree of action-orientation in the individual organizations.

Theories concerning the division of tasks may be expressed in terms of ideologies, as exemplified above, or they may be incorporated into organizational structures. If individual organizations are seen as part of an organization hierarchy, with the state at the top for instance, this can provide further legitimation for specialization. As in the individual organization, the top can conduct politics while the lower levels concentrate on specialized action. This can be effected either by state ownership of companies, as in Socialist countries, or by the state creating national plans (whether they are implemented or not), as in France and many other European countries.

But if theories on the division of tasks are weak or non-existent, organizations may be forced into generalization, into including a wider range of norms and values in their structures and processes and ideologies. Every organization then has to reflect in itself the inconsistencies in the conception of the public good, becoming more self-sufficient and possessing greater autonomous legitimacy. Politics is conducted not only at society's top level but also at the level of the individual organization, where it hampers vigorous action. According to this hypothesis, politics at the organizational level could be expected to be particularly strong in countries such as Scandinavia and West Germany, where state ownership, national planning and capitalistic theory are particularly weak.

IMPLICATIONS FOR ORGANIZATIONAL STAKEHOLDERS

The typical organization has many stakeholders, people who are affected by it and who therefore have an interest in influencing its behaviour. A good understanding of how organizations work is a necessary although not a sufficient condition for success in steering organizations in a desired direction. In this context organizational stakeholders could make use of the analysis

218 THE DYNAMICS OF HYPOCRISY

presented here. It is difficult to wield influence in organizations of a pronounced political nature, if one regards the organization as a system exclusively geared to organized action or to the ideal rationality model. An attempt to exert control based on an analysis that does not fit the realities of the situation is liable to be ineffective, and any results it achieves may be quite different from those intended. In the following sections I shall discuss some more specific normative implications for people in different positions desirous of influencing an organization. I shall start with those in positions of leadership.

Solutions for Leaders—Controlling Without Confronting

There is an abundance of normative ideas and models to tell us how leaders should control their organizations. Some of these models assume that the leader's task is to partake directly in the organization's activities; many more assume that it is to ensure that action takes place and to control its content. This is a natural task for the leaders of any organization that acquires external support solely on account of its products; the activities resulting in these products are obviously of crucial importance. Thus in the action model there is no inherent contradiction between the task of controlling action and the task of creating legitimacy.

Normative models usually include various organizational structures and processes and ideologies which serve to facilitate control. But if as well as affecting organizational action these structures and processes and ideologies also represent independent outputs which might affect external support, the situation becomes more complicated. As I have argued in this book, it is not at all certain that the structures, processes and ideologies that are acceptable in a legitimacy perspective will also be good at producing action efficiently or even at producing the action that management wants. Political elements in organizational structures, processes and ideologies are difficult to combine with a desire to promote action. This makes it difficult for leaders to be both good at producing politics and to control the content of the organization's actions.

A common response to the problem of combining action and politics is to separate them, often between a leadership group that conducts politics and an administrative or producing organization that concentrates on action. But, as we found in the case studies described in Chapters 3 and 4, this type of leadership has difficulty in asserting itself in its relations with the action-oriented parts of the organization. Nor is this altogether surprising. In fact the opposite notion appears more astonishing: that a suborganization (leadership) which is marked by conflict, ideological variety, problem awareness, rationality, criticism and generalization should take on the task of controlling another suborganization (the administration) which is characterized by unity, ideological homogeneity, a solution orientation, irrationality and specialization. The leaders of the organizations described here resorted to making decisions in the situations that faced them, but their decisions served to confirm and legitimize the actions of the administrative suborganizations rather than to control them. The will of the leadership, its ideas about the direction in which it wanted to go, and the action it wanted to see, was largely determined in intimate interaction between itself and the administration, whereby it was informed by the latter of various existing needs and opportunities. Many control models assume that the supply of control is greater than the demand for it: that leaders are eager to control people who try to avoid being controlled. In the cases I have described the opposite appeared to be true: the demand for control on the part of those who were to be controlled was greater than the control exerted by their leaders. The actors in the administrative suborganizations were trying to persuade their leaders to decide on the actions which they, the administrators, wanted to perform or already had performed, and to assume the responsibility for them.

It may be important for an organizational management to create legitimacy for the actions of its organization, perhaps by making decisions about them, but this task threatens another one, namely the creation of legitimacy for the organization as such. And whereas the legitimation of action calls for consistency between talk, decisions and action, legitimizing an organization often requires inconsistency. Leaders have to strike a suitable balance between manifest support and responsibility for individual actions and compensation for other actions by using talk and decisions.

The job of the leaders is even more difficult if they genuinely want to control action, and not just to look as though they are doing so. Given a strong desire to control, a strategy that might naturally suggest itself would be to try to increase and improve interaction with the controlled. This is a dubious strategy on two counts, as we have seen in Chapters 4 and 5: it does not seem very likely to succeed, and it reduces the chances of being able to legitimize the organization.

In the following pages I shall suggest a few leadership principles which can help to promote the organization's legitimacy in an inconsistent norm environment, while also underpinning the leaders' control over the organization. These are the principles of distance, morality, responsibility and reform. My normative ambitions are modest. The principles are hypothetical in character, and I shall not try to prove that they work. On the other hand, they do not seem to be far removed from organizational practice. This suggests that they may be workable, but it also indicates a certain lack of novelty. Such novelty as there is emerges in comparison with some of the norms more commonly invoked rather than in comparison with practice. The principles are also agreeably abstract; I shall not try to deal with all the difficulties that might arise in trying to apply them. To put it in non-normative terms, the principles are really hypotheses about what would be done by perceptive leaders desirous of exerting control and creating legitimacy.

The Principle of Distance

Instead of interaction between leaders and led, I would like to recommend distance. The distance between management and actors (and action) reduces the risk of management being controlled by the actors, and makes it easier for them to maintain inconsistency between talk, decisions and action. Distance also reduces the risk that management might obstruct action by involving its own conflicts and its problem orientation and rationality in the action, thus undermining its force.

Distance can be created by the way in which management handles its own right to make decisions. For reasons of legitimacy it may sometimes be necessary to make decisions that contradict the actions performed. If these decisions are taken before or during the performance of the action, they might interfere with the process. This motivates a certain chronological distance, whereby decisions succeed actions. For example, firm decisions can be taken to counteract the negative effects which the critics of a particular action are invoking. Distance can also be based on subject areas: the decisions can refer to areas other than the one in which action is taking place. If management is forced to make decisions without any chronological or subject distance, it can try instead to make its decisions so vague that internal or external actors can interpret them in the opposite way.

Management should not give way to demands from actors for a closer link between decisions and the actions desired or already being carried out. If decisions about actions are linked to decisions about resources, for example, management risks paying a high price, it risks being controlled by economics. Instead management should refrain from coupling decisions about resources to decisions about actions.

To be able to decouple decisions and actions, it is necessary to decouple evaluations and sanctions from decisions. Evaluations and audits are often regarded as formal investigations in which actions and results are compared with decisions and goals, with a view to imposing sanctions. Some evaluation methods can be quite dangerous to organizations which want to demonstrate talk and decisions that are inconsistent with their actions. And yet in a control perspective it may be necessary to know what is really happening in the organization. This suggests that a useful evaluation should not get itself talked about—should not, for instance, lead to management's criticism; and it should restrict itself to fairly independent descriptions of what has actually happened rather than comparing actions with talk and decisions. Nor should it be associated with sanctions. If it is not intended that decisions should be followed, it is not very sensible to punish people who do not follow them. A system of sanctions will simply encourage actors to involve themselves in talk and decisions, to ensure that these are steered towards the realistic and feasible.

Distance can also be maintained by the formulations of the organizational structure. Management's role can be described as being closely or loosely linked to action. Distance in this context means that management is not directly involved in controlling individual actions, and various forms of decentralized organizational structure can be used to ensure this. In a decentralized structure management is responsible for operations as a whole, but it has no influence over everyday affairs, i.e. over the actions performed.

Thus, organizational structures with a built-in distance between leaders and led are to be preferred to those that lack such an arrangement. Large divisionalized organizations are better than small compact ones. Organizations which see themselves and are seen by others as federations or networks are in a better position here than those which are regarded as hierarchical. When an organization is subject to inconsistent demands, its management can be expected to favour decentralization. Decentralization is an instrument of politicization.

Distance does not necessarily mean that leaders should not meet their subordinates; 'management by wandering around' (Peters and Waterman 1982) can easily be combined with decoupling decisions from actions.

Thus distance can promote inconsistencies and can prevent lower levels in the organizations from controlling their own management. On the other hand, distance does not in itself provide management with an effective method for controlling action. And so we have to look for methods of control which can be applied at a distance, methods that operate indirectly by controlling the conditions within which the action occurs. It may be a question of structuring the formal organization at lower levels, of allocating resources to different parts of the organization concerned with different tasks, or of controlling recruitment and promotion. Or control can be exerted indirectly through external individuals or groups, such as customers. The management of a hotel chain which decrees that guests can ask for their money back if their hotel room is not in perfect order is using the customers as a means of controlling the quality of the service supplied by the individual hotels, while keeping management at a distance. Lastly, management can proceed by influencing ideology, an approach which I shall be discussing in more detail below.

The Principle of Morality

An organizational management that keeps its distance from action and from the concrete conditions of action acquires instead excellent opportunities for thinking big. It can generate and establish lofty principles and goals and visions, which then become associated with the organization. This production of high morality is important, to show the rest of the world the organization's good intentions. But it can also be used for control.

Realistic goals are goals adjusted to what the actors regard as feasible, such as the goal that 85% of the products should pass a quality test. Realistic goals are often evidence that the actors are controlling the management. Unrealistic goals—for instance that all products should be of the highest quality— on the other hand can encourage actors to change the boundaries of what they regard as feasible. If this supposition holds, then unrealistic goals imply a higher type of influence than the one generally presented in traditional models, in which control consists largely of a choice between possible alternatives. A management that exerts influence by means of unrealistic goals is playing a more important role than traditional control models allow; it is exploiting its own unique position at far remove from the action.

By establishing high-flown principles, management is suggesting that the organization can strive to produce more, rather than less. Instead of explaining regretfully why the organization cannot achieve more, management encourages external stakeholders to expect greater things. This can trigger a search for improvement, sometimes far beyond what management, for all its visionary zeal, would have dreamt of, and more than the actors in traditional control situations would feel any call to seek.

This type of leadership is probably vital when greater efficiency is the goal. An important interactive means of control in such cases is the budget. But, as we have seen in Chapter 5, budgeting may turn out to be a way of improving financing rather than promoting efficiency. The interaction between management and actors in the budget process provides people with a splendid opportunity for explaining why greater efficiency is impossible. Improvements in efficiency call for the exploitation of knowledge at the action level, but if this knowledge is to be used to raise efficiency rather than to favour financing then actors should be given incentives to pursue the first and be denied the opportunity to pursue the second—both of which would be achieved more easily with the help of unrealistic goals and no interaction. For instance, the managements of American car manufacturers employ the latest techniques of rational analysis to establish the optimal size of stocks. There is no reason to try to reduce stocks below this level. Japanese managements entertain the unrealistic goal of keeping stocks as small as possible and continual efforts are made to cut them down. American car manufacturers' stocks are far larger than their Japanese equivalents (Imai 1986).

High moral principles and sanctions do not go together. People cannot be punished for failing to fulfil impossible demands. If management wants to introduce sanctions, the splendid goals will probably be the first victims; sanctions presuppose realistic goals.

The Principle of Responsibility

The principle of morality demonstrates once again the importance of maintaining a certain distance between managers and managed. But there is a danger lurking in this distance, namely that people will perceive management as having little or no control over the organization's actions. The perception may be correct, but it also means that management has no responsibility. If management has no responsibility, then it cannot reasonably help to legitimize the organization, and its own *raison d'être* disappears. Thus a management that employs the principles of distance and morality must be careful to ensure that its responsibility does not get lost.

The standard way of assuming responsibility is to claim influence. In the management model which I have outlined here, it is difficult for management to claim that it has any direct control over individual actions. Instead it has to lay claim to influence of a more general and indirect type, emphasizing that all its activities as the central pivot of a decentralized organization—making weighty decisions, designing plans and strategies, dealing with crucial issues, and promoting goals and visions—are all good ways of achieving influence. There may, as we have noted, be some truth in all this, but such a modest claim is not enough to entail responsibility; the efficacy of the methods has to be dramatically exaggerated.

Several normative management theories provide useful help here, since they emphasize the powerfulness of just these tools. Ultimately the rational model is the most useful, as it tells us that the one who establishes goals and makes decisions also has influence over what is actually done. These theories probably draw their strength and persistence from the fact that they attribute responsibility to organizational leaders by portraying them as wielders of influence.

If management wants to assume responsibility also for events outside its organization, it will in the same way have to exaggerate its own or the organization's importance in the eyes of the world. This seems to be a typical characteristic of highly political organizations. Because of their lack of active drive, they often make little impact on happenings in their environment. At the same time it is extremely important to them that many groups in the environment should believe in their power. Governments make decisions and thus assume responsibility for many things over which in reality they have little or no control.

A second way of assuming responsibility is to claim responsibility but to acknowledge one's lack of influence. It is not usually difficult to prove the lack of influence; the difficulty is to demonstrate the responsibility which has to be done clearly and in some dramatic way, perhaps by a visible personal sacrifice, such as resignation from a position at the top when things have gone badly wrong.

The Principle of Reform

The discrepancy between morality and action makes it reasonable to expect repentance and the promise of reform. Attempts to improve should be made at least, otherwise credibility will be lost. Reform should not be aimed directly at people's behaviour, as this would involve a form of interactive control. But behaviour can be influenced indirectly, by the introduction of new management techniques or new organizational conditions for the actors. This type of reform is concerned with formal structures, rules of behaviour and ideologies. An organization undergoing reform inspires hope; the very attempt staves off despair. Reform also demonstrates management's power to act, without their interfering in day-to-day activities. Redesigning organizational charts need not disturb organizational activities. Reforms give management a chance to fulfil their intention to generate action.

How much opportunity there will be for starting reforms will depend on the supply of problems, solutions and forgetfulness: there have to be problems which can be used to motivate reform, there have to be new solutions which can be suggested, and the actors should somehow have forgotten how difficult it was to implement their previous reforms, so that they are willing to try again (Brunsson 1988). Politics guarantees at least a supply of difficult or insoluble problems. The discrepancy between intentions and results is one such problem, Here the action model provides the promise of a solution. But there is no likelihood that this solution can be implemented; the reform naturally fails and provides a fine new platform from which to launch new attempts. Forgetfulness is also easily achieved: most organizations thrive happily on the fact that almost all reforms look better *ex ante* than *ex post*. Reforms are often launched as simple slogans which attract and inspire, while the actual work of reform tends to reveal the complications and drawbacks. So it is easy to argue that the new reform now being proposed is better than the old one already tried, and a new attempt is always worthwhile.

Management or Leadership

The leadership principles which I have presented above have been formulated in extremely general terms. Nonetheless they suggest one thing: if they are right we have to conclude that leadership in the kind of situations we are concerned with here is not the same as 'control', and 'management' is not a good label for what leaders do. On the contrary, the role of the leader as I have described it above contradicts any idea of firm control or management. Leaders should systematically refrain from direct control. And yet the notion of control and management is useful, since it provides a basis for the assumption of responsibility. Management models based on rational concepts do not seem to provide useful normative models or result models, either in the exercise of leadership or in the execution of organizational action. Rather, they are useful as presentation models—models which indicate the responsibility of the leadership.

Organizational Intermediators

In spite of what has been said above, organizational leadership can be regarded as a simple undertaking in the sense that it can concentrate on a single aspect of the organization: the political. A similarly simple situation faces those who concentrate on action and who are normally located at the lower levels of the organizational hierarchy. If 'managers' and 'actors' are kept sufficiently separate, life is easier for both parties. But the situation may be much more complicated at intermediate organizational levels. In many organizations which embrace important elements of politics and action, there is a group of employees whose work relates to both, and who may be understandably uncertain as to which game they are playing. This situation can generate much confusion, frustration and depression—states of mind that are not uncommon in organizations of this kind.

As was shown in Chapter 3, it is easy for people to become confused and frustrated when they have to try to adapt to two contradictory norm systems. People at intermediate levels may find it more difficult to delegate (either up or down) the norms and tasks that are inappropriate to themselves than people at the levels above or below them. They may be forced to think or act in both systems, i.e. to sustain double standards and double talk and produce hypocrisy. In anyone with a low level of tolerance for such situations or little schizophrenic capacity for keeping disparate roles clearly apart, depression is likely to set in. One way of escape could be to choose sides: to try to belong to one system only. And when the action model functions as the presentation model, the natural choice would be action rather than politics.

But employees in this sort of intermediate situation may also evolve a role of their own, in which they avoid the difficulties of both politics and action. They may try to substitute their own consistent professional norms for management's inconsistent prescriptions. Accountants employ general accountancy norms for the design of accounting systems, investigators employ special norms for the conduct of analyses and audits, and planners apply their special norms for good planning. Employees become experts—experts in relating management and action.

All these professional norms imply certain strongly held assumptions about management and the connection between management and action. Although they may often be clothed in descriptive form, they are usually normative in the sense that they build not upon realistic perceptions of how management works in practice but on ideas about how the particular profession would like—or feels it ought—to perform its tasks. These perceptions often relate to the rational action model—to its idea of the close connection between thought and action, its notion of hierarchy, its assumption that ideas control action, and its conception of decisions. The task of accounting is said to consist of giving objective and fair information to those who are to make decisions, and as a means whereby management can check that its·directives are being followed (Mellomvik *et al.* 1988). Investigations are supposed to follow the rational model of decision-making, and planning literature is full of ideas about how politicians and other leaders should act in order to make planning possible (Jantsch 1972). For instance, they should make their objectives clear, and they should stick to the task of making decisions and not participate in other parts of the planning process (Dror 1971). When descriptive studies show that accounting is not used in the manner prescribed (Johnson and Kaplan 1987, Mellomvik 1988, Chapter 5 above), that information gathered in investigations is not used (Feldman and March 1981), or that leaders do not behave as they are supposed to in planning and implementation processes (Pressman and Wildavsky 1973), this does not mean that the norms have changed or that the activities are perceived as meaningless (Feldman 1989), since they easily acquire the stamp of truth and are supported by researchers of a normative bent.

Professional norms make it possible for people to identify with something outside their organizations, and this helps to protect them to some extent from the disorder they perceive in the organization and the inconsistent signals that are produced there. The discrepancies between professional norms and organizational reality may trigger a call for organizational reform, and the professional norms can then also serve as a signpost to the intent and content of the reforms. Reforms can help to arouse hope, not only in external stakeholders but also in those members of the organization who find the prevailing situation intolerable.

It is of course vital to the organization as a whole that reforms are initiated and carried out, and the driving function of the intermediators is thus an important one. For the intermediators themselves, however, a more radical remedy against confusion and frustration would be a better understanding of the conditions of management and action, of the fundamental difficulty of linking these two in an inconsistent world, and of the value of being able to decouple them.

Problems and Solutions Outside the Organization

All the advice given so far has little comfort to offer to those outside the organization, who are less interested in its survival and success and more interested in its production of certain results that suit their particular interests. Organizations with a strong element of politics are constantly facing claims from a great many different groups. Just because the organization has opened itself to external demands, it also raises the expectations that the demands will be met. And the ambitions and expectations of external groups may be substantial. Further, the knowledge that organizations do handle insoluble problems and inconsistent norms may even lead people to think that the insoluble problems can be solved or that inconsistent norms can be met. Organizational reforms promising a future which will be better than the past all add to this hope. Some organizations even spread a hope of democracy, that external groups can control or actually control the organization.

The political nature of organizations makes them more adaptable to external demands in one respect, but less so in another. They become more adaptable in the sense that they produce talk and decisions to agree with external demands. They become good listeners, open to suggestions; they are ready to acknowledge their mistakes (or at least the internalized critics or opposition are). It is in this ability to adapt to 'impossible' situations and contradictory demands that the strength of powerfully political organization lies.

But this ideological flexibility makes the organization less ready to adapt or alter its products. Ideological flexibility makes such adjustments both less necessary and more difficult; to change products is a difficult organizational action, and action is the weakness of organizations whose main strength is politics. External groups which are eager for products to be changed, are likely to be disappointed, but their disappointment can perhaps be softened or counterbalanced by the production of ideologies. Even physical products and services can be supplied with suitable ideological superstructures to make them more appetizing. This applies particularly to services whose results are difficult to measure, such as education and medical care, and which are sometimes provided by powerfully political organizations. No reform aimed at promoting an action orientation can be allowed to succeed, because, if it did, it would threaten the organization's ability to handle the inconsistent claims that are being made upon it.

But the problem of adapting to external groups becomes less dramatic if the number of such groups is not too great; and since the political nature of the organization means internalizing parts of the environment by including in its own management representatives of groups that were formerly external, the number of groups which are still external tends to be automatically reduced. Internalized groups are more likely to worry about the survival and success of the organization, and this in turn may moderate their demands for adjustments to meet their own specific interests. The demand for a change in products, for instance, may be subordinated to an interest in the organization's well-being, while those still outside can now direct their complaints to their own representatives instead of to the organization as a whole, or when disappointed can turn to them for comfort and consolation.

If the consolation offered is not enough, all that remains for the external claimants to do is to reduce their level of aspiration. Demands can be satisfied more easily if they are based on realistic expectations of what the organization can achieve. We have already noted that politics in organizations is liable to raise rather than reduce aspirations, so if these are to be kept within realistic bounds too much attention should not be paid to organizational talk and decisions. It is better to recognize that insoluble problems really are insoluble, that all inconsistent claims cannot be fully met, and that reforms geared to increasing action in a world of inconsistencies cannot be expected to materialize. The idea that the organization is controlled by its environment can .serve to make the environment responsible for the organization's activities, and this can be an important way of maintaining the legitimacy not only of the organization in question but of political and economic systems in general. But to take these ideas as a basis for action and expectations is of course to run a very high risk of disappointment. Democracy should mean that the environment (the electorate) has a certain degree of control over the composition of the leadership. In addition, powerful interest groups can sometimes stop or seriously impede organizational action either by their own efforts or through their representatives. One way of doing this is to increase the rationality of the decision processes that may precede the action, perhaps by making the organization consider more preferences or alternatives or consequences. But the step from there to steering organizational action is a long one.

Observers of Organizations

The analyses in this book also have implications for students of organizations, those who want to understand organizations whether or not they have any desire to influence them. All the illusions and paradoxes discussed here present students of organizational life with a number of important problems, and indicate several possible traps. One such trap consists of confusing organizational talk and decisions with the actions they describe. Observers might make the mistake of supposing that organizational statements and decisions agree with organizational actions, that people refer in interviews to actions that have actually happened, and that organizational decisions really have been or will be implemented. For instance, if we assume that a government's description of its disastrous economy exactly corresponds to the amount of money it possesses, or that budget cuts in themselves actually affect events, we may persuade ourselves that more money is really needed and fail to recognize that we are being subjected to a common financing strategy. Perceptions that put ideology and action on an equal footing certainly confirm traditional models of organizations, but they are likely to be poor reflections of reality. Talk and decisions are important in organizations, but they should be analysed as autonomous activities.

Another possible trap consists of confusing organizational display with organizational results, or intentions with effects. Organizational leaders may be striving for consistency, action, influence or rationality, but this does not automatically mean that they achieve them. It does not even necessarily mean that they should achieve them, or that they ever could, or that they should not try. Sometimes the opposite effect is achieved, but this does not necessarily mean that it was intended either. Rather, in observing an organization it should always be remembered that the purposes, causes and effects associated with organizational structures, processes and ideologies may not always correspond to those expressed by the organizations themselves or recommended in normative theories. Decisions, rationality, budgets, reforms and failures may all be entangled in purposes and causes and effects that resemble neither one another nor those indicated in the standard descriptions. And the situation is further complicated by the fact that we cannot simply do without all our myths about intentions, or causes and effects; many of them have important functions, although telling the truth is not one of these.

The Morality of Hypocrisy

Is it also possible to raise some more fundamental normative questions than those discussed so far: are the political characteristics that I have described in this book examples of organizational dysfunctions or abnormities; are they something evil that should be exorcized? Or are they necessary or even benevolent qualities that should be preserved? In an action perspective it might be tempting to assign politics to the debit side: since the action model is a powerful presentation model, it may easily appear to provide a norm and an argument for organizations to concentrate on efficient action only. And if organizations do have to handle inconsistent norms, then they should arrange trade-offs between them and thus furnish themselves with a consistent preference function to guide their actions.

But such arguments are not indisputable. Morality is not automatically on the side of action. Organizations which conduct politics are less forceful when it comes to action, but vigorous organizational action is by no means always a positive thing. The history of the twentieth century has shown that the behaviour of increasingly vast and powerful organizations often has devastating consequences for individual people.

It could also be claimed that the handling and maintenance of norms and values is more important than acting. If morality is a question of promoting human happiness, then action certainly doesn't seem to provide an obvious way of achieving it. Happiness is an idea, an ideology, and it is not always necessary to tackle material conditions in order to influence an ideology: it may be safer to tackle the ideology direct. Many problems are insoluble on any material plane and are accessible to ideological handling only, and it is in just such situations that a political element in organizations is particularly valuable. And what problems could be more important than those that are insoluble?

But the way in which values are handled is also important. It is important that the values are not destroyed in the handling, even if they are inconsistent. Important high-level values can be better maintained if they are not relativized. The economists' notion of arranging trade-offs between conflicting values implies a normative stance, whereby values are reduced or abandoned in order to promote collective action. If we want to preserve high and inconsistent values we must be prepared to handle them on more procedural lines, rather than linking them to the achievement of action and results; values are better suited to handling in talk than in action, and by reference to the future rather than the present. If we are to be able to maintain high values, we must not adapt them to reflect our actions. We seldom reflect high values in action, and because of their unreal elevation and their internal inconsistencies our best values cannot be adequately reflected in action. The maintenance of high values involves sin, i.e. a discrepancy between values and actions. And if norms which are not or cannot be adapted to action are to be advocated, some hypocrisy is called for. Sin and hypocrisy are necessary to the creation and preservation of high morals. Those without sin or hypocrisy are those who pursue or advocate realizable goals, trading in their morality in exchange.

None of this means that we should strive for sin and hypocrisy; they belong not to the presentation model but to the result model. High morality should characterize our intentions, our talk and our decisions even if it cannot imbue our actions.

High values, sin and hypocrisy—all these help to explain the role of responsibility. Responsibility is more important when things go badly than when they go well; it is more important when sin is present than when values are lowered to the level of action. We can accept responsibility, but we can also be relieved of it if someone else accepts it, even someone who is 'innocent', i.e. without influence. High values, sin and hypocrisy also necessitate repentance and reform if any hope of progress is to be maintained, i.e. the hope that the values might be approached or even attained at some time in the future.

Thus both the problems and the solutions that have been described here are related to existential problems of a more general kind, and the solutions resemble traditional Christian solutions. Ideas concerning sin, hypocrisy and responsibility in the human being have their roots in the classical Greek and Christian concept of the individual, of man as a separate and unique entity, comparatively independent of his context—a view that conflicts with many pre-classical and non-Western conceptions, which see man as nothing more than the different roles he plays in different contexts. The ideas are similarly meaningless in an organizational context, if the organization is regarded solely as a host of chaotic networks and arenas for the independent actions of its members. Organizations can only be regarded as bearers of sin, hypocrisy and responsibility if they are perceived as single wholes, as individuals, i.e. as entities acting collectively under their leaders in order to achieve certain goals. Once again the action model is important as a presentation model. It is by presenting itself as a coherent entity that the organization can handle qualities which have traditionally been assigned to the human being.

Thus the problems and solutions discussed here are not new. What is new is the notion that in our modern and highly secularized societies even the most mundane production organizations have to reflect and deal with them. The tendency in secularized societies to explain the world in terms of man endows man and his organizations with a strong significance: managements and organizations can occupy the divine role of accepting responsibility even though they are innocent of the contents of the action. Organizations which accept responsibility help to relieve others of it, which may make it easier for these others to live and also to act. By producing both politics and action, organizations can also help to maintain the beautiful myth of rationality, of the unity between thinking and doing and the paramountcy of ideas over actions.

Maintaining high values, accepting responsibility and producing hope are no mean tasks, surely as significant to society as producing organized action. The vital question then is whether we have not let our organizations and their leaders become too important, too 'crucial' to society as a whole and to us personally. It seems worth reflecting on the consequences of this importance and considering what alternatives there may be.

References

Ansoff, H. Igor, Declerck, R.P. and Hayes, R.L. (eds) (1976) *From Strategic Planning to Strategic Management.* New York: John Wiley & Sons.

Argyris, Chris and Schön, D. (1978) *Theory in Practice.* San Francisco: Jossey-Bass.

Aristotle (1984) *The Nichomachean Ethics.* Oxford: Oxford University Press.

Arnold, Thurman W. (1935) *The Symbols of Government.* New Haven: Yale University Press.

Baier, Vicki E., March, J.H. and Saetren, H. (1986) Implementation and ambiguity. *Scandinavian Journal of Management Studies,* Vol. 2, No. 3–4, 197–212.

Barnard, Chester (1938) *The Functions of the Executive.* Cambridge, Mass.: Harvard University Press.

Bower, Joseph L. (1970) *Managing the Resource Allocation Process: A study of corporate planning and investment.* Boston: Harvard University, Graduate School of Business Administration.

Brorström, Björn (1982) *Planeringspolitik eller resultatpolitik.* Lund: Doxa.

Brorström, Björn (1985) Uppföljning och framförhållning—om bokslut och ekonomisk planering i storstadskommuner in Wiberg, Sven: *Ledarskapets förnyelse.* Lund: Doxa.

Brown, Richard H. (1978) Bureaucracy as praxis: Toward a political phenomenology of formal organizations. *Administrative Science Quarterly,* Vol. 23. No. 3, 365–382.

Brunsson, Nils (1981) *Politik och administration.* Stockholm: Liber.

Brunsson, Nils (1982) The irrationality of action and action rationality. Decisions, ideologies and organizational actions. *Journal of Management Studies,* Vol. 19, 29–44.

Brunsson, Nils (1985) *The Irrational Organization*. Chichester: John Wiley & Sons.

Brunsson, Nils (1988) Organizational Reforms. Paper presented at the SCANCOR conference on organizations. Hemsedal, Norway.

Brunsson, Nils and Jönsson, S.A. (1979) *Beslut och handling*. Stockholm: Liber.

Brunsson, Nils and Malmer, S. (1978) Värdering av produktutvecklingsprojekt. Paper presented at the conference on Product Development, Lidingö, Sweden.

Cohen, Michael, March, J.G. and Olsen, J.P. (1972) A garbage can model of rational choice. *Administrative Science Quarterly*, Vol. 17, No. 1, 1–25.

Cyert, Richard M. and March, J.G. (1963) *A Behavioral Theory of the Firm*. Englewood Cliffs, N.J.: Prentice-Hall.

Danielsson, Albert and Malmberg, A. (1979) *Beslut fattas*. Stockholm: SAF.

Dror, Yehezkel (1971) *Design for Policy Sciences*. New York: Elsevier.

Edelman, Murray (1971) *Politics as Symbolic Action*. New York: Academic Press.

Edwards, Rem B. (1969) *Freedom, Responsibility and Obligation*. The Hague: Martinus Nijhoff.

Epstein, Edwin M. and Votaw, D. (1978) *Rationality, Legitimacy and Responsibility*. Santa Monica: Goodyear.

Fayol, Henri (1916) Administration industrielle et générale. Prévoyance. Organisation. Commandement. Coordination. Controle. Extrait du *Bulletin de la Societe de l'Industrie Minérale Paris*: Dunod (ed.).

Feldman, Martha (1989) *Order Without Design: Information Production and Policy Making*. Stanford: Stanford University Press.

Feldman, Martha and March, J.G. (1981) Information in organizations as signal and symbol. *Administrative Science Quarterly*, Vol. 26, 171–186.

Fincham, F. and Jaspers, J. (1980) Attribution of Responsibility: From man the scientist to man as lawyer, in Berkowitz, Leonard (ed.): *Advances in Experimental Social Psychology*. New York: Academic Press.

French, Peter A. (1984) *Collective and Corporate Responsibility*. New York: Columbia University Press.

Geertz, Clifford (1973) *The Interpretation of Cultures*. New York: Basic Books.

Gluckman, Max (ed.) (1972) Moral Crises: Magical and secular solutions, in: *The Allocation of Responsibility*. Manchester: Manchester University.

Gustafsson, Jeppe and Seeman, J. (1985) *Små institutioner i store systemer— tilpasning og påvirkning*. Aalborg: ALFUFF.

Hanf, Kenneth and Scharpf, F.W. (eds) (1978) *Interorganizational Policy Making*. London: Sage Publications.

Hannan, Michael T. and Freeman, J. (1977) The Population Ecology of Organizations. *American Journal of Sociology*, Vol. 82, 929–966.

Helkama, Klaus (1981) *Toward a Cognitive–Developmental Theory of Attribution of Responsibility*. Helsinki: Suomalainen Tiedeakatemia.

Hernes, Gudmund (1978) *Forhandlingsøkonomi og blandingsadministrasjon*. Bergen: Universitetsforlaget.

Høgheim, Sven, Monsen, N. Olsen, R. and Olson, O. (1989) The two worlds of management control. Forthcoming in *Financial Accountability and Management*.

Huysmans, Jan, H. (1970) The effectiveness of the cognitive style constraint in implementing operations research proposals. *Management Science*, Vol. 17, No. 1, 92–104.

Imai, Masaaki (1986) *Kaizen*. New York: Random House.

Jansson, David (1987) *Investeringskalkylker i empirisk investeringforskning*. Research report. Stockholm: EFI.

Jantsch, Erich (1972) *Technological Planning and Social Futures*. London.

Jepperson, Ronald L. and Meyer, J. (1989) Politics, actors, functions and organizing, in Powell, Walter W. and Dimaggio, P. (eds): *The New Institutionalism in Organizational Analysis*. In press.

Johnson, H. Thomas and Kaplan, R.S. (1987) *Relevance Lost*. Boston: Harvard Business School Press.

Jones, Edward and Nisbett, R. (1972) The actor and the observer: Divergent perceptions of the causes of behaviour, in Jones, Edward, Kanouse, D., Kelley, H. *et al.: Attribution*. Morristown: General Learning Press.

Jönsson, Sten A. and Lundin, R.A. (1977) Myths and wishful thinking of management tools, in Nystrom, Paul C. and Starbuck, W.H. (eds): *Prescriptive Models of Organizations*. Amsterdam: North-Holland.

Kahneman, Daniel and Tversky, A. (1973) On the psychology of prediction. *Psychological Review*, Vol. 80, No. 4, 237–251.

Kelley, Harald (1972) Attribution in social interaction, in Jones, Edward, Kanouse, D., Kelley, H. *et al.: Attribution*. Morristown: General Learning Press.

Kingdon, John (1984) *Agendas, Alternatives and Public Policies*. Boston: Little Brown & Co.

Lawrence, Paul R. and Lorsch, J.W. (1967) *Organization and Management: Managing differentiation and integration*. Boston: Harvard University Press.

Lipman-Blumen, Jean and Schram, S. (1984) *The Paradox of Success: The impact on priority setting in agricultural research and extension*. Washington: United States Department of Agriculture.

Lipset, Seymour and Schneider, W. (1983) *The Confidence Gap*. New York: Free Press.

Lorange, Peter and Vancil, R.F. (1977) *Strategic Planning Systems*. Englewood Cliffs, N.J.: Prentice-Hall.

Lundberg, Erik (1957) *Produktivitet och räntabilitet.* Stockholm: SNS.

March, James G. (1976) The technology of foolishness, in March, James G. and Olsen, J.P. (eds): *Ambiguity and Choice in Organizations.* Bergen: Universitetsforlaget.

March, James G. and Olsen, J.P. (1975) The uncertainty of the past: organizational learning under ambiguity. *European Journal of Political Research*, Vol. 3, 147–171.

March, James G. and Olsen, J.P. (1984) Organizing political life: What administrative reorganization tells us about government. *American Political Science Review*, Vol. 88, 281–296.

March, James G. and Simon, H.A. (1958) *Organizations.* New York: John Wiley & Sons.

Martin, Joanne, Feldman, M. Hatch,. M. and Sitkin, S. (1983) The uniqueness paradox in organizational stories. *Administrative Quarterly*, Vol. 28, No. 3, 438–453.

Mayntz, Renate (1976) Environmental policy conflicts: The case of the German Federal Republic. *Policy Analysis*, Vol. 2, 557–587.

Mellomvik, Frode, Monsen, N. and Olson, O. (1988) Functions of accounting: a discussion. *Scandinavian Journal of Management*, Vol. 4, No. 3–4, 101–119.

Meyer, John (1983) Innovation and knowledge use in American public education, in Meyer, John and Scott, R. (eds): *Organizational Environments.* Beverly Hills: Sage Publications.

Meyer, John and Rowan, (1977) Institutionalized organizations: Formal structure as myth and ceremony. *American Journal of Sociology*, Vol. 83, No. 2, 340–363.

Meyer, John and Scott, R.W. (1983) *Organizational Environments: Ritual and rationality.* Beverly Hills: Sage Publications.

Meyer, Marshall W. and Zucker, L. (1989) *Permanently Failing Organizations.* London: Sage Publications.

Micheletti, Michele (1987) Toward interest inarticulation. Paper presented at 1987 Annual Meeting of the American Political Science Association.

Nisbett, Richard and Ross, L. (1980) *Human Inference.* Englewood Cliffs, N.J.: Prentice-Hall.

Olsen, Johan P. (1971) Local budgeting: Decision-making or a ritual act. *Scandinavian Journal of Political Studies*, Vol. 5, 85–118.

Olsen, Johan P. (1983) *Organized Democracy.* Bergen: Universitetsforlaget.

Persson, Bo (ed.) (1977) *Surviving Failures.* Stockholm: Almqvist & Wiksell International.

Peters, Thomas J, and Waterman, R.M. Jr (1982) *In Search of Excellence.* New York: Harper & Row.

Pfeffer, Jeffrey (1981) Management as symbolic action: The creation and maintenance of organizational paradigms, in Cummings, L.L. and

Staw, B. (eds): *Research in Organizational Behavior*, Vol. 3. Greenwich, Conn.: JAI Press.

Pressman, Jeffrey and Wildavsky, A. (1973) *Implementation*. Berkeley: University of California Press.

Renck, Olov (1971) *Investeringsbedömning i några svenska företag*. Stockholm: EFI.

Rombach, Björn (1986) *Rationalisering eller prat?* Lund: Doxa.

Ross, A. (1975) *On Guilt, Responsibility and Punishment*. London: Stevens & Sons.

Sahlin-Andersson, Kerstin (1986) *Beslutsprocessens komplexitet*. Lund: Doxa.

Simon, Herbert (1965) *Administrative Behavior*. New York: Free Press (originally published 1947).

Spiro, Herbert J. (1969) *Responsibility in Government: Theory and practice*. New York: Van Nostrand Reinhold.

Starbuck, William, H. (1976) Organizations and their environments, in Dunnette, Marvin D. (ed.): *Handbook of Industrial and Organizational Psychology*. Chicago: Rand Mcnally, 1069–1123.

Starbuck, William H. and Nystrom, P. (1981) Designing and understanding organizations, in Starbuck, William H. and Nystrom, Paul (eds): *Handbook of Organizational Design*, Vol. 1. New York: Oxford University Press.

Starbuck, William H., Greve, A. and Hedberg, B.L.T. (1978) Responding to crises. *Journal of Business Administration*. Vol. 9, No. 2, 111–137.

Tell, Bertil (1974) *Investeringskalkylering i praktiken*. Lund: Studentlitteratur.

Van der Ven, Andrew H. (1983) Book review of Peters and Waterman *In Search of Excellence*. *Administrative Science Quarterly*. Vol. 28, No. 4, 621–624.

von Bertalanffy, Ludwig (1968) *General Systems Theory*. New York: G. Braziller Inc.

van Gunsteren, Herman R. (1976) *The Quest for Control*. Chichester: John Wiley & Sons.

Weick, Karl E. (1969) *The Social Psychology of Organizing*. Reading, Mass.: Addison-Wesley.

Wildavsky, Aaron (1972) The self-evaluating organization. *Public Administrative Review*, Vol. 32, No. 5, 509–520.

Wildavsky, Aaron (1974) *The Politics of the Budgetary Process*. Boston: Little Brown & Co.

Wildavsky, Aaron (1975) *Budgeting. A comparative theory of budgetary processes*. Boston: Little Brown & Co.

Wolff, Rolf (1986) *Organizing Industrial Development*. Berlin: de Gruyter.

Zajonc, Robert B. (1960) The process of cognitive tuning in communication. *Journal of Abnormal and Social Psychology*. Vol. 61, 159–167.

INDEX